BPM Excellen in Practice 2010
in Practice 2010
Successful Process Implementation

BPM Excellence in Practice 2010

Successful Process Implementation

Award-winning Case Studies in Workflow and Business Process Management

Edited by

LAYNA FISCHER

Future Strategies Inc.
Lighthouse Point, Florida, USA

BPM Excellence in Practice 2010: Successful Process Implementation
Copyright © 2010 by Future Strategies Inc.
ISBN13: 9780981987064

Published by Future Strategies Inc., Book Division
3640-B3 North Federal Highway, #421, Lighthouse Point FL 33064 USA
954.782.3376 / 954.719.3746 fax
www.FutStrat.com
books@FutStrat.com

Publisher's Cataloging-in-Publication Data
ISBN: 978-0981987064
Library of Congress Control Number: 2010934219

BPM Excellence in Practice 2010: Successful Process Implementation /Layna Fischer (ed)

p. cm.

Includes bibliographical references and appendices.

1. Technological Innovation. 2. Organizational Change. 3. Business Process Management. 4. Information Technology. 5. Total Quality Management. 6. Management Information systems. 7. Office Practice-Automation. 8. Knowledge Management. 9. Workflow. 10. Process Analysis

Fischer, Layna. (ed)

Table of Contents

Introduction
BPM Excellence in Practice 2010
Successful Process Implementation

Layna Fischer, Global Awards Executive Director

The prestigious annual **Global Excellence Awards for BPM and Workflow** are highly coveted by organizations that seek recognition for their achievements. Now evolved into their 18th year, originally starting with, and moving through, imaging, documentation, knowledge management and more, as our industry moved forward, these awards not only provide a spotlight for companies that truly deserve recognition, but provide tremendous insights for organizations wishing to emulate the winners' successes.

These winners are companies that successfully used BPM in gaining competitive advantage within their industries.

CRITERIA

The criteria for submitting an entry are fairly simple: the project should have been operational for six months prior to nomination, and have been installed within the past two years. The submission guidelines, however, are more detailed. To be recognized as winners, companies must address three critical areas: excellence in *innovation*, excellence in *implementation* and excellence in strategic *impact* to the organization. Details at www.bpmf.org.

Innovation

Innovation encompasses the innovative use of technology for strategic business objectives; the complexity of the underlying business process and IT architecture; the creative and successful deployment of advanced workflow and imaging concepts; and process innovations through business process reengineering and/or continuous improvements.

- Innovative use of BPM technology to solve unique problems
- Creative and successful implementation of advanced BPM concepts
- Level of integration with other technologies and legacy systems
- Degree of complexity in the business process and underlying IT architecture

Implementation

Hallmarks of a successful *implementation* include extensive user and line management involvement in the project while successfully managing change during the implementation process. Factors impacting the level of difficulty in achieving a successful implementation include the system complexity; integration with other advanced technologies; and the scope and scale of the implementation (e.g. size, geography, inter-company processes).

- Successful BPM and/or workflow implementation methodology
- Size, scope and quality of change management process
- Scope and scale of the implementation (e.g. size, geography, inter-and intra-company processes)

Impact

Impact is the bottom line, answering the question, "What benefit does BPM deliver to my business? Why should I care?"

- Extent and quantifiable impact of productivity improvements

- Significance of cost savings
- Level of increased revenues, product enhancements, customer service or quality improvements
- Impact of the system on competitive positioning in the marketplace
- Proven strategic importance to the organization's mission
- Degree to which the system enabled a culture change within the organization and methodology for achieving that change

Using BPM for Competitive Advantage

Examples of potential benefits include: productivity improvements; cost savings; increased revenues; product enhancements; improved customer service; improved quality; strategic impact to the organization's mission; enabling culture change; and—most importantly—changing the company's competitive position in the market. The visionary focus is now toward strategic benefits, in contrast to marginal cost savings and productivity enhancements.

While successes in these categories are prerequisites for winning a Global Excellence Award, it would reward all companies to focus on excelling in *innovation*, *implementation* and *impact* when installing BPM and workflow technologies. Companies must recognize that implementing innovative technology is useless unless the organization has a successful approach that delivers—and even surpasses—the anticipated benefits.

SUBMIT AN ENTRY

Submissions for the annual **Global Excellence Awards for BPM and Workflow** open in the September timeframe. The Awards program is managed by Future Strategies Inc., the Awards Director is Layna Fischer in collaboration with Derek Miers of BPM Focus.org, with sponsorship from WfMC, OMG and BPM.com.

General information and guidelines may be found at www.bpmf.org or contact:

Layna Fischer, Layna@FutStrat.com

Future Strategies Inc., www.FutStrat.com

Phone +1 954 782 3376, Fax +1 954 719 3746

Contents and Chapter Abstracts

Guest Chapters:

PRIMITIVES AND STYLE: A COMMON VOCABULARY FOR BPM ACROSS THE ENTERPRISE

Dennis Wisnosky, Business Mission Area Chief Architect & CTO, ODCMO, US DoD and Linus Chow, Oracle, USA

The US Department of Defense (DoD) is leading the way in the Federal Government for Architecture-driven Business Operations Transformation. A vital tenet for success is ensuring that business process models are based on a standardized representation, thus enabling the analysis and comparison of end to end business processes. This will lead to the re-use of the most efficient and effective process patterns (Style Guide), comprised of elements (Primitives), throughout the DoD Business Mission Area (BMA).

TRANSFORM BUSINESS PROCESSES THROUGH BUSINESS ANALYTICS

Clay Richardson, Senior Analyst, Forrester Research, USA

If you're reading this, odds are you're either knee deep implementing an enterprise-wide BPM program, or you're exploring the potential impact and value of standing up a BPM program for your organization. If neither of these apply, then maybe you're just bored and figured, why not learn about a new and exciting topic. Regardless which bucket you fall into, at some point you'll come face-to-face with BPM's multiple-personality disorder.

This is a conversation I've been having more and more with business process professionals. Some define "business process management" as a management discipline, while others define BPM as a technology. And still, others define BPM as a capability for transforming the culture of an organization. Most BPM experts—including yours truly—agree that BPM is broad enough to house all three of these paradigms. However, I'm always amazed to see the knock-down, drag-out fights that take place over three simple words: "What is BPM?"

TRANSFORMING SECURITY THROUGH EA AND BPM

Christine Robinson, Christine Robinson & Associates, LLC, USA

This Enterprise Architecture (EA), Business Process Management (BPM), and security approach offers the potential to dramatically transform security on all levels, providing leadership and practitioners alike the tools to benefit from a strategic to a granular level. Security often suffers from cultural barriers, inadequate funding, insufficient attention, bolting it on the back end, lack of understanding, lack of uniformity, and many more ills. This approach enables organizations to plan and implement security throughout an enterprise and beyond using EA frameworks and integrated business process management (BPM) software as an enabler.

Section 1: Europe

FACULTY OF MANUFACTURING TECHNOLOGIES—TUKE, SLOVAKIA

Finalist, Europe. Nominated by Czestochowa University of Technology, Poland

Faculty of Manufacturing Technologies as part of Technical University of Košice has recently decided to modernize library services through the use of advanced technologies and methods of work with a focus on providing specialized information resources. In our solution we have integrated a commercial automated library system CLAVIUS with RFID technology that improves the flaws of the traditional paper card and the bar code. As known RFID tags embedded in books enable automatic management of library items within libraries, but other possibilities to automate workflows in a library are more or less uncovered. This study focuses on the process-based library service modularization at the conceptual stage of development and adoption of RFID technology for library process automation in the above mentioned project.

HOMELOAN MANAGEMENT LIMITED (HML), EUROPE

Silver Award, Europe. Nominated by Lombardi Software, Limited, UK.

HML is a financial outsourcing company and the UK's largest mortgage servicer, providing outsourced mortgage administration solutions to over 30 UK and Irish lenders, and operating out of four UK locations – Skipton (North Yorkshire – head office), Padiham (Lancashire), Londonderry (Northern Ireland) and Glasgow. The company was established in 1998 and is a wholly-owned subsidiary of Skipton Building Society. The client portfolio includes some of the largest players in the UK and US financial markets and currently the company is managing in excess of £50bn of assets.

SNS BANK, NETHERLANDS

Silver Award, Europe. Nominated by Red Hat, Netherlands

SNS Bank, Netherlands, has made a strategic decision to empower its customers on-line by fully automating its business processes. The ability to automate these service channels is achieved by applying Business Process Management (BPM) techniques to existing selling channels. Both the publicly available and internal processes are being revamped into full scale Straight Through Processing (STP) services. This extreme use of online STP is the trigger in a shift that is of crucial importance to cost-effective banking in an ever turbulent and changing financial world. The key elements used in implementing these goals continue to be Free

Open Source Software (FOSS), Service oriented architecture (SOA), and BPM. In this paper we will present an industrial application describing the efforts of the SNS Bank to make the change from traditional banking services to a full scale STP and BPM driven bank that can survive on the Financial Crisis front lines.

SWISSCARD AECS, SWITZERLAND

Gold Award, Europe. Nominated by Action Technologies Inc., USA

The liberalization of the credit card market in Switzerland in 1997 paved the way for American Express and Credit Suisse AG to establish the joint venture company Swisscard AECS AG and to merge their credit card activities. Swisscard ideally combines the complementary strengths of the founding companies, with American Express being the global leader in card management and Credit Suisse providing strong national sales channels. On behalf of Credit Suisse, Swisscard offers the world-famous American Express card within Switzerland. It is thus the sole issuer in Switzerland with all three major brands (American Express, MasterCard and Visa) in its product portfolio.

Section 2: Middle East and Africa

ABU DHABI COMMERCIAL BANK, UNITED ARAB EMIRATES

Finalist, Middle-East-Africa. Nominated by Newgen Software Technologies Ltd., India

Newgen provided the bank with a BPM-enabled workflow platform, which not only helped bank to automate its processes, but also allowed seamless integration of the BPM solution with its existing applications. Abu Dhabi Commercial Bank (ADCB), with a strong presence in Consumer and Corporate is a leading provider of technology-enabled services. In its objective towards complete automation of processes, the bank was in urgent need for a solution that would enable end-to-end automation of their key business processes and also provide integration with its existing applications. Newgen provided the bank with a BPM-enabled workflow platform, which not only helped bank to automate its processes, but also allowed seamless integration of the BPM solution with its existing applications.

NAFITH LOGISTICS PSC, MIDDLE EAST AND AFRICA.

Nominated by TraxAware Software LLC, Jordan.

Nafith Logistics Services is a company that delivers logistics support and trade facilitation services on a national and regional level, and one of the main branches of the company within Jordan is NAFITH-Aqaba. NAFITH-Aqaba is a 250 employee organization spread over 39 remote locations working on a 24/7 shift structure to manage and control all trucks going in and out of the city of Aqaba. The NAFITH Truck Control System (TCS) is a public private partnership project with a 10 year concession from the Aqaba Special Economic Zone Authority with the primary objectives of eliminating congestion, pollution, and increasing road safety. The purpose of this document is to layout the overall success elements of implementing the NAFITH Online Intranet Portal (NOIP) for the Nafith-Aqaba operation.

NOKIA SIEMENS NETWORKS, UAE

Gold Award, Middle East and Africa. Nominated by Appian, USA

Nokia Siemens Networks was created in 2007 through the merger of the former Networks Business Group of Nokia and the carrier-related businesses of Siemens. Today, NSN is one of the world's largest network communications companies – with 60,000 employees, a leading position in all key markets across the world, and total sales of more than €15 billion a year. The Consulting and Systems Integration (CSI) unit within NSN is an organization of 4,000 staff, with sales of over €500 million a year. CSI desperately needed to get an established set of processes in place very quickly because without end-to-end visibility, fast and effective decision-making to drive the business was hampered, if not impossible. CSI looked to BPM technology to drive quick, highly-configurable, higher-value/lower cost process solutions to meet its business goals.

SOUTH AFRICAN POST OFFICE

Silver Award, Middle East and Africa. Nominated by Pétanque Consultancy, South Africa

The case study is about how key business processes were mapped to deliver on strategy, embracing the elements of strategy, people, process and IT, within the framework of innovation.

The South African Post Office (SAPO) needed change on a number of levels: a fresh strategy agreed to in 2007 resulted in a new business model. This strategy was driven by the need for the South African Post Office to respond to changing markets and re-position itself as a major player in the region. This required SAPO to become more accessible, more customer-focused, more innovative in generating revenue and finding new and better ways of providing services to the urban and rural communities it services. The new model needed the right processes and people to eventually deliver on strategy. Through VizPro®, an innovative approach to process documentation and improvement, a number of challenges were overcome and resulted in benefits ranging from enterprise wide buy-in through transparency and participation, role clarity on who needs to do what to bring about the changes needed, along with capturing immense volumes of corporate knowledge in process maps that reflect the *business* view of the step by step activities needed to ensure achievement of strategic goals in storyboard format process maps that are easy to use and easy to follow.

Section 3: North America

AMERISOURCEBERGEN, U.S.A.

Silver Award. Nominated by Metastorm, USA.

AmerisourceBergen is a global organization that has embraced BPM technology. As part of the competitive and complex pharmaceutical industry, the company was faced with critical challenges like maintaining high standards while managing growth, creating efficiencies, making better and faster decisions and ensuring regulatory and legal compliance. Company leaders recognized that BPM can help them meet these demands – while delivering extremely significant impact and ROI.

Today AmerisourceBergen has established a BPM Center of Excellence, having deployed and optimized nearly 200 processes through-out the enterprise with approximately 3,000 global users. Total an-nual benefits are in the tens of millions of dollars. This nomination will showcase AmerisourceBergen's enterprise-wide BPM success, with specific mention of one of its most innovative BPM implementations.

LINCOLN TRUST COMPANY, USA

Gold Award, North America. Nominated by Lincoln Trust Company, USA

This paper describes the experiences of implementing an enterprise wide BPM program at Lincoln Trust Company. The program was constituted in early 2007 with an initial goal of managing core processes related to physical paperwork and an ultimate goal of using BPM technology to manage all strategic processes of the organization. When the program began the company was receiving over 100,000 client documents each month with limited to no control over these instructions. Initial, overwhelming success with an enterprise wide implementation of BPM technology to workflow-enable document centric processes led to the strong de-sire of company management to move quickly to our next goals of understanding, improving, and automating other strategic processes. By doing so we've been able to open our back office process for collaboration with a strategic outsourcing partner, drive processes to the web, reduce costs and risks, improve customer satisfaction, and completely turn around a damaged relationship between IT and the business.

PINELLAS COUNTY CLERK OF THE CIRCUIT COURT, FLORIDA, USA
Finalist, North America. Nominated by Global 360, Inc. USA

Supporting the most densely populated county in the state of Florida with a population of nearly one million residents, the Pinellas County Clerk of the Circuit Court office needed a process and document management solution for the Probate Division of the Clerk's office. This solution needed to not only make all court files and their supporting documents electronically available to all Pinellas County judges, lawyers, office staff, the public, and the entire County judicial system, but provide improved court file workflow and create an improved audit trail within the system. Moreover, the Clerk's office wanted to position itself to be in compliance with the state's legislative mandate requiring them to support e-filing and make records publicly available via the Internet.

SAN FRANCISCO PUBLIC UTILITIES COMMISSION, USA
Finalist, North America. Nominated by Interfacing Technologies, Canada

The retirement of baby boomer workforce is putting companies' productivity and readiness to the test. How quickly and efficiently companies rearrange their operations to the generational swap will set their competitive edge in the next years. Creativity and determination are crucial to overcome the challenge. The San Francisco Public Utilities Commission (SFPUC) implemented a business process management and workflow solution to drive change efforts across its organizations. The SFPUC deployed innovative ways to capture the baby boomers' knowledge and transmit it to the new generation; without missing a step in service efficiency and quality, the SFPUC prepared itself for major challenges such as environmental preservation.

COUNTY OF SAN JOAQUIN, CALIFORNIA
Silver Award, North America. Nominated by Oracle USA

The County of San Joaquin Information Systems Division is the central IT organization serving the County of San Joaquin, which is a midsize California county with a population of more than 650,000. The county's information systems division supports its systems serving general government, human resources, law and justice, and health services. To better serve our county and support the California Administrative Office of Courts (AOC) modernization initiatives we initiated a modernization effort using Business Process Management (BPM) and Service Oriented Architecture (SOA) technologies.

In our first phase we have successfully added SOA, BPM/BPEL & BAM, an Application Development Framework (ADF), J2EE appserver/webserver, RAC and Databases to our Enterprise Architecture (EA). Furthermore, during this first 18 months we developed an application for local warrants which has 30 modules and local admin console integrated with LDAP, CUPS, ActiveX, CLETS, CJIS and CAD systems. The Law and Justice application for Warrants has been live for over 18 months and has accumulated 30 million transactions with the application supporting over 6,600 employees, 18 Law and Justice Agencies in County of San Joaquin and integration with CLETS and Police Mobile car units. This success has been recognized by the California AOC and is published as a best practice success on their website.

Section 4: Pacific Rim

AEGON RELIGARE LIFE INSURANCE CORPORATION, INDIA
Finalist, Pacific Rim. Nominated by DST Global Solutions, USA

AEGON Religare Life Insurance Company Ltd, is a joint venture between AEGON, one of the world's largest life insurance and pension companies, Religare, one of India's leading integrated financial services groups and Bennett and Coleman, India's largest media house.

The company was launched across pan-India with multi-channel operations in July 2008 with over 30 branches spread across India. The business philosophy for AEGON Religare is to help people plan their life better.

RELIANCE LIFE INSURANCE, INDIA
Silver Award, Pacific Rim. Nominated by Savvion Inc., USA

Life insurance is a hugely completive industry in India. It is also seasonal with the bulk of policies purchased during the end of the year. Reliance Life Insurance (RLIC) is an associate of Reliance Capital Ltd. which ranks among the top 3 financial services firms in India. In just two years of operation, Reliance Life Insurance has exceeded 2 million policies and is among the country's fastest growing life insurance firms in new business premiums with a year-over-year growth rate of 195 percent.

However, its technology infrastructure systems were not keeping pace with its rapid rate of development, limiting its growth, proving to be a bottleneck and preventing the company from scaling fast enough. A number of processes were manual and resulted in lack of visibility into operations. The absence of automation was impacting productivity and the ability to book revenue in a timely manner. RLIC needed to find a solution that could improve process control, enhance visibility, reduce policy turn around time, as well as accelerate time to market and agility

SOUTH AUSTRALIA DEPARTMENT OF THE PREMIER AND CABINET, AUSTRALIA
Gold Award, Pacific Rim. Nominated by HandySoft, USA

The Department of the Premier and Cabinet (DPC) is the principal government agency in the state of South Australia responsible for strategic planning and policy development. Under the leadership of the Premier and Executive Council, these matters of state business require collaboration and negotiation across more than 20 directorates and agencies with more than 40,000 potential participants. The workload, as a result, became highly dynamic, heavily paper-based, and prone to security breaches.

Rolled out in 2009, the Electronic Cabinet Online (ECO) system is DPC's answer to streamlining business processes, improving the quality of work and ensuring information security. The fundamental purpose of ECO is to create a paperless government.

Section 5: South and Central America

QUALA SA, COLOMBIA
Gold Award, South and Central America. Nominated by PECTRA Technology, USA

Quala, a multinational mass-consumption corporation dedicated to the production and commercial distribution of food, implemented a technology plan which included the adoption of a process management philosophy and the incorporation of a BPM tool to gain agility in front of market changes and greater scalability in the operations of: logistics, human resources, promotions and prices, with the same organizational structure. The BPM project allowed for integration of all the members of the value chain associating tasks from over 500 users in six Core processes. Time reduction (-250%) and a productivity increase (145%) stand out among the main benefits in human resources processes and expense reduction in the purchase of materials (USD 55,000 monthly).

Section 6 Appendix

AWARD WINNERS AND NOMINATORS CONTACT DIRECTORY

FURTHER READING, ASSOCIATIONS,

Guest Chapters

Primitives and Style: A Common Vocabulary for BPM across the Enterprise

Dennis Wisnosky, Business Mission Area Chief Architect & CTO, ODCMO, US DoD and Linus Chow, Oracle, USA

The US Department of Defense (DoD) is leading the way in the Federal Government for Architecture-driven Business Operations Transformation. A vital tenet for success is ensuring that business process models are based on a standardized representation, thus enabling the analysis and comparison of end to end business processes. This will lead to the re-use of the most efficient and effective process patterns (Style Guide), comprised of elements (Primitives), throughout the DoD Business Mission Area (BMA).

A key principle in DoD Business Transformation is its focus on data ontology. The Business Transformation Agency (BTA), under the purview of the Deputy Chief Management Officer (DCMO), has been at the forefront of efforts to develop a common vocabulary in support of business enterprise interoperability through data standardization. The use of Primitives and re-use of patterns will reduce the construction cost, duplication and waste of building and maintaining enterprise architectures. By aligning The Department of Defense Architecture Framework 2.0 (DoDAF 2.0) with Business Process Modeling Notation 2.0 (BPMN 2.0) and partnering with Industry, the BTA is accelerating the adoption of these standards to improve government agility.

Organizations struggle with understanding and aligning their business activities with departmental, management, and enterprise processes. As standards in technology and methodology have evolved, it provides opportunities to solve this dilemma.

Figure 1.1: Making sense of the Enterprise is not easy

The US DoD is arguably one of the largest and most complex organizations in the world today. The Secretary of Defense is responsible for a half-trillion dollar enterprise that is roughly an order of magnitude larger than any commercial corporation that has ever existed. DoD estimates that business support activities—the Defense Agencies and the business support operations within the Military Departments—comprise 53% of the DoD enterprise.

A Small Slice of the As-Is

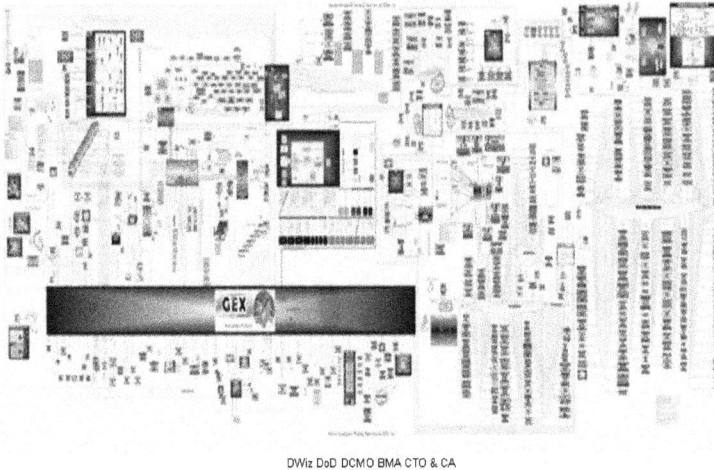

DWiz DoD DCMO BMA CTO & CA

Figure 1.2: A Small Slice of DoD Enterprise Complexity

There is enormous pressure on the US DoD to manage its processes and information in real time mission critical scenarios. The growth in data transactions are increasing exponentially, and will continue to grow.

2025 SOA Forecast: >1,000 Billion Transactions / Hour

Generation	Period	Missions for National Security Systems	Interoperability: Number of Data Sources
1	1955 - 1975	Automate Separate Applications	100
2	1975 - 1995	Automate Separate Processes	1,000
3	1995 - 2005	Integrate Processes within a Function	100,000
4	2005 - 2015	Integrate Functions within an Organization	10 Million
5	2015 - 2020	Innovate Processes As Needed	1 Billion
6	2025 -	Sense and Respond	1,000 Billion

DWiz DoD DCMO BMA CTO & CA

Figure 1.3: Estimated SOA Transaction Growth

The DoD and the Intelligence Communities (IC) share these challenges and are leveraging Service Oriented Architecture (SOA) to transform the way they operate. It is the most efficient way they can meet the ever changing mission and keep up with the growth in collaboration and interoperability requirements.

"The DoD and IC share a vision for a services-based environment that leverages technologies to provide access to information and business processes, and interoperable infrastructure and standards to enable discovery, availability and trust." DoD Memorandum from the Assistant Director of National Intelligence, Chief Information Officer, and the Assistant Secretary of Defense for Networks and Information Integration, Chief Information Officer, Subject: Department of Defense (DoD) and Intelligence Community (IC) Commitment to an Interoperable Services-Based Environment, dated July 13, 2007.

DWiz DoD DCMO BMA CTO & CA

Figure 1.4: Net-Centric Strategy

SOA provides a technology platform to enable an enterprise services environment, but it does not solve ability to understand and align all the processes across the organization. As a result, the use of Primitives and development of a DoD BMA Enterprise Common Vocabulary can be considered game changing innovations.

If we can precisely state requirements and precisely describe data/services, we will be able to find them and know how to use them to facilitate Integration and Interoperability. We must describe both the data/services and requirements with enough precision to accomplish the goal.

To accomplish this we can use Business Process Modeling Notation (BPMN)/Primitives for business mission descriptions and OWL and RDF for domains, services, data, capabilities and requirements descriptions.

Other Disciplines Can Do It!

Not This

But This:

Resistor symbol

Capacitor symbol

This agreed upon representation of electrical engineering allows a common understanding...

Primitives!

DWiz DoD DCMO BMA CTO & CA

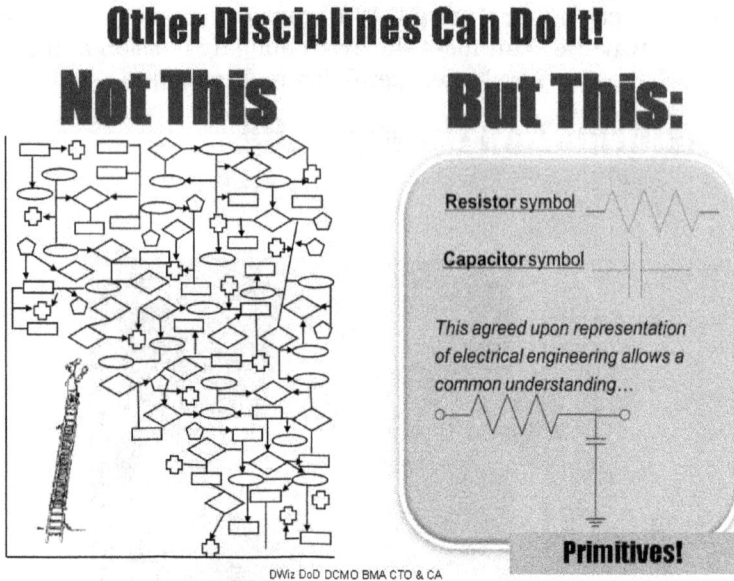

Figure 1.5: Primitives provide a standard representation that all can understand

Building Common Vocabularies

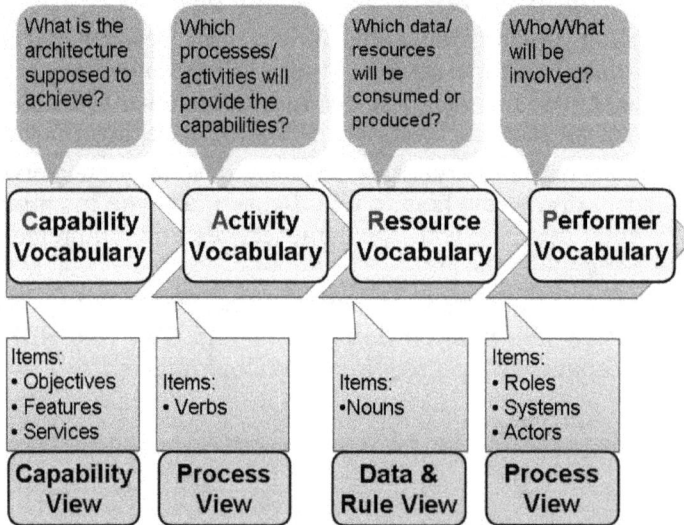

What is the architecture supposed to achieve?

Which processes/ activities will provide the capabilities?

Which data/ resources will be consumed or produced?

Who/What will be involved?

| Capability Vocabulary | Activity Vocabulary | Resource Vocabulary | Performer Vocabulary |

Items:
• Objectives
• Features
• Services

Items:
• Verbs

Items:
•Nouns

Items:
• Roles
• Systems
• Actors

| Capability View | Process View | Data & Rule View | Process View |

DWiz DoD DCMO BMA CTO & CA

Figure 1.6: Common Vocabulary Enables Enterprise Visibility & Understanding

Using Primitives and a Common Vocabulary allows sharing and collaboration without confusion and misinterpretation. It can be likened to sheet music written in the US and then played in a concert in Germany. The musician can play the song without misunderstanding or having to ask for clarification from the song writer.

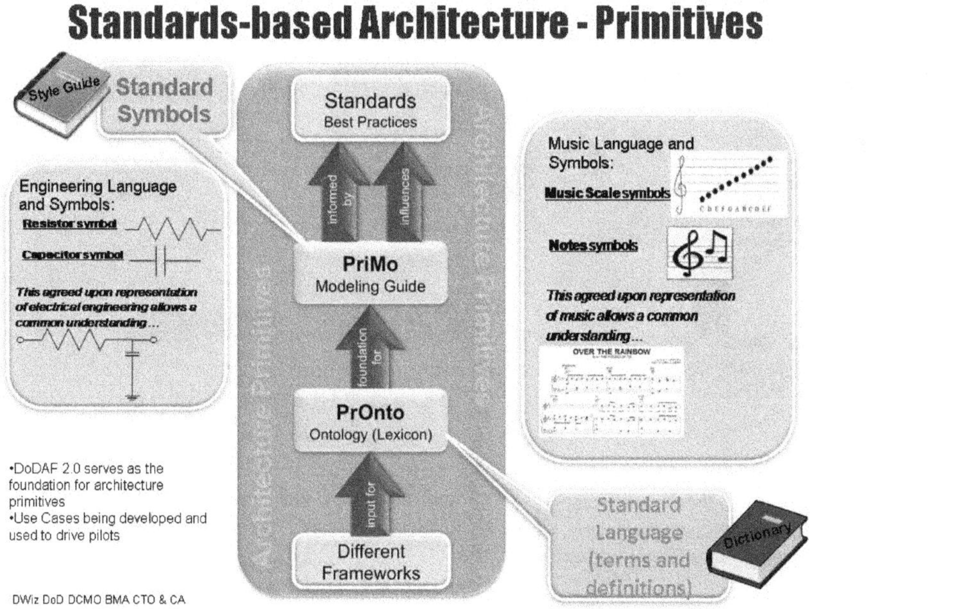

Standards-based Architecture - Primitives

Figure 1.7: Instilling a Standards-based Architecture using Primitives and a Common Vocabulary

The standards bodies and vendor communities are taking notice of the US DoD's thought leadership and see the strategic value of this program.

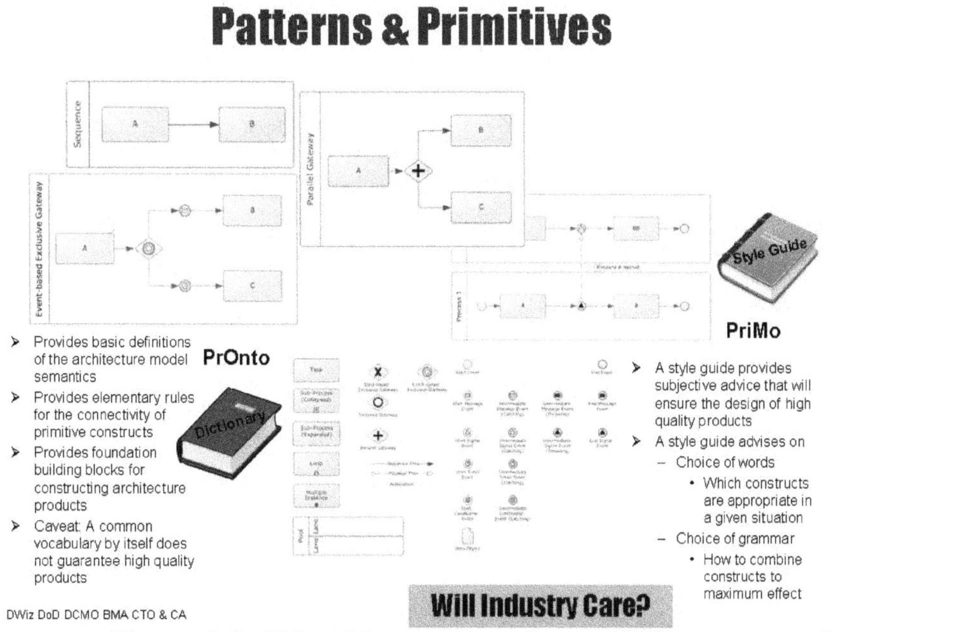

Patterns & Primitives

Figure 1.8: Object Management Group (OMG) manages the BPMN 2.0 standard

The OMG selected DoD Primitives to be included in the BPMN 2.0 conformance class. Also, Oracle, in addition to already supporting BPMN 2.0 in its BPM product, has also agreed to support this vision and specific DoD requirements in its product roadmap.

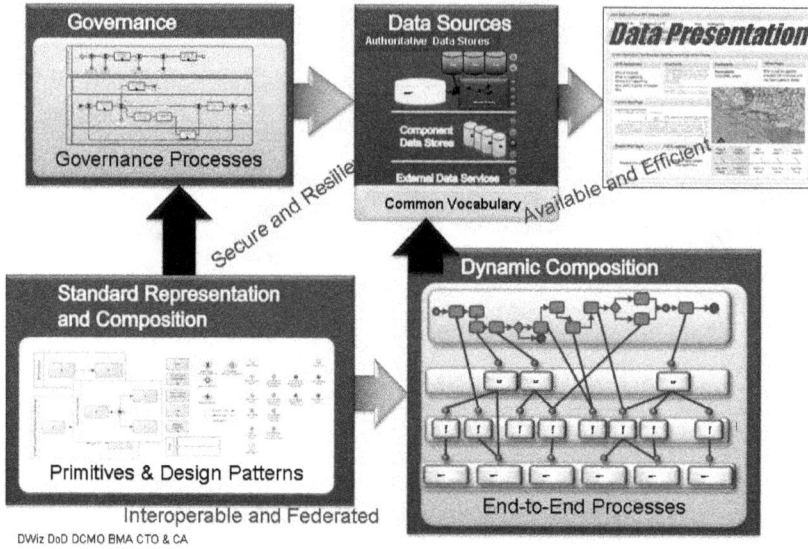

Figure 1.9: Now all the pieces fit together

This initiative is extremely well received as a path toward a more modern, efficient and effective enterprise, especially by the government. Presented and published at many conferences and leading publications, this strategic DoD initiative is gaining momentum not only DoD-wide, but also across organizations world-wide. With OMG and Oracle on-board, the DoD is rapidly moving from concept to reality.

For more information on the DoD BMA Primitives and Enterprise Common Vocabulary efforts visit:

http://www.bta.mil/products/bea_7_0/BEA/html_files/federation.html

Transform Business Processes Through Business Analytics

Clay Richardson, Forrester Research, USA

If you're reading this, odds are you're either knee deep implementing an enterprise-wide BPM program, or you're exploring the potential impact and value of standing up a BPM program for your organization. If neither of these apply, then maybe you're just bored and figured, why not learn about a new and exciting topic. Regardless which bucket you fall into, at some point you'll come face-to-face with BPM's multiple-personality disorder.

This is a conversation I've been having more and more with business process professionals. Some define "business process management" as a management discipline, while others define BPM as a technology. And still, others define BPM as a capability for transforming the culture of an organization. Most BPM experts—including yours truly—agree that BPM is broad enough to house all three of these paradigms. However, I'm always amazed to see the knock-down, drag-out fights that take place over three simple words: "What is BPM?"

Before proceeding any further, it's probably a good idea to share Forrester's official definition of BPM:

> "Business process management (BPM) is a discipline that focuses on continuous
> improvement of end-to-end, cross-functional mission critical business processes."

Ultimately, it's safe to say, BPM means different things to different people. It all depends on your perspective and the internal business issues you're trying to tackle. The one thing that all process professionals—novice and expert alike—agree on is the "improvement" imperative that forms the foundation of BPM. When I'm refereeing—or more often when I'm teeing up—a heated debate on "What Is BPM", I always see heads shake in agreement that "improvement" is an essential ingredient for BPM, no matter which process approach is being followed. And once agreement is reached on "improvement", these conversations then focus on the role "analytics" plays in driving process improvement activities.

Although "analytics" is the new term du jour in the business technology world, it really has become the glue that ties the different BPM perspectives together. And for good reason: analytics support better analysis and also form the basis of insight on how best to improve business processes. It's fair to say that without analytics, it would be time consuming and painful to identify and carry out process improvement.

In 2008, Forrester published a report highlighting the pivotal role analytics plays in driving optimization efforts. In this visionary report, authored by Forrester analysts Boris Evelson, Colin Teubner, and John Rymer, we outlined how the convergence of business rules, business process management, and business intelligence disciplines would help companies respond quickly to rapidly changing business conditions[i]. This convergence, coined as the "Three B's", painted a future where:

- BPM automates flows of work and information –
- Analytics help drive business processes –
- Business rules automate key process decisions –

- Business intelligence powers optimization—

I can already see you shaking your head saying "What's so visionary about this? Businesses have been doing this for a while now." The key here is that these activities have typically been done separately in silos—where one group may emphasize business rules and process automation, and another group might emphasize process automation and business intelligence. Here, we're saying to truly reap the benefits of optimization it really requires all three of these disciplines—business process management, business rules management, and business intelligence—to come together and work seamlessly.

However, when the "Three B's" report was published, business process professionals faced many hurdles in leveraging analytics across these three areas to drive process improvement. The most obvious hurdle was that many teams still buried their processes, policies, and business rules in custom application code—making it almost impossible to mine for process analytics.

Another barrier for the "Three B's" at the time was the lack of standards for defining analytics across BPM, BI, and BRE environments. I recall one process professional's experience meeting with his company's BI team for the first time and commenting "I have no idea how we're going to bring these two worlds together!" While this process professional saw the need and mandate for business process and business intelligence to co-exist, he wrestled with defining metrics and standards for bridging the gaps between his firms BI, BPM, and BRE environments.

In addition to the hurdles mentioned above, technology vendors offered little in the way of a combined framework for tying analytics to process improvement, business intelligence, and business rules initiatives. So most teams, if they tried to blaze a trail towards the "Three B's", were left stuck developing custom integration across these three environments—which was costly, time consuming, and risky.

Recently, another Forrester analyst, James Kobielus, and I joined forces to revisit what's changed since the "Three B's" report was published. Our primary focus was to identify whether many of the hurdles to the "Three B's" had been removed and we also explored how teams are applying the "Three B's" as part of their standard methodology for process optimization.

At Forrester's Spring 2010 Information Technology Forum, James and I joined two additional Forrester analysts, Craig Le Clair and Boris Evelson (one of the original authors of the "Three B's" research) in panel discussion to highlight what's changed since the report was published in 2008. We highlighted key trends and themes that make the "Three B's" more accessible to business process professionals, including:

- **Never let a good recession go to waste.** The recession highlighted the need for organizations to develop more dynamic environments that could sense and respond to rapid change. While most organizations knew they needed more agile business environments, the recession accelerated the shift to embrace analytics as a foundation to drive process improvement, business intelligence, and business rules activities.
- **Steady consolidation and convergence of key technologies.** Over the last two years, we've seen significant consolidation and convergence across business process management, business rules, and business intelligence market. Now, leading stack vendors, such as IBM and Oracle offer comprehensive suites that cover BPM, BI, and BRE environments. And, they're working hard to deliver unified offerings that leverage the same

analytics and standards across all three areas—in the end, this will appear seamless to business process professionals and business stakeholders.

- **Increased focus on process quality and data quality.** Before teams can trust the insights offered up by analytics, they first must trust the underlying data and business processes. Forrester highlighted this as a major challenge for business process professionals in a 2009 report that focused on the connection between process quality and data quality[ii]. Teams are beginning to understand the important link between BPM and MDM, which is essential to improve the quality of automated decisions executed by business rules and manual decisions based on business intelligence.

Additionally, during the panel discussion, we highlighted specific patterns we seeing for customers adopting the "Three B's" within their environments. Based on conversations with process professionals, we've identified three dominant patterns for using analytics to transform business processes.

The first pattern we identified is "predictive process analytics." In this pattern, we're seeing teams leverage a unified "Three B's" environment to detect specific process-related patterns and to automatically implement business rules changes that impact how the process executes. This is a common scenario we're seeing used in the insurance space. While insurers already used analytics for fraud detection, some insurers are taking this one step further to flag potentially fraudulent claims in real-time while the agent is on the phone gathering information from the person filing the claim. This connects BPM, BRE, and BI to highlight the probability that the claim is fraudulent as the information is being gathered.

The second "Three B's" scenario we're seeing teams adopt is around "automated process discovery." This involves mining existing application data for process metrics to better understand business processes that are buried across multiple applications and legacy environments. Using this approach, teams are able to glean key process analytics without conducting lengthy process modeling and analysis exercises. In some ways, this approach short-circuits the traditional approach to "AS-IS" modeling, since the model is literally generated based on existing application data. One team we spoke with uncovered hidden insights into their real process challenges by showing team members how the actual process was executing through different underlying legacy applications.

And finally, we're seeing business process professionals leverage analytics to deal with unstructured and ad-hoc business processes. For most business process professionals these types of processes are very difficult to get their hands around—literally. Unstructured processes are impossible to model and are often exceptions that must be handled at run-time. But process professionals also realize that allowing these unstructured processes to be handled at run-time introduces the possibility of losing valuable insight into how the overall process is executing. Leading BPM teams are using analytics to keep tabs on execution of unstructured business processes and provide management with insight on how these processes are executing. Analytics are also used to alert users when SLA's or KPI's are not being met for unstructured activities.

While we're seeing more teams leverage analytics and the "Three B's" still more work needs to be done. At the conclusion of our panel presentation, I walked away asking myself what's still missing to take this—the convergence of BPM, BRE, BI—to the next level. The key ingredients are there: The technology is now in place, some standards are coming into play, and the enterprise has the proper motivation to embrace analytics and the "Three B's". In order to take full advantage of the "Three B's" process professionals will need methodologies that support best practice for bringing together analytics with BPM, BRE, and BI activities.

This is the next phase of the "Three B's" that we're focused on at Forrester. We've already identified some early key best practices, including:

- **Develop shared glossary of performance metrics.** Often, BI and BPM teams work together to identify key metrics and performance measure that both are tracking. However, very few of these teams turn this into a shared glossary that can be used by both teams to establish performance reporting standards for both initiatives. In leading teams, we're seeing an emphasis on developing a common vocabulary for performance metrics that is shared across BI and BPM environments.

- **Empower business users with self-service analytics.** For the most part, analytics has remained the domain of data architects, report writers, and business intelligence experts. However, some organizations are delivering self-service analytics to front-line workers. These self-service environments allow front-line workers to do deep analysis and generate sophisticated reports based on exposed analytics, allowing them to make better informed and higher-quality decisions.

- **Synchronize BPM and MDM activities.** As previously mentioned, poor data quality leads to poor process quality and poor decisions. To effectively leverage process analytics, business process professionals must first link their BPM and MDM efforts. This keeps upstream and downstream data clean and allows teams to trust process-related and business-related analytics.

No matter how you decide to approach transforming your business processes, you will find analytics and the "Three B's" essential ingredient to success. If you're just starting to explore analytics as part of your BPM program, we recommend starting small by identifying street-level opportunities—for example, maybe a small group of users are interested in robust self-service analytics. Once you have success with the street level opportunity, and then look to expand process analytics to encompass additional teams and other scenarios.

---

i If your enterprise wants to move beyond mere efficiency and productivity improvements for back-office processes and seeks instead to optimize (and even transform) the business, look to the convergence of the "three B's" to serve as the foundation. See May 14, 2008 report "How The Convergence Of Business Rules, BPM, And, BI Will Drive Business Optimization"

ii If you are seeking to reduce complexity and move to optimization, link BPM and MDM activities to gain "one version of the truth" as a key foundation for business process transformation efforts. See September 21, 2009 report "Warning: Don't Assume Your Business Processes Use Master Data"

Transforming Security through Enterprise Architecture and BPM

Christine Robinson, Christine Robinson & Associates, USA

ABSTRACT

This Enterprise Architecture (EA), Business Process Management (BPM), and security approach offers the potential to dramatically transform security on all levels, providing leadership and practitioners alike the tools to benefit from a strategic to a granular level. Security often suffers from cultural barriers, inadequate funding, insufficient attention, bolting it on the back end, lack of understanding, lack of uniformity, and many more ills. This approach enables organizations to plan and implement security throughout an enterprise and beyond using EA frameworks and integrated business process management (BPM) software as an enabler.

An EA/BPM approach provides business-rule driven process automation offering visibility, access across stovepipes, accountability, and transparency into security operations according to a need to know. We can truly cut across stovepipes to see the composite security posture. This applies to governance, planning, design, and operations. Improved security could potentially help facilitate telework and cloud computing adoption. Cyber security, physical security, biometrics, business continuity and disaster recovery, and more can benefit from rule-driven process automation that provides the ability to automatically anticipate, defend against, and create new processes in real time. We can address some of the unique characteristics of the Next Generation U.S. Airspace, energy, and health care, which are some of the U.S. and world's largest information-sharing environments and integral parts of the country's critical infrastructure.

INTRODUCTION

Security, and particularly cyber security, represents some of the most critical challenges to security from a personal level as well as national and international levels. This is really a people problem. We currently have the skills and technologies today to transform our approach and effectiveness to security. It's how we put this all together. Today, we can capture institutional knowledge in software, manage regulatory and legislative compliance activities, pre-define human and system responses that can anticipate and defend against threats, and offer real time capabilities to modify or create new security processes. Security solutions integrated throughout all the business processes and integrated technologies can provide us far greater power, focus, precision, flexibility, and effectiveness. BPM's proven history of success in other areas provides the precedent for its use for security. We can improve transparency, access, and visibility into operations for leadership and practitioners alike using an EA/BPM approach. Why should security be any different?

SECURITY DEFINED

Security covers a broad spectrum of disciplines. Each segment of security has legions of "specialists" with associated technology solutions often little understood by people in other disciplines. For example, the Transportation Security Agency, responsible for safeguarding U.S. transportation systems, must manage myriad security systems, has a presence at 457 U.S. airports, screens two million people per day, and employs nearly 50,000 security officers. Security requirements cross myriad disciplines, involve many complex processes, and necessitate multiple technology solutions.

The news bombards us with reports of viruses and worms spreading to businesses, grids, networks and households alike. We can identify, capture, and address our vulnerabilities through business rules and processes captured in technology just the same as we can provide case management, emergency management, call center, and other BPM capabilities.

EA AND BPM DEFINED

Enterprise Architecture (EA), simply defined, means all of the business processes and supporting technologies that enable an organization to perform its mission. The Federal Enterprise Architecture (FEA), Department of Defense Architecture Framework (DODAF), federal segment architecture (FSAM), The Open Group Architecture Forum (TOGAF), and other frameworks provide powerful sets of tools with which to assimilate information, draw relationships, and create roadmaps for improvement. These frameworks allow an organization to optimize existing structures, incrementally retire those that are no longer suitable or efficient as they need to be, and build new ones that better enable the organization to succeed and thrive. BPM integrated across stovepipes can become the EA's enabling mechanism.

POTENTIAL BENEFITS OF AN EA AND BPM APPROACH

BPM has proven to be of great value in industry and government. According to the Gartner Group, BPM is becoming more and more often a component of most major IT implementations. An EA/BPM approach can help transform security and EA from necessary evils and compliance exercises into strategic resources. This allows us to capture and define best security practices that may vary widely between organizations, optimize them, standardize across communities of interest, and share proven practices.

An EA/BPM approach can cross organizational boundaries to supply chains, customers, government entities, and others. Specialists can manage highly detailed security processes and leadership can see across the EA, managing security operations more effectively. Building security up-front can help drive out human inefficiency, avoid differences of opinion during critical operations, and reduce or eliminate lag time. BPM can automatically initiate predefined responses to lock down network infrastructure access, direct human resources and other assets, and provide access to systems based on a need to know.

CHALLENGES TO PROVIDING IMPROVED SECURITY

Improving our security has significant challenges. Cultural challenges top the list. Stovepipes, system access, inadequate visibility, secrecy, fear of adverse publicity, insufficient funding, for compliance only, magnitude, and reluctance to share information are just some of many concerns.

OPPORTUNITY TO TRANSFORM SECURITY OPERATIONS THROUGH EA AND BPM

Governance

An EA/BPM approach can help manage conformance to such as the Federal Information Security Management Act (FISMA), Sarbanes Oxley, and the Health Information Portability and Accountability Act (HIPAA) of 1996. For example, one of the leading BPM software packages is used to automate Sarbanes Oxley governance processes for testing and security. Agencies could use BPM to capture and automate the vast number of processes associated with FISMA requirements. This could include everything from automatic notification to interfacing disparate systems and running test scenarios.

Security operations

An EA/BPM approach building security up-front into all the business processes and technologies can enhance both normal operations as well as automatically set in motion contingency operations. EA/BPM can facilitate enterprise security operations with vastly increased transparency and visibility across stove-piped disciplines as different as cyber security to biometrics and identity management. This sets the stage for optimizing, sharing across domains, standardizing, and many other possibilities.

EA/BPM can facilitate information-sharing environments with multiple instances of BPM security in different organizations under a "federated environment." Federated solutions would be especially useful in large information-sharing environments such as the Next Generation U.S. Airspace, energy, and health care where security issues compound exponentially.

Cyber security

Cyber threats can develop quickly and propagate instantly around the world. They can wreak terrible damage to our personal information, economy, intellectual property, government systems, and potentially anything else that is connected to the internet or otherwise accessible. The theft and ransom of 36 million patient prescription records and eight million Commonwealth of Virginia patient records offers a highly publicized example of a cyber threat to a government entity and to a segment of Virginia's population. [1]

An EA/BPM approach could help achieve dramatic improvements on a variety of fronts. Predetermined rules and processes can anticipate and instantaneously respond to cyber threats. Linking up-to-the-minute information coming from the SANS Institute and other sources about new cyber threats could allow BPM to instantly notify personnel to respond to a new threat.

Identity Management and credentialing

AN EA/BPM approach can help provide interoperability, standardization, substantial cost savings, and improved performance for identity management and credentialing. Strong Identity Management and credentialing for transactions over the Internet provide a chain of "trust" foundation for individuals, devices, software code, application servers, and more to offer a few examples for industry and government. We can govern identity management via BPM rule-driven process automation. BPM can capture and manage

---

[1] Thomas Claburn, "Virginia Health Data Potentially Held Hostage," Information Week, (May 4, 2009).

agreements, policies, standards, and technologies to help create a federated environmental where identity credentials become portable between many organizations. For example, the first responder communities can recognize and share credentials with federal agencies and vice versa and the government can also recognize and share credentials with industry partners.

Cryptographic Tokens and Biometrics

Multiple factors of identification increase the probability that a person is really who he or she claims. Established standards, policies and procedures define the proper use and integration of these various technologies, all of which EA/BPM can facilitate. We can achieve "three factor identification" with tokens and biometrics combined.

- Pin codes or passwords provide one-factor authentication.
- Two-factor authentication requires both something one knows such as a pin or password and something one possesses such as a smart card or something one is (biometric).
- Three-factor authentication requires something one knows, something one *has*, **and** something one *is*.

Forensics

Forensics represents another critical aspect of security that is a prime candidate for an EA and BPM approach. Often tremendously backlogged, crime labs perform their functions in similar ways. West Virginia University is presently exploring business transformation for crime labs and EA/BPM could become a key enabler. Crime labs everywhere could potentially benefit from integrated EA/BPM to help facilitate their internal and external processes, without having to reinvent the wheel for every different crime lab. EA/BPM could help save money, improve efficiency, replicate across local, state, and federal levels, and above all, facilitate the testing and availability of reliable forensic evidence. We have a personal and societal stake in prosecuting criminals and protecting the innocent.

AREAS WHERE ENHANCED SECURITY CAN PROMOTE ADOPTION

Telework

Telework requires strict security policies to prevent the loss or theft of critical information, as employees are able to work at a variety of remote locations. EA/BPM could help facilitate telework adoption by defining, capturing, and automating the security rules and processes enabling workers to perform their work at remote locations. The adoption of telework in industry, government, and other areas holds vast implications for our environment, quality of work life, productivity, morale, safety, economy, efficiency, and other potential offshoots.

According to Darren Ash, Chief Information Officer of the Nuclear Regulatory Commission (NRC), NRC has standardized on strict security policies for its teleworkers as much of its data may be sensitive.[2] NRC employees are only allowed to use phone company wireless air cards and does not allow access to public wireless, which can be insecure.

---

[2] Darren Ash, Telework Exchange conference, 8 April 2010

Cloud computing

Security in cloud computing environments is often one of the top concerns. This security approach can help more effectively manage security for cloud computing services. Organizations will need to carefully think through the sensitivity of their information before determining if cloud computing is right for them. For example, sensitive defense and law enforcement information has vastly different security requirements than sales lead information.

ENHANCING SECURITY FOR CRITICAL INFRASTRUCTURE

Information Sharing Environments

We increasingly need to integrate among larger and larger information-sharing environments. For example, the Suspicious Activity Reporting System established after 9/11 and created through participating local, state, federal and international entities, provides information to the law enforcement community. This led to the National Information Exchange Model's common vocabulary for the exchange of information. Security complexity for these large environments expands exponentially. Three of the largest ones with great impact on the U.S. and the world are the Next Generation (NextGen) U.S. Airspace, energy, and health care.

NextGen

NextGen, with a congressional mandate to place all U.S. airspace operations over net-centric operations by 2025, represents the world's largest and one of the most complex information-sharing environments requiring an IT implementation of unprecedented magnitude. NextGen is key to U.S. economic prosperity and continued dominance in international aviation.

Representatives from multiple agencies work together at the Joint Program Development Office (JPDO) to oversee the development of everything from the commercial airspace, homeland defense, military defense, commercial interests, and more, all with varying levels of criticality and needs for security.

"NextGen has some unique security requirements that are much more complex than other types of environments," according to Patty Craighill, who is in charge of overseeing the guidelines for developing all of NextGen net-centric operations. "Our stakeholder community extends from public to private sector, across security domains, and warrants special protections for data types such as law enforcement, intelligence, and privacy data."[3]

Health Care

Health care represents another of the U.S. largest information-sharing environments with stringent security requirements at all levels. We must assure that health care information doesn't fall into the wrong hands, yet make it available to those who need access to the information. Electronic health care records could help prevent dangerous or even fatal drug interactions, share information about pre-existing conditions, provide a composite history of health care information available to individuals throughout their lifetimes, and provide the health care community a vast research knowledge base.

An EA/BPM approach to health care could accelerate the gains in health care modernization and provide many more individual and collective bene-

---

[3] Patricia Craighill, Personal interview, 7 April 2010.

fits. BPM can help direct and manage the workflow for all of the security requirements to include managing individual patient data, satisfying legal and regulatory requirements, and helping manage health care systems on a larger basis for hospitals, local and other jurisdictions, health care networks, government, and many others. For enterprising organizations that develop them, EA/BPM models of varying purposes and sizes could be replicated, shared, packaged, and sold across the country and around the world to help us realize advantages from an individual to a national or even international basis.

Energy

Energy represents yet another one of the most critical and most vulnerable aspects of our critical infrastructure. In addition to monumental physical security required to secure nuclear and other utility systems, our energy infrastructure depends upon computer systems and the Internet. This includes utilities, the Department of Energy (DOE) environmental cleanup efforts, protecting nuclear facilities and nuclear materials around the world, scientific advancement, developing wind and solar power, and vastly more.

Some people believe that hackers caused the Northeast blackout and, whether it is true or not, the potential exists to cause immense damage by attacking our energy critical infrastructure. Cyber criminals who hack into our energy systems could wreak havoc, causing loss of life and economic chaos as has occurred during major outages.

An EA/BPM Approach for Security Holds Vast Potential

Our personal security, our homeland security, and national defense are at undue risk unless we adopt new and better ways of approaching security such as described in this EA/BPM approach. EA/BPM offer the framework and the means through existing practices and technologies to develop far more effective and repeatable solutions for providing security on all levels. Because of BPM's proven history in business and government we know that we can apply this to security. We can capture institutional knowledge in software, manage governance activities, predefine rule-driven responses that can anticipate and defend against a security threat, and provide real-time responses to new and different threats.

This approach can provide leadership and practitioners alike with the powerful means to achieve transparency, access, and visibility into operations to vastly improve our security capabilities. We can use BPM to integrate across stovepiped security disciplines with particular benefit to three of the largest information-sharing environments with critical impact on the nation: NextGen, health care, and energy. This holds true for physical security, cyber security, and any other type of security.

Acknowledgment

A major contributor to this paper, Daniel Turissini, founder and CEO of Operational Research Consultants, and Christine's co-author of another paper about security, also provided greatly expanded expertise and information in their joint paper featured in the "2010 BPM & Workflow Handbook."[4]

---

4. Published by Future Strategies Inc., Florida, USA. July 2010

Section 1

Europe

Faculty of Manufacturing Technologies—TUKE, Slovakia

Finalist, Europe
Nominated by Czestochowa University of Technology, Poland

1. EXECUTIVE SUMMARY / ABSTRACT

Faculty of Manufacturing Technologies as part of Technical University of Košice has recently decided to modernize library services through the use of advanced technologies and methods of work with a focus on providing specialized information resources. In our solution we have integrated a commercial automated library system CLAVIUS with RFID technology that improves the flaws of the traditional paper card and the bar code. As known RFID tags embedded in books enable automatic management of library items within libraries, but other possibilities to automate workflows in a library are more or less uncovered. This study focuses on the process-based library service modularization at the conceptual stage of development and adoption of RFID technology for library process automation in the above mentioned project.

2. OVERVIEW

The Technical University of Kosice (TUKE) was established in 1952 and during its history and up to now has been recognized as an important provider of higher education in the Slovakia. In addition to a small Faculty of Arts the University offers a wide range of technical disciplines in eight faculties. In addition TUKE has several university-wide departments, namely Languages, Social Sciences, Physical Education, and Engineering Pedagogy. The university is located in Kosice, the most important city in eastern Slovakia. It is of note that this region has one third the GDP per capita of western Slovakia. TUKE is a public university and the second largest technical university in Slovakia. Business process management technologies that were implemented from top to bottom at our University are basically widely adopted also across our Faculty.

The previous library service within our faculty was based on small central library without any information system. Usually faculties in bigger universities do not establish own libraries because this self-academic service is ordinarily centralized into large libraries for all faculties. As mentioned above, our faculty is dislocated from the university campus and is situated in another town. Because faculty library development evidently fell behind the central library progress, the issue regarding its continuation has become topical. Our team from Manufacturing Management Department came with a good idea to revitalise of the faculty library and has written a project proposal on "Increase education and R&D quality at Faculty of Manufacturing Technologies by establishment of alternative specialized library" within the framework of the national fund call, which was focused on education and research support by use of innovative approaches. Subsequently, based on project evaluation report, our project proposal met with a positive response and an approval for financing. Thanks to that we could implement our intention to build up modern small library utilizing recent management concepts including exploitation of information and identification technologies. Duration oft the project was set up from April to October 2009.

3. BUSINESS CONTEXT

No everyone agrees with the position of University-as-business firm. Moreover, most faculties do not agree with the point to define students as customer of education, since it refers to assumption that "customer is always right" [1]. On the other hand it is obvious that education institutions should have to be competitive, and it also means to be student-oriented rather than discipline-oriented. One of conditions for achieving such goals is to provide to students and teachers high-quality library services. Moreover, university library systems might be respected as a core institution activity, because scholarly processes are changing rapidly in learning and research. In accord with this contention, we have embarked to on a project to modernize our library system.

There were also several additional motivations behind this initiative. Firstly, it was a generally known fact that information searching approaches used by students were changed. Expectations are that all library services should be represented on the website. Accordingly, library users including students are increasingly expecting workflow-related systems for searching and discovery. Secondly, a central university library (UL) of our University is situated out of the affiliated residence of the Faculty of Manufacturing Technologies and physical connection between the Faculty and UL requires using time wasted travelling. Third reason for a motivation was the reality that, our team at the Manufacturing Management Department has recently established RFID laboratory to adopt this automatic identification (Auto ID) technology to manufacturing processes. Because RFID (Radio Frequency Identification) technology is frequently used in library management systems, it was strong challenge to expand our research activity also to this area.

3.1 Approach to the business process management

To describe our approaches, we will firstly concentrate our attention on business process management concept development. Naturally, utilization of business process modelling methodologies varies depending on a particular purpose or activity. After analysing business content we decided to apply modified IDEF (Integration Definition) modelling technique [2]. There are several types of IDEF models. The most familiar are IDEF0 diagrams that model the tasks performed by an organization at a high level of abstraction. Process mapping by this technique begins with the description the system as a whole at the highest level and then decomposing this model level by level to describe each of the sub-systems within the system hierarchy. The IDEF0 notation was standardized in 1993 by the National Institute of Standards and Technology of the USA [3]. Use of this standard permits the construction of models comprising system functions (activities, actions, processes, and operations), functional relationships, and data (information or objects) that support process integration and consistency.

Workflow models in the so called modified IDEF0 version we classified to the three basic diagrams:
- System diagram,
- Sequence flow diagrams-describing content of top–level processes,
- State transition diagrams-describing content of sub-processes.
- System diagram that models the structure of top-level processes performed by an organization at highest level of abstraction.

Subsequently, relations between them and the enterprise environment are specified. The environment is represented in a System diagram by External entities, with which the system communicates, while their content is not a subject of analysis in the following steps. Even though, further these relations are analysed.

They usually represent the initial source of sequence flows, or their end consumer. Fig. 1 shows System diagram describing real model of our library named „Library of Manufacturing Technologies and Management" (further only LMTM, available at http://www.kniznica.tk/.)

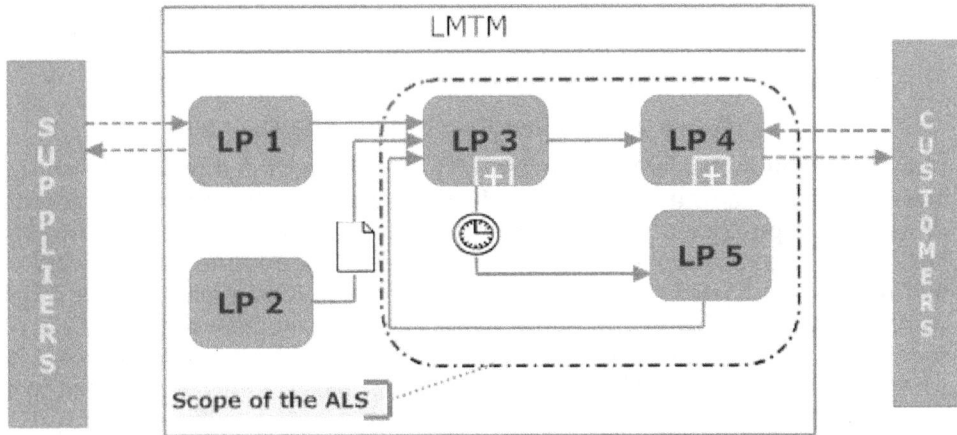

Figure 1. System diagram

Library system in this diagram is represented by four autonomous processes (called also as parent processes with accordance to BPMN modelling and reference guide [4]), which are:

- LP 1 Acquisition of library fond units
- LP 2 Data structure definition of library documents
- LP 3 Cataloguing
- LP 3 Providing of library services
- LP 4 Revision of library fond

Three of library processes (LP 3, LP 4, and LP 5) are automated through automated library system CLAVIUS. The library information system (LIS) is able to manage also library process LP1, but in this time we don't capitalize its all functions. Speaking about the LIS, only few basic characteristics are perhaps needful to summarize.

Automated library system CLAVIUS has been developed in 1998 by the company LANius which will be described at the end of this case study. In present time this system is widely implemented in many libraries in Czech Republic and Slovakia (see http://www.CLAVIUS.cz/odkazy.htm). Library system core application works on the Windows operating system and interacts with SQL database and web server. Its main advantage that determinate our selection decision is that it has potential to cope with radio frequency identification (RFID) technology which is main innovative element of LMTM library processes automation.

External environment of LMTM consists of library suppliers (book vendors) and customers who are students and teachers of our faculty.

Figure 2 which represent second level of diagram models, describes structure of library process LP2. This structure consists of the following workflow steps:

- LP 3.1 Data dictionary management
- LP 3.2 RFID tags printing
- LP 3.3 Tagging of library units
- LP 3.4 Moving of library units into shelving storage.

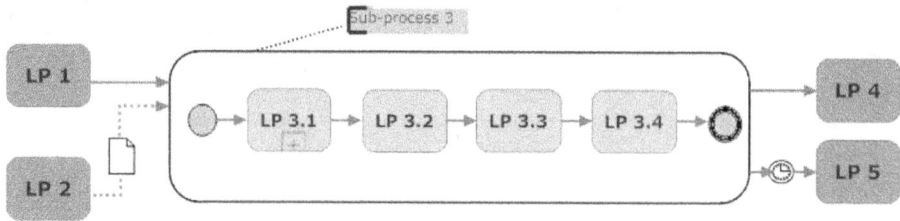

Figure 2 Sequence flow diagram of the LP 3

Due to the reality that library process LP3.1 is the most compounded from sub-processes depicted in above diagram, further content of the process is described in Fig.3. The purpose of this procedure is transforming data of physical library item (either a book, magazine, CD, or video) to the library automation system. Its first step is automated verification whether given unit is already present in the database system of Slovak National Library and in databases of CLAVIUS software users. If yes, relevant data are copied and applied for creation of library item document record (LIDR). Library item document record can be generated in five formats after search (Fig. 4):

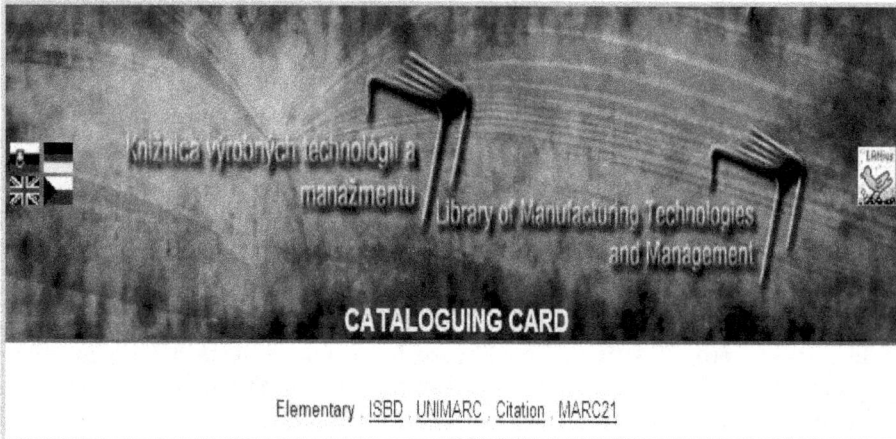

Figure 3. State transition diagram of the Library Process 3.1

- Elementary document record,
- ISBD (International Standard Bibliographic Description),
- UNIMARC (Universal machine-readable catalogue),
- Citation,
- MARC21.

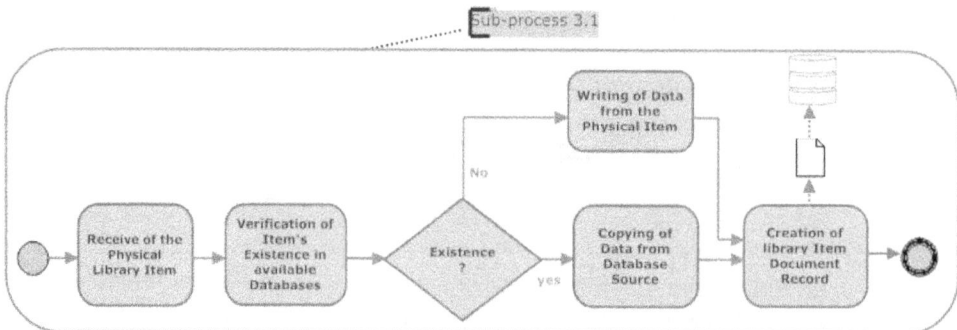

Figure 4. Menu of alternative formats for Library item document records

From the all autonomous library processes, LP 4 process can be considered as the most decisive from a user viewpoint. Its decomposition is shown in the Fig. 5. In this process the following important workflow sequences can be identified:

- Client registration
- Searching of library documents and identification of availability by clients either through internet or the touch terminal
- Checking item availability at Google Books from Elementary Catalogue Card format (it is directly visible without clicking on the link)
- Sending the order to the librarian through library system
- Change of book availability to state "Out now" in the automated library system
- Completing of physical library items by librarian for clients
- Feedback announcement to client by e-mail (in case if needed)
- Reading of client's RFID card
- Linking of client's RFID card number with library document RFID number into ALS.

Library process LP 5 – Revision of Library Fond can be very effectively carried out by use of portable RFID reader/writer. Gathered data from RFID readers regarding a presence of the books are automatically compared against all.

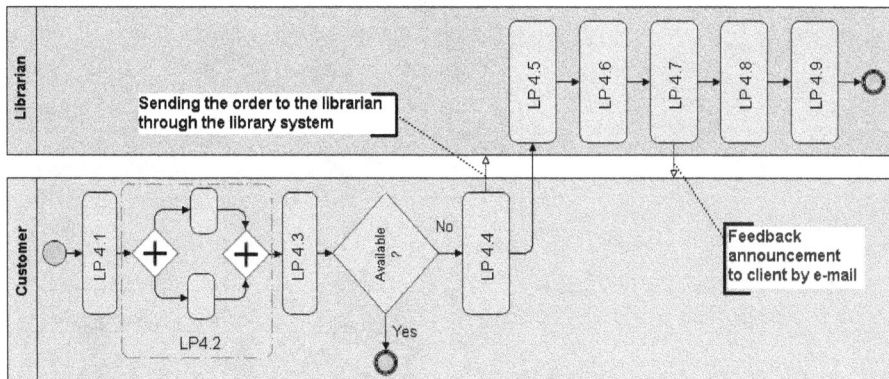

Figure 5. Sequence flow diagram of the library process LP 4

3.2 Description of technical solution

Obviously minimal equipment requirements for implementation of commercial software products are always defined by software vendors. Our aim was to technically equip our library for sustainable development.

Hardware conception of LMTM library system is connected with chosen software platforms like MS Windows server, Linux and applications running on these operating systems as IIS (Internet Information Services), MySQL, CLAVIUS software and proprietary RFID software. The core of the hardware is application server which operates CLAVIUS software. Library document records are stored in MySQL database server. Finally, web server is used in this concept to serve clients by providing access to the database and library document reservation system. In order to enhance the security of stored library document records, the database server is connected to the application server. This information connection flows exclusively through the second network card of application server with just one open port used for communication furthermore secured by password. In case of electricity power failure, servers are supplied by UPS up to one hour running time. After that time, automatic and safe shut down is initiated. When the electric power is again on, all servers turn automatic on. Above mentioned systems and BIOS configuration ensures that no data will be lost by power failures. Beside this, data stored on the hard disks are either mirrored by use of RAID1 mode or parity is shared on all disks in RAID5 mode. This hardware configuration of disks enables hot plug-in and plug-out of defective disks and reduces server off time during the maintenance. Firewall is also inherent part of this configuration which is shown on Fig.6

Beside the servers itself, hardware configuration includes intranet switch, touch terminal for easy access of students to the library system, RFID printer and wireless barcode/RFID reader used for fond revision. Finally RFID readers/writers supplement the whole configuration.

RFID readers in general work in various frequencies, radiation powers and are using different protocols. For our library an 13,56 MHz band readers have been chosen from the following reasons:

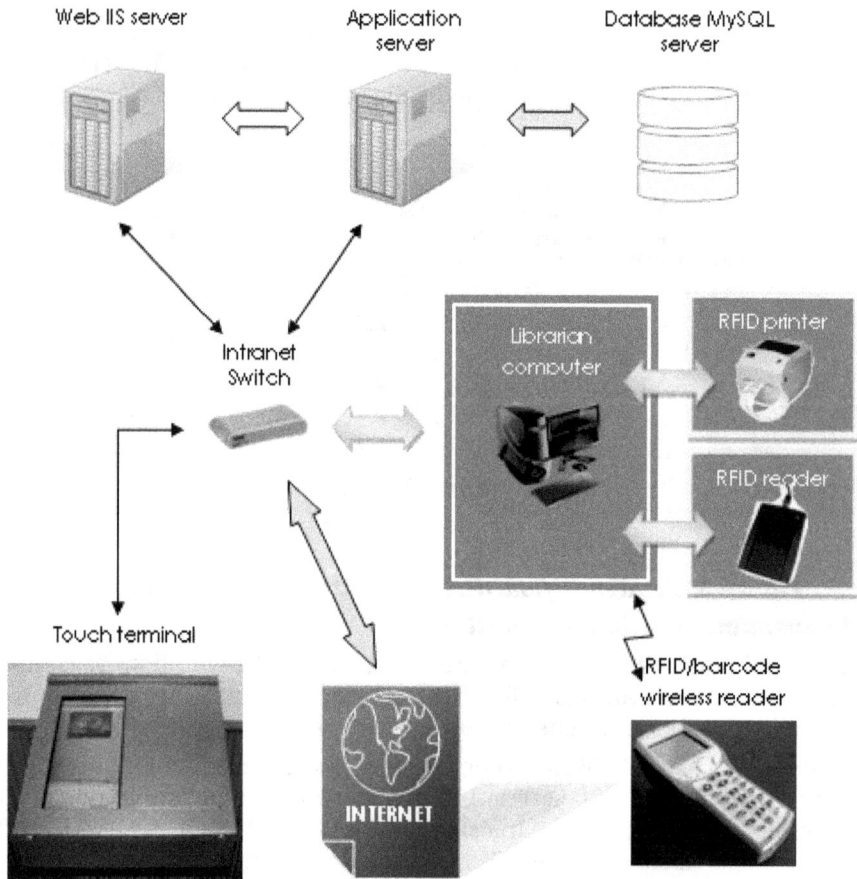

Figure 6. Technical configuration of LMS

- Students and teachers identification cards operate on this frequency
- Tags on this frequency operate up to 10 cm so no accidental tag reads can occur
- Our working team has already enough experiences with this technology since they are RFID laboratory staff members

- This frequency readers and tags are widely spread and are quite cheap
- This readers are already described in ISO14443A
- Proprietary software development could be easier carried out by our staff due to familiarity with 13,56 MHz RFID technology.

4. THE KEY INNOVATIONS

RFID applied in library management system, said in simplified form, provides alternative method of identification technology. Since there is no need for line of sight, RFID rapid read of items making the LMS more users friendly and is able to carry out a wider scope of functions.

4.1 Business innovation

The prevalence of RIFD installations as security systems in libraries reducing antisocial behaviour present only limited potential for benefits. Other effects can be achieved in a number of different ways. Goal of library business is customer orientation and satisfaction. Based on presented solution, now students and teachers have comfortable online access to the library fond either through internet or through the touch terminal that is situated on public accessible faculty place. All information regarding fond and news can be updated in real time. Clients are not discouraged to utilize library services due to waste of their time. To satisfy customer (library client) needs it is essential to have latest books, journals and other information/knowledge sources. This requires continuous searching of financial sources. If library doesn't dispose with modern technical solution it is practically impossible to be successful in this effort. As regards to operational costs, new technical solution does not demand additional finances in compare with previous status.

4.2 Process innovation

Library management sustainability and development requires not only technically oriented solution, but also respecting of so called soft approaches that include process oriented management. Consequently we evenly paid attention to this aspect during architecture design of library system. For this purpose we used approved modelling technique to describe workflows in library system. In previous solution above mentioned aspects have been undertaken.

4.3 Organization of work

Presented solution have enhanced library functionality on one side, on the other didn't demanded higher personal needs. Naturally it was necessary to train existing staff. However staff trainings present common activities that are part of lifelong learning. Furthermore work load of the worker has decreased even if the library fond is currently much bigger. Accordingly after adoption of new work organization, our librarians wouldn't wish to have to revert to the old way of working. Moreover, by documentation of library processes and workflows these work organization is easier repeatable.

5. HURDLES OVERCOME

Adoption of new technology into new function areas is frequently accompanying with unexpected hurdles like in our case. Applied software product doesn't count with the possibility that student or/and teacher card ID could be coupled with yet existing institution database information and automatically used for direct data entry into library registration sheet. In order to automate the process of registration to employ existing institution database information it was necessary to gain access to the University database. This administration process took approximately two months and according by our opinion obstacles was caused by typical behaviour of administration workers to solve not routine tasks.

Another bottleneck during implementation was problem with supplier quality services of RFID components. For instance, the same supplier that delivered us RFID printer, subsequently delivered us tags, but with not compatible frequency with printer. Our explanation of this embarrassment is that given distributor was not technically educated in area of RFID.

6. BENEFITS

Overall, we are convinced that RFID application in our library provides a platform for improving of customer satisfaction and gradual technical enhancement. Even though initial investment seem to be generally higher (in compare with barcode), our experience proved that this solution makes financial savings of operation costs. Savings of initial costs in our case have been achieved mainly thanks to decision to design and implement the workflow solution solely by our internal team. Considering the ubiquity of the barcode in everyday applications companies tend to prefer this type of identification against RFID. Our case proved that in our specific conditions the barcode reading would be at least twice slower and manual identification would be couple of times slower than RFID. Assuming that the rate of growth in the use of RFID by libraries around the world rapidly increases, this identification technology can be seen as a significant tool that enables library managers to transform and modernize their services.

7. THE TECHNOLOGY AND SERVICE PROVIDERS

LANius s.r.o. was founded in 1996 as specialized library Software Company with residence in Czech Republic. Few years later LANius library system software became the most used system in public libraries across the Czech Republic. At the moment this software vendor is successful also in Slovak Republic. More information, available only in Czech Language, can be found at http://www.lanius.cz .

8. REFERENCES

Michael, R.K., Sower, V.E. and Motwani, J. (1997), "A comprehensive model for implementing total quality management in higher education", *Benchmarking for Quality Management & Technology*, Vol. 4 No.2, pp.104-19.

Modrák, V. (2008) Case on Modeling of Manufacturing Systems by Modified IDEF0 Technique. ICEIS International Conference on Enterprise Information Systems, Barcelona, pp. 306-310.

Anon. (1993) Integration Definition for Function Modelling (IDEF0). Draft Federal Information Processing Standards. Publication 183.

White, S. A, and Miers, D. (2008). BPMN Modeling and Reference Guide. Future Strategies Inc., ISBN 978-0-9777-5272-0.

9. CASE STUDY AUTHORS

Vladimír Modrák and Peter Knuth

Homeloan Management Limited (HML), Europe

Silver Award, Europe
Nominated by Lombardi Software, Limited, UK.

1. Executive Summary / Abstract

HML is a financial outsourcing company and the UK's largest mortgage servicer, providing outsourced mortgage administration solutions to over 30 UK and Irish lenders, and operating out of four UK locations – Skipton (North Yorkshire – head office), Padiham (Lancashire), Londonderry (Northern Ireland) and Glasgow. The company was established in 1998 and is a wholly-owned subsidiary of Skipton Building Society. The client portfolio includes some of the largest players in the UK and US financial markets and currently the company is managing in excess of £50bn of assets.

In 2007, HML recognised the need to Improve, Streamline and increase overall control of the processes within the Credit Management area. The key drivers for this were the need to respond quickly to the changing market conditions and the need to maintain focus on regulatory requirements The CREWS Programme was initiated to address these needs alongside the introduction of LEAN techniques.

2. Overview

The CREWS programme objective was to automate repeatable, efficient, consistent Credit Management strategies across the client base. The Programme structure utilized closely integrated business and IT members all working collaboratively towards a common goal. This team worked closely with Lombardi, who implemented the business process management toolset, to ensure a robust and responsive system.

The workflow functionality enables us to model and automate the complex credit management strategies of each of our clients, comprising over 50 different strategies. The tool has 400 business rules, uses 100 data attributes as the basis for its decisions and will be used by over 350 HML credit management consultants.

By moving more capabilities to this world-class platform, the credit management process is streamlined, made more efficient and consistent.

3. Business Context
- The Credit Management function was heavily focussed on manual tasks to drive the collections process.
- Staff had to run reports from the core system and split this work by process area. The reports were exported to excel spreadsheets, manually manipulated and pushed out to staff.
- Report segmentation was also used to identify data to populate outbound calling strategies within the dialler system.
- Operational Management Information was produced using reports and Excel spreadsheets.
- Letter production was equally manual with staff working from lists and manually requesting letters using screens in the core system.

Due to the high degree of manual intervention this opened up risks around human error and the possibility of accounts 'falling through the gaps'.

4. THE KEY INNOVATIONS

4.2 Business

Engagement with HML's client base has significantly improved by working closely with them to understand their Credit Management strategies in detail and how these translate into process models.

4.3 Process

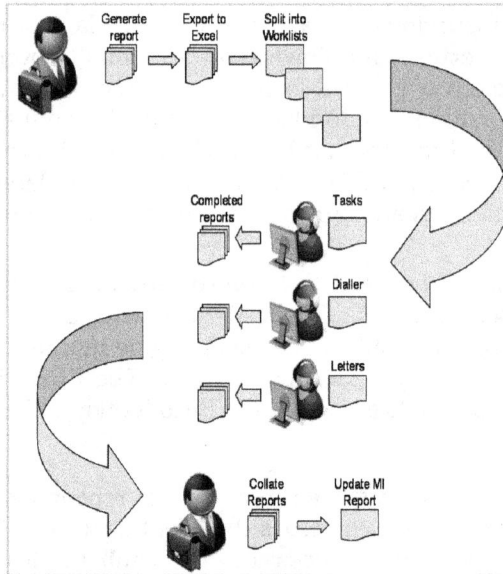

Before

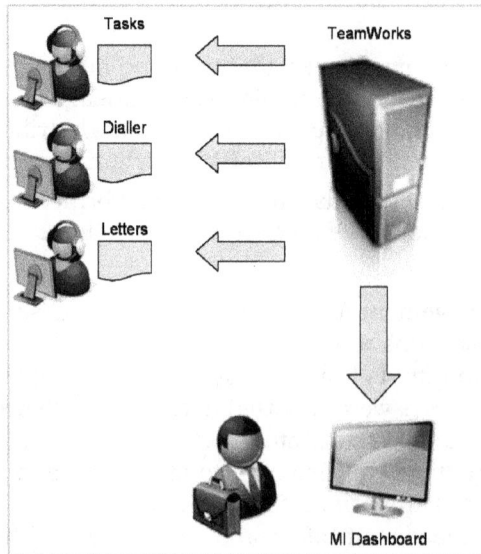

After

4.4 Organization

- Staff training is now much easier, thanks to the way in which process are clearly defined, and the use of 'coaches' to guide staff through work items based on the specific task they are working.
- By automating non value add manual processes such as the identification and distribution of work items, staff have more time to liaise with customers to achieve positive results. This has therefore resulted in an increase in staff morale and overall engagement.
- Managers now have access to real time dashboard reporting which gives an instant view of key data such as SLA reporting. This enables resource allocation based on work levels.

5. HURDLES OVERCOME

Management

The key management challenge was the timescales set for deployment and roll out to our clients. Having a single team enabled dedicated Subject Matter Experts from the business, IT and Testing resource to fulfill our clients expectations.

Business

The key business challenge was increasing their understanding and accepting that the current process had real scope for optimization. Also, it was necessary to dispel the myth that BPM is a replacement for staff. To counter these issues, change champions were nominated from the impacted areas. They were provided with detailed information and involved in the business readiness activity, which in turn aided operational buy in at the user level.

Organization Adoption

With CREWS being the first implementation of BPM technology in the organization, a centre of excellence was created. This is made up of modelers, developers and testers following documented best practice and strict standards.

At a high level, the organization has embraced BPM and sees it as an enabler for process change, control and efficiency. This provides flexibility in resource deployment to manage workloads.

6. BENEFITS

6.1 Cost Savings

The CREWS project has achieved savings of 22 FTE's due to the elimination of manual tasks. This translates to a cost saving of £400,000 per year.

6.2 Time Reductions

Speed of change to strategies is key to HML's clients in the current market place. CREWS has provided a platform to quickly manage this change without the need for lengthy development, test and deployment.

6.3 Increased Revenues

HML's Clients benefit from a number of features:

Due to the elimination of manual intervention, HML can guarantee greater adherence to client strategies in terms of how to manage their assets. This means that HML has been able to eliminate the type of errors that arise from manual intervention, and ensure consistency and accuracy, making sure that all borrowers are treated in accordance with the client's strategies, or those developed through HML's analytics, and within a strict TCF framework.

Elimination of manual intervention also means improved compliance, so that strategies and processing are both effective and fully in accordance with FSA regulations;

Clients benefit from better credit management results, with the aim of getting pre-litigation accounts to 'cure' – get back to a point where there are no arrears. Automation leaves our consultants more time to liaise with customers and field counsellors and achieve positive results;

Teamworks offers HML increased flexibility, with the system able to respond quickly to any changes in client strategies by updating the relevant business rule.

7. BEST PRACTICES, LEARNING POINTS AND PITFALLS

7.1 Best Practices and Learning Points

- ✓ Business Sponsorship
- ✓ Robust Change Control
- ✓ Integrated business and IT team is crucial
- ✓ Keep It Small & Simple
- ✓ Select a process that crosses humans and systems
- ✓ Measure the baseline process
- ✓ Speed – How long does the process take
- ✓ Cost – What is the cost of the process
- ✓ Experience – What value does the process bring
- ✓ Involve everyone the process touches
- ✓ Top-level buy-in
- ✓ Appoint a process owner
- ✓ Set Expectations
- ✓ Speed – What time improvements are expected?
- ✓ Cost – What cost reductions will be made?
- ✓ Experience – How will the user experience change?
- ✓ The person responsible for the process outcome has to 'own' the process
- ✓ Ownership is important for collaboration purposes
- ✓ Collaboration takes place when designing the process and within the process
- ✓ Perform a dress rehearsal of the implementation in a controlled 'like for like' test region to increase confidence in the actual implementation process, timescales and flush out last minute bugs.
- ✓ Close partnership with your BPM provider and 3rd party resource providers.

7.2 Pitfalls

- ✗ Know your baseline to enable clear measurement of improvements.
- ✗ Perform meaningful proof of concept and pilot prior to full scale project roll out.
- ✗ Be prepared to manage the flexibility requirements versus the performance requirement. Manage both to arrive at a suitable level of each.

8. COMPETITIVE ADVANTAGES

In an environment where arrears are a rising problem and the FSA frameworks in which to deal with them are increasingly strict, CREWS enables HML to guarantee their clients a consistent service in accordance with TCF, and an approach which they are confident will have the optimum success rate in terms of getting borrowers back on track. HML are so confident in the efficiency of their workflow systems that they offer clients a pay by results pricing structure – whereby clients pay by accounts cured, whereby typically servicers are paid by activity levels.

CREWS is part of the structure that enables HML to say 'our competitors charge on number of accounts in arrears, we charge for number of arrears accounts cured'.

9. TECHNOLOGY

The key elements of the CREWS solution are;

Lombardi Teamworks. This has been used to develop the Credit Management Strategies and fully automates the management of the processes that implement those strategies.

HML's Core System. This is the legacy system which maintains the detail of accounts, takes payments, registers arrears etc.

HML peripheral applications. These handle such actions as sending letters and automatically dialing customers.

These elements have been fully integrated using Web Services, allowing each system to focus on what it does best. The systems exchange information in real time, ensuring that all decisions are made on up-to-the-minute data. The credit management strategies and associated business rules are held in the Teamworks system in the form of Business Process Definitions, allowing users to create and make changes to the strategies using the highly productive and intuitive Teamworks graphical interface. We have also developed a number of key, reusable components in Teamworks, which, combined with the graphical interface, ensure that coding and development effort is kept to a minimum.

The data relating to the position of an account is held in the core system, and is passed, via Web Services to the Teamworks system in real time. The Teamworks system assesses the account and moves it through the relevant strategy, automating actions wherever possible. Many of these actions involve interacting with other HML systems, for example sending a letter, or placing an account into the automatic dialing system – and again the integration has been completely automated using web services. Once in Teamworks, an account will be fully monitored by the system until it is either cured or moves to the litigation stage.

10. THE TECHNOLOGY AND SERVICE PROVIDERS

Lombardi is a leader in business process management (BPM). Our passion for process performance is changing the way companies compete. We offer award-winning BPM technology and services to help our customers, partners and government agencies around the world succeed with their process improvement initiatives by putting "Business First."

Lombardi is behind some of the largest, most successful BPM implementations in the world. Our customers span a wide variety of industries including the automotive, education, energy, financial services, government, healthcare, insurance, manufacturing, retail, services, technology and travel & leisure sectors. For more information, visit www.lombardi.com.

SNS Bank, Netherlands

Silver Award, Europe
Nominated by Red Hat, Netherlands

EXECUTIVE SUMMARY / ABSTRACT

SNS Bank, Netherlands, has made a strategic decision to empower its customers on-line by fully automating its business processes. The ability to automate these service channels is achieved by applying Business Process Management (BPM) techniques to existing selling channels. Both the publicly available and internal processes are being revamped into full scale Straight Through Processing (STP) services. This extreme use of online STP is the trigger in a shift that is of crucial importance to cost-effective banking in an ever turbulent and changing financial world. The key elements used in implementing these goals continue to be Free Open Source Software (FOSS), Service oriented architecture (SOA), and BPM. In this paper we will present an industrial application describing the efforts of the SNS Bank to make the change from traditional banking services to a full scale STP and BPM driven bank that can survive on the Financial Crisis front lines.

OVERVIEW

The Dutch SNS Bank is making a strategic move to automate its support and selling channels to provide its customers with modern on-line services. Realizing that it will take more than just an on-line web shop to excel in the financial world, the bank has also moved to automate many internal processes. The key elements used in implementing these goals are full scale Straight Through Processing (STP) [1] and Business Process Management (BPM) [2].

In this paper we present the efforts made to change from traditional banking services to a full scale STP and BPM driven financial institution during the current world wide Financial Crisis. We begin by clarifying what the various concepts mean to us and why they are of importance to the future of SNS Bank. We will provide some insights into the application of STP with BPM within an open source development environment, discuss the component architecture, take a look at our process modeling steps, examine how we utilized customer testing, and conclude with an overview of some general empirical data. We will present our experiences, both good and bad, in dealing with a large BPM implementation. As can be expected, there will always be challenges to be met when such an expansive shift in strategy is being implemented, and we start our tour of the issues encountered in the project. We will also discuss the brighter side, outlining the positive impact that this project has had in the technical realm. This will leave the reader with a good idea of the challenges involved, hopefully helping in implementing other industry BPM applications. Finally, we look at applying the lessons we have learned to survival on the Financial Crisis front lines.

The application of STP with BPM is not a new phenomenon in the financial industry, with other banks having reported some success with relatively straight forward on-line financial solutions [3, 4]. Some are even dreaming of taking on the more challenging processes within the banking industry, such as mortgage processes [5]. The difference between these types of solutions and the one presented here concerns complexity. We offer the following definitions:

Definition 1 (Business Process Management) Business Process Management concerns aligning business processes to the customers want and needs by applying relevant methods, tools and solutions.

This is a simple and straight-forward look at how we intend to apply BPM within our organization.

Definition 2 (Straight Through Processing) Processing a business transaction automatically, without requiring people to be involved in the process. The purpose of STP is to create efficiency, eliminate mistakes, and reduce costs by having machines instead of people process business transactions.

This definition is in line with most of the definitions we have encountered in the financial world [6, 7, 8]. It will work fine as a beginning definition of how we construct our processes, but we need to refine it a bit for real world financial business processing.

Definition 3 (Full Scale STP) A straight through process (STP) implementation that requires the solution to encompass a wide range of system integration and will include human tasks which embody the complex decision making that automation either cannot legally implement, or is precluded by technical limitations.

We exclude cost as a factor to determining if an implementation is full scale STP or not. We feel that cost, in terms of time, money, or other value risk, is a business concern that is not related to complexity, but rather to some current operational or environmental situation (i.e. budgets, deadline pressures, politics, environment, etc.).

The drive to push for full scale STP with BPM is multifaceted. The leading goals are cost reduction, manpower reduction in business processes, removing potential (human) mistakes, and channel independent processing. Users should experience such processes as transparent, quick, simple, directly usable, and should be able to complete their task in one attempt.

SNS Bank is targeting effective and efficient processing where as much human intervention as possible has been removed. The customer will be kept informed at crucial process steps, communication always being an important factor in customer experience. For the cases that are exceptions or fall out of STP processing, there will be clear and predefined processes to ensure expeditious handling. Last but not least, the entire communication process is as paperless as can be. This encapsulates the SNS Bank's idea of full scale STP processing.

As Heckl and Moormaan [9] concluded "...long term success cannot be achieved without the development of new business ideas, innovative products and services, and customer retention." We believe that such success can only be achieved if BPM techniques are fully integrated. Full scale STP with BPM will continue to be expanded on and implemented throughout the range of products, sales channels, and business processes that affect both customer and customer support. We believe that the time for full scale STP with BPM is now.

BUSINESS CONTEXT

The initial state of the organization was one that took over two weeks to completely process a customer's request for savings products. This article shows the transition from two weeks back to an average of two days to process a new savings product for an existing customer. This was but the first step on the way to automating much of the SNS Bank's internal processes and external selling channels.

The driving motivation for initiating the change program was cost reduction, manpower reduction in business processes, removing potential (human) mistakes, and channel independent processing. Users should experience such processes as transparent, quick, simple, directly usable, and should be able to complete their task in one attempt.

THE KEY INNOVATIONS

In the beginning of 2007 the first full scale STP project at SNS was launched, with the goal of putting four new savings products on-line at the start of 2008. This project is known as *STP Purchasing* and will provide us with a case for closer examination of full scale STP with BPM. This section will present the component architecture, take a look at how the process was modeled, show how customer testing was used to verify the solution, and provide some empirical data of the results.

Overview

The goals for this project were for a customer to be asked as few questions as possible during the purchasing process, that the entire process would be completed within a maximum of five clicks in the on-line website, and that the customer would be kept informed during all crucial steps in the process with clear, directed communication relevant to a specific purchasing process. A further desire was to maximize paperless communication with the customer. It was essential to maintain as short a processing time as possible, with processes involving human action stages causing no more than one-day delay. It should be volume independent, deliver reusable processes, reusable services, be multi-label, and multi-channel. Above all, the project should provide a full scale STP solution with a maximum degree of automation.

With our definition of full scale STP [definition 3] in mind, we already assume that the process is not free from human tasks. There are several instances in which we could not avoid having human interaction as part of this process. The resulting challenges will be discussed in more detail later on in this section. The project resulted in a general end-to-end purchasing process, initially for savings products, and a new process for document scanning and storage. A purchasing request database implementing the data model for each processing request was delivered along with a BPM process flow; a web front end was created for the initial savings products and the relevant SOA services. A new department was created, called *Process Management Evaluation and Processing*. Total project IT investment was 14,000 hours.

4.2 Business

A key concept in the vision of this solution is that the customer must be central to the process. A customer centric business model is not new [9], but we feel that aligning the entire strategy to empower one's customers is breaking the mold. As strategic products are made available through full scale STP with BPM we are able to adjust easily to customer needs. Products and product lines can be introduced into existing business processes in a cost effective manner. The flexibility to combine extends beyond products, product lines, and selling channels to become a very effective tool to reach customer bases in a timely and personalized fashion.

Customer communication can be personalized and tailored to specific processes, products, and customers' personal needs as the data generated by their behavior within the processes is documented. There have been very positive reactions from customers with regards to the speed, quality, and the level of detail in communications.

4.3 Process

The SNS implementation environment for full scale STP with BPM is one of pure Java [10]. The emphasis is on building solutions within the bank's own IT department, making use of Free Open Source Software (FOSS) where possible, achieving re-usability of existing applied solution components, and using best of breed components when forced to shop outside of our existing code base.

There was a shift in component strategy in 2004 from three main commercial suppliers to one where FOSS components are preferred when possible. Open source is now quite pervasive throughout the solution architecture of all SNS projects. Furthermore, the development environment and tooling used to implement the solution consists of almost only FOSS. This is outside the scope of this paper and will therefore be excluded from further discussion. The component architecture as shown in Figure 1 (UML package-style visualization) is a very generic and high-level view. We will discuss the components as shown, from left to right.

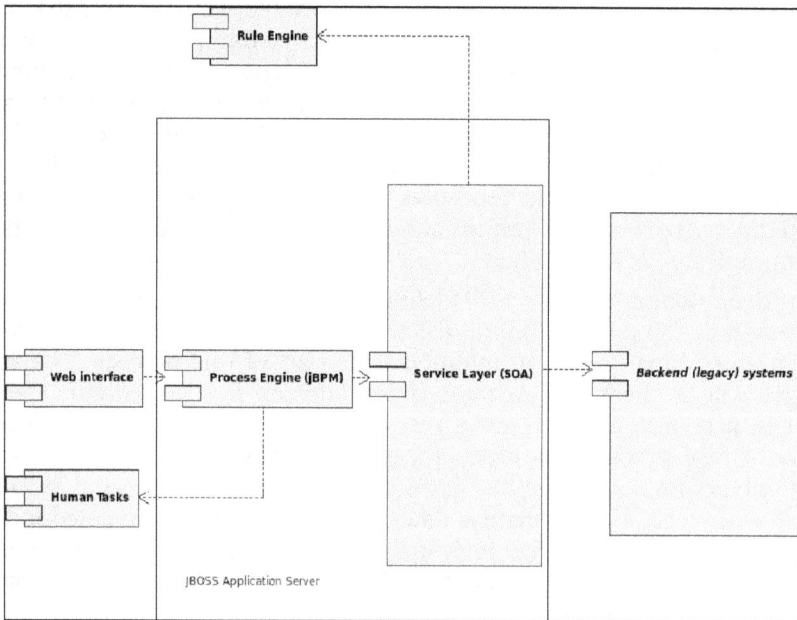

Figure : STP Purchasing architecture

Web interface

The entry point for any full scale STP application is the web interface as seen by the customer in the on-line banking website. This is a Java based website that makes use of a content management system. In the STP Purchasing project it provides the user with the option to apply for one of four saving products. If placed, a request is gathered together with user information, verified through various web services, and then using a web service it is deposited into the *Request Database*.

One might expect that a request is submitted directly to the jBPM process engine, but each request is put into a database to ensure that no single customer request is every lost due to the process engine begin unavailable. This is required by a banking regulation that ensures that no risks are taken with customer-submitted information. We must and will always be able to trace and audit every single step in the chain of events from customer request to product delivery. This small design step has been left out of the component diagram as it happens underwater and is of little importance to industries where intensive risk protection is not needed; we mention this in the interest of completeness.

Human tasks

A human action interface was implemented to provide functional administrators with the ability to deal with tasks as they drop out of the automated process for various reasons. Furthermore, Service Center employees provide input to the system through another interface with the document monitoring section of the process flow. Communication with the customer can require for a human task to be performed, such as customer's reply to questions which needs to be judged on completeness, correctness, and validity. This input to the jBPM process flow causes pending processes to be triggered into their next stages, to be stopped, or to be restarted. The interfaces have been created in-house by the project development team.

Within the project process definition it is always possible to encounter problems, planned or not, that need human intervention to be solved. This intervention is called a human task, where the process is dumped into a task bucket for further action by an authorized person. We refer to the need to invoke human tasks as having the process *fall out* of the process flow. This fall out can then classified as either technical or functional. The first is often related to some error in processing a request within a process step, the latter is related to a problem in the application flow logic. When we look at full scale STP we are concerned with processes that by definition contain planned functional fall out points in their process descriptions.

STP Purchasing supplies a web-based Java interface that enables humans to manipulate the tasks that they have been authorized to view. This component makes use of web services in the SOA layer to retrieve and manipulate process data located in various locations. It is mostly concerned with the *Request Database* where we find the complete request data structure that is maintained during the process life-cycle. One example of a functional fall out is a planned review of the applying customer credit rating results. This process might legally require that more than one person must review the customer's rating results before approving them as new bank customers.

Rule engine

This is a non-FOSS component supplied by a third party which we access from STP with BPM projects for business rules. This allows the business entity to maintain their own rule set regarding their businesses unit within the financial organization. For example, within a savings product you will have various rules and regulations as to the various conditions that must be met before a customer can be allowed to purchase that specific product. These rules and regulations can change over time or due to a special offer on that product during a specific time frame. It is often a wish from the contracting business unit to be able to manipulate these rules and regulations without having to contact the software vendor (i.e. project team).

JBOSS: jBPM and Service Layer (SOA)

The application server is an open source component called JBOSS [11], from the JBOSS component family we have adopted the jBPM engine [12] and its process definition language (PDL) implemented in jPDL [13]. These are the main FOSS components in our project solution and are considered core components in the enterprise architecture.

The jBPM process engine is used for all BPM projects, so component selection was not an issue. The BPM process flows are defined by the information analyst together with the business customer for the application. It is a process involving workshops and use cases. It provides the lead developer of the project with a starting point, in the form of a process flow. This is mapped almost one-to-one into the process definition language, which delivers a jPDL file. The resulting process definition is used for matching nodes to business services. In most cases this again is a one-to-one mapping and the design of the services is the most time consuming part of the implementation. Should there be any technical details that call for adjustment to the flow, consultation ensues with the information analyst, and eventually with the business customer. Individual developers are then given technical designs based on use case realizations that allow them to integrate their implementations into the proper process steps.

The project was completed using only simple nodes that contain all business logic in plain Java. Basic service calls were combined in the Java code to achieve what later could be implemented as a more complex business service. There were no nodes implemented as actual wait states, where the process can wait for action from an external system. Our back-end systems are not yet set up to trigger jBPM process instances to allow for real wait states. To facilitate wait states, a polling mechanism was used at points in the process were external systems need to be checked for completion of a task. For example, while waiting for a customer to correctly identify herself by returning a signed contract with a copy of a valid identification, the process will use a scheduler to periodically poll the back-end system via a web service to determine if the identification has been completed. Once completion is detected, the scheduler triggers the process via a web service. Furthermore, there are the standard decision nodes, transitions, and human task nodes within the project's process implementation.

We have implemented a standard Service Oriented Architecture (SOA) [14], referred to in-house as our Service Oriented Architecture Layer (SOAL). Granularity of the services in this layer have been defined as basic services, business services, and some very simple composite business services (CBS) [15]. A basic service brings the existing transaction out of the back-end system and makes it available through a web service. For example, to validate a postcode, the basic service *postcodeCheck* has been created to expose the back-end mainframe transaction that checks if a given postcode is valid. The business services handle more complex processing that may consist of one or more basic services. One of the more complicated issues is that of allowing the existence of CBS's in our SOA layer. These are business services that can contain not only calls to basic services, but to other business services, if the business service being called is in the same classification category as the caller.

The SOA layer deploys web services with versions. If a new release of the SOA layer contains services with interface changes, then the version of the release will be increased. To support backwards compatibility, a total of three versions are maintained for production applications to use. This allows for applications to upgrade to the newer versions over time.

Back-end systems

These systems can be anything in the wide variety that exists within our banking infrastructure: banking applications that provide and interface, external third party services, legacy systems, or some form of data storage like a data warehousing solution. It should be noted that these systems are always approached from our projects via the SOA layer in the form of a web service. We will provide the three most important back-end systems that are used in STP Purchasing.

A *request database* was implemented for tracking each purchasing request as it migrates through the BPM process flow. This was the direct implementation of our purchasing request data model. As stated in context of the *web interface* and *human task* components, this database is filled with the initial request data, manipulated by the process as it migrates through the various steps, and directly affected when technical or functional fall out occurs. Access is arranged by a very specific service dedicated to accessing, reporting, and updating data in the database works for the web interface, the human task interface, and from inside the process itself.

Another important component in the back-end is the *customer information system*, used to maintain all customer and prospect contact information. This is a marketing data pool and there is a specific service dedicated to accessing and updating the information kept here.

A central system in our back-end network is a legacy COBOL mainframe. This is where the bank customers are managed and it is accessed via web services that make use of a Java communication layer. This layer bridges the gap between Java and COBOL mainframe functions which are provided when functionality is exposed from the mainframe.

Customer testing

From the very beginning of the project, customer input was sought. An initial prototype was created for which four customers and four internal customer support personnel were invited to conduct usability testing in a controlled environment. These eight sessions were 90 minutes long, each dealing with a single respondent and a task assignment walk-through. The walk-through was done by the respondent with verbal communication accompanying all actions which were recorded by an observer sitting in a different room with a hidden view.

Even though it was a small usability test, it did provide relevant details which led to advice for the development team in the areas of information structure, interaction, navigation, content, graphical information, style, layout, and features. Our view is that any steps taken to improve customer satisfaction should be exploited to the fullest.

Another customer test took place before the project was released into production. It was a last test that the business users took to examine the entire project. The testing users were guided by a test leader during the earlier project iterations to develop functional stories. These were then set up in the databases to allow them to test actions on submitting new requests, handling functional fall out, schedulers, and other such actions as deemed necessary for project acceptance. This is a standard practice in our project release cycle and it remains a valuable feedback loop for finding functional problems before the project hits production status.

Hurdles Overcome

Even though the use of business process models is proving itself successful at SNS Bank, there is room for improvement concerning the activities of conceptualization, communication, and engineering that are part of the ongoing development process.

Quality of business process models is a notion that has many aspects and thus is quite complex [16]. Engineering-oriented, mathematics-based aspects are involved (correctness, formal expressiveness, and various more specialized aspects such as mentioned by Vanderfeesten et al. [17]), but also social aspects (validation, agreement through collaboration, and common understanding [18]).

For high quality process models to be realized, sufficient investment in detailed knowledge exchange and discussion is required. The main challenge is a common one: the business (analysts, managers) have the best knowledge of detailed processes to be supported/automated, and have the authority to decide about them, yet are neither willing nor able to be too actively and intensively involved in high-quality, detailed, engineering-like specification of business processes, which they consider a "technical" job. Technicians, on the other hand, resent being forced to guess at details required for successful implementation and point out that "technical" is not the same as "involving detailed, precise, and well-conceived descriptions". This is mostly a cultural issue [18], but therefore also a deeply rooted one.

In an ideal situation, we would still need the people with the proper knowledge and authority concerning the business to describe and/or design products and processes. How this can be realistically achieved in the short run is an open question yet. Possible options include:

- Teach business people to read (at least) and create (less likely) formal modeling techniques.

- Find and use alternative ways to represent formal process models; verbalization, perhaps, or alternative (simpler) schemes.

- Encourage and allow business-oriented stakeholders to get involved in more detailed process modeling.

Arrange for discussion and negotiation about process models to be optimally collaborative from the start, i.e. involve all relevant stakeholders at an early point and create explicit agreement (e.g. in workshops). The more divergence occurs in this phase, the more the diverging parties will fight for the survival of their initial ideas later on, and the harder it will be to reconcile alternative models. Discussion should take place, certainly, but not because effort and authority has been invested in particular diverging positions.

BENEFITS

Empirical data providing results concerning running STP Purchasing in production since February 2008 is presented in Table 1. The numbers represent the total number of processes per month, with a rather large spike in the months starting in September 2008. This was the beginning of the worldwide Financial Crisis, which lead many Dutch citizens to spread their savings to different financial institutions.

Table 1: Production process overview – 2008/2009 monthly

Month	Requests
Feb	750
Mar	2750
Apr	2000
May	1200
Jun	1100
Jul	1500

Aug	850
Sep	4250
Oct	2250
Nov	1000
Dec	2340
Jan	3715
Feb	3210

Taking a look at Table 1, we can clarify some of the dips and peaks in the numbers. In February 2008 the project was released half way through the month, resulting in a low start number. It picked up steam and was pretty steady until August 2008, which we believe is due to the vacation period when most Dutch people tend to be on their holidays and away from computers. In September we see the explosion of interest due to the Financial Crisis, followed by a leveling of interest. At the end of November 2008 the second set of five *deposito products* hit production. Logging shows us that the number gains for December 2008 to Feb 17th 2009 can indeed be attributed to the new *deposito products*, which were almost exclusively purchased. It should be noted that at the time of this publication, the numbers were climbing steadily each month. This could be attributed to the competitive interest rates being offered, by the worsening of the Financial Crisis, or a combination of both. More time will be needed to evaluate the eventual results and we plan to continue to track them during the remainder of the Financial Crisis.

Table 2: Status overview of customer processes

Status	Percentage
Completed on time	52%
Rejected for various reasons	8%
Human action (functional)	0.7%
Human action (technical)	0.3%
Currently in a fall out status	4%
In Document Monitoring	12%
Taken out of STP flow, completed by hand	23%

Another view of results is given in Table 2, which shows us percentages of the various statuses a process can be in. We must take into consideration that our metrics are limited and that we are only able to report on process totals. Even so, it is encouraging that the amount of functional and technical fallout that needs attention is both less than one percent of the total. Also encouraging is that over 50 percent of all processes are completing on time. The ones that do not complete on time and are listed in *Document Monitoring* tend to be waiting for customer response to documentation problems as previously discussed. We have a timer running that ensures a customer receives reminders several times. Should the customer not reply at all, we eventually abort the request. The category listing 23 percent of processes taken out of the engine and completed by hand needs more explanation. This feature was added to allow special cases to be handled in the original manner, by hand.

With only eight percent being rejected due to various reasons, it appears we are hitting the target audience and providing a process that is effective.

Development process improvements

The initial STP Purchasing project has provided a starting point for the IT department to build on for future full scale STP with BPM projects. Lessons learned and best practices are being applied, resulting in some interesting improvements to the process.

To our initial surprise, BPM process definitions can be easily changed with a minimal impact on the development time. The work is not in the process definition, but in the business services and basic services in the underlying structure.

A standard way of implementing process nodes and testing has made this part of the development process much less critical. It is important to focus on what we call the *Happy Flow* during initial development. This is the backbone of the process flow which represents a positive test case that processes as expected. For example, we would focus in the STP Purchasing project on a single savings product being requested by a verified and known customer of the bank. This means that you do not have to deal with any exceptions during the initial run through your process implementation. The focus of the first iteration of development is to get this Happy Flow working. By providing a quick working Happy Flow, the business can be shown tangible progress in the project at an early stage.

With an ever growing base of BPM process definitions it is clear that the time to market for similar products is much quicker. We have projects with estimates ranging from one third to one half of the initial development hours put into STP Purchasing. This is quite a big improvement. One thing of note here would be that the development of business services should always be carefully considered, as they tend to be the focus point of complexity.

The initial process definitions as provided by the information analysts and business analysts are not in our process definition language. Much depends on the quality of this process flow model, but with some care and attention to this step it is not too much trouble to map the process flow model to our process definition language. The generated image of the flow is a very good communication tool with the business. No better way to let them see the business services and understand where the development time is spent. Bringing the business closer to the development team with regards to communication about the process flow has been a positive experience that we would like to see continued.

BEST PRACTICES, LEARNING POINTS AND PITFALLS

7.1 Best Practices and Learning Points

- ✓ *standardize process development with clear guidelines for how processes implemented.*

- ✓ *develop a process repository, enable reuse of these processes.*

- ✓ *initial business process design should be reflected in initial top level technical process design*

- ✓ *hide implementation details below the highlevel process design*

- ✓ *test early, test often, and enable your business contact/users to provide feedback easily/often in the development process*

- ✓ *process design will change, allow for this during the development cycle when selecting your BPM tooling*

✓ attack BPM process development in steps; implementing the 'happy flow' (a perfect run through the process), then expand on exception paths

7.2 Pitfalls

✗ process design done by part of the development team, usually a lead or architect

✗ spending enough time on usage scenario's as it is very easy to implement incomplete processes or miss exceptions

✗ modeling business processes without business unit commitment or active involvement

✗ starting a BPM project without knowledgeable people, that have experience in creating BPM solutions

COMPETITIVE ADVANTAGES

In this paper we presented the efforts of a Dutch bank at migrating from traditional banking services to a full scale STP with BPM driven financial institution during the current world-wide Financial Crisis. The components being used to realize the STP Purchasing project were described and some basic resulting empirical data were presented for evaluation. The issues and benefits were covered along with the challenges yet faced by the IT organization. The large shift in strategy has started to deliver the desired results and we expect these will continue to roll in as future full-scale STP with BPM projects are implemented.

The positive effects on customer interaction, improvements on accelerating product deployment, and more flexible product/customer support channels have energized some internal ideas about becoming a facilitator to external third party enterprises. Imagine a future where individual entrepreneurs would be able to open a banking store with complete full scale STP with BPM selling channels for products and services.

We hope that our experiences, lessons, and observations will be of value to the industry as a whole. This is a financial industry story as we experience it on the front lines, but it could be applied to many different situations to help you survive the current Financial Crisis.

TECHNOLOGY

See section 4.3, built on JBoss technology, specifically, jBPM for BPM.

The initial STP Purchasing project has provided a starting point for the IT department to build on for future full scale STP with BPM projects. Lessons learned and best practices are being applied, resulting in some interesting improvements to the process.

To our initial surprise, BPM process definitions can be easily changed with a minimal impact on the development time. The work is not in the process definition, but in the business services and basic services in the underlying structure.

A standard way of implementing process nodes and testing has made this part of the development process much less critical. It is important to focus on what we call the *Happy Flow* during initial development. This is the backbone of the process flow which represents a positive test case that processes as expected. For example, we would focus in the STP Purchasing project on a single savings product being requested by a verified and known customer of the bank. This means that you do not have to deal with any exceptions during the initial run through your process implementation. The focus of the first iteration of development is to get this Happy Flow working. By providing a quick working Happy Flow, the business can be shown tangible progress in the project at an early stage.

With an ever growing base of BPM process definitions it is clear that the time to market for similar products is much quicker. We have projects with estimates ranging from one third to one half of the initial development hours put into STP Purchasing. This is quite a big improvement. One thing of note here would be that the development of business services should always be carefully considered, as they tend to be the focus point of complexity.

The initial process definitions as provided by the information analysts and business analysts are not in our process definition language. Much depends on the quality of this process flow model, but with some care and attention to this step it is not too much trouble to map the process flow model to our process definition language. The generated image of the flow is a very good communication tool with the business. No better way to let them see the business services and understand where the development time is spent. Bringing the business closer to the development team with regards to communication about the process flow has been a positive experience that we would like to see continued.

THE TECHNOLOGY AND SERVICE PROVIDERS

Below table shows technology used, development by internal IT organization.

bpm (JBoss, http://www.jboss.com)

document management (internal system)

workflow (JBoss, http://www.jboss.com)

business process (JBoss, http://www.jboss.com)

process management (JBoss, http://www.jboss.com)

business process management (JBoss, http://www.jboss.com)

filenet (n/a)

business processes (JBoss)

work flow (JBoss)

REFERENCES

1. Khanna, A.: Straight Through Processing For Financial Services: The Complete Guide. Academic Press, Burlington, MA. (Nov 2007)

2. van der Aalst, W.M.P., Hofstede, and A.H.M, Weske,M: Business Process Management: A Survey. In: van der Aalst, W.M.P., Hofstede, A.H.M., and Weske, M. (eds) BPM 2003, LNCS, vol. 2678, pp. 1–12. Springer, Heidelberg (2003)

3. Brahe, S.: BPM on Top of SOA: Experiences from the Financial Industry. In: Alonso, G., Dadam, P., and M.Rosemaan (eds) BPM 2007, LNCS 4714, pp. 96–111, Springer, Heidelberg (2007)

4. Guerra, A.: Bloomberg Aims To Simplify Straight-Through Processing. On: InformationWeek, On http://www.informationweek.com/817/bloomberg.htm (18 Dec 2000)

5. Strickland, R., Aach, D.: Getting to straight-through processing: in theory, there is a way to deliver faster and better service in the mortgage lending business. On: BNet Business Network,

http://findarticles.com/p/articles/mi_hb5246/is_/ai_n29277448 (Feb 2006)

6. The Free Dictionary, http://encyclopedia2.thefreedictionary.com/Straight+Through+Processing (10 Feb 2009)

7. Answers.com, http://www.answers.com/topic/straight-through-processing (10 Feb 2009)

8. Investopedia, http://www.investopedia.com/terms/s/straightthroughprocessing.asp (10 Feb 2009)

9. Heckl, D., Moormann, J.: Matching Customer Process with Business Processes of Banks: The Example of Small and Medium-Sized Enterprises as Bank Customers. In: Alonso, G., Dadam, P., and M.Rosemaan (eds) BPM 2007, LNCS 4714, pp. 112–124, Springer, Heidelberg (2007)

10. Java Technology. 18 March 2008, http://java.sun.com (19 March 2008)

11. Jboss.org: Community Driven. http://labs.jboss.com (19 March 2008)

12. jBPM Overview. http://labs.jboss.com/jbossjbpm/jbpm overview (19 March 2008)

13. Welcome to jBPM jPDL. http://labs.jboss.com/jbossjbpm/jpdl (19 March 2008)

14. Erl, T.: Service Oriented Architecture: Concepts, Technology and Design. Prentice-Hall, Englewood Cliffs (2005)

15. Neuman, S.: Composite Business Services. IBM Global Business Services, http:// www-935.ibm.com/services/us/index.wss/offering/gbs/a1027243 (25 October 2008)

16. Recker, J.: Towards an Understanding of Process Model Quality. Methodological Considerations. In: Ljungberg, J., Andersson, M. (eds.) Proceedings 14th European Conference on Information Systems, Goeteborg, Sweden (2006)

17. Vanderfeesten, I.T.P., Cardoso, J., Mendling, J., Reijers, H.A., van der Aalst, W.M.P.: Quality Metrics for Business Process Models. In: Fischer, L. (ed.) BPM and Workflow handbook 2007, pp. 179–190. Future Strategies Inc., Mississauga (2007)

18. Hoppenbrouwers, S.J.B.A.: Community-based ICT development as a multi-player game. In: Conference proceedings of What is an Organization? Materiality, Agency and Discourse, May 2008, University of Montreal, Canada (2008)

Swisscard AECS, Switzerland

Gold Award, Europe
Nominated by Action Technologies Inc., USA

EXECUTIVE SUMMARY / ABSTRACT

The liberalization of the credit card market in Switzerland in 1997 paved the way for American Express and Credit Suisse AG to establish the joint venture company Swisscard AECS AG and to merge their credit card activities. Swisscard ideally combines the complementary strengths of the founding companies, with American Express being the global leader in card management and Credit Suisse providing strong national sales channels. On behalf of Credit Suisse, Swisscard offers the world-famous American Express card within Switzerland. It is thus the sole issuer in Switzerland with all three major brands (American Express, MasterCard and Visa) in its product portfolio.

In 2007, Swisscard issued its one-millionth credit card. Swisscard employs approximately 500 staff in total. We aim to offer the best possible card solutions to all our customer groups. In order to meet this challenge, we continuously analyze the needs of our customers and develop new products and services based on these findings. Innovation and its time-to-market are thus crucial: the foundation of our success lies in the permanent alignment of our business requirements with best-of-breed information technology. Our business is to act as a service center provider for our corporate and private customers. The quality and processing time of our former transaction-processing platform and host systems were not sufficient to serve our new products and services. We were also confronted with increasing regulatory and risk issues concerning internal credit card application processing, from both consumers and customers placing orders using handwritten, signed paper forms.

To improve these situations, we initiated a project to implement electronic workflows for the business processes involved – covering external document scanning with integral handprint recognition and data exchange services, as well as host and robotics integration – with the final objective of end-to-end automation, thus reducing human intervention to a minimum. This resulted in what we call electronic participant-to-participant (P2P) workflow, whereby workflow participants are treated uniformly whether they are humans or machines. Today we are capable of integrating, or rather socializing, host and robotic systems in such a way that they act as software agents just like human actors in SwisscardNet, the Swisscard workflow system.

This case study presents new methods and inventions that combine business process management (BPM) principles and software agent technology to minimize the costs, time and management overhead disadvantages faced when extending workflow boundaries to include external customers. Furthermore, we discuss the management of business process management with a generic meta-case approach as a valuable alternative for defining processes and activities.

OVERVIEW

Credit Suisse AG hired Swisscard AECS AG to handle the product development and management, marketing and sales, customer services, risk management, card processing and development/management of additional services and customer loyalty programs for all credit cards offered by Credit Suisse and its co-branding partners. Consumer Services ensures that our more than 30 card products are offered, acquired and marketed optimally. Corporate Services helps national and international companies to significantly and sustainably reduce their expenses, travel and purchase costs by optimizing processes, preparing reliable management reports and making invoicing more efficient.

As merchant acquirer, Swisscard is responsible for expanding and handling the American Express network of participating businesses in Switzerland. We ensure that American Express customers can use their cards wherever they want to. At the same time, our contracting parties benefit from the advantages of cashless payment transactions and access to attractive new customers. Altogether this makes us the current market leader in Switzerland:

- 25% market share
- No. 1 in frequent flyer and business traveler cards
- No. 1 in the discerning private customer business
- No. 1 in the corporate customer business
- No. 1 in the co-branding business (TCS, Miles & More)

To realize and strengthen this leadership, the Swisscard CEO, who had been a key stakeholder in the award-winning ServiceNet application at Credit Suisse, thought to replicate ServiceNet's cost, speed and quality benefits within a substantially smaller organization. The result of a process improvement study produced an action plan that electronically extended workflow support to our external contracting parties and automated overall processing as much as possible, thus reducing human intervention to a minimum. The close integration of our external contracting parties into our internal processing maximizes customer retention and reinforces our market leadership.

This report to the Workflow Management Coalition discusses the results of Swisscard's unique participant-to-participant BPM system.

BUSINESS CONTEXT

Swisscard responded to its substantial growth by increasing centralization, maximizing work automation and extending internal business process boundaries to our external contracting parties.

Optimizing was required for complicated processes with many media breaks, the permanent growth of informal communication with order nature, and inefficient monitoring due to complexity and physical separation.

In addition, we were confronted with increasing regulatory and risk issues, especially concerning the back offices' internal processing of credit card applications from consumers and contracting parties, which were made using handwritten paper forms. Furthermore, business process implementations were too slow and insufficient to fulfill our business demands for flexibility, agility, time and cost. We were forced to radically change the way we implemented and deployed our business processes.

Spawning process boundaries and integrating third-party technology (such as document scanning, handprint recognition and rule-based application validation) into the workflows was a key decision for successfully managing and orchestrating the new business-processing platform.

Out-sourcing Paper intensive Procedures

We outsourced the document management procedures, including scanning and handprint recognition, to a third-party company. We did so in order to completely automate data entry from paper forms, thus increasing throughput and the quality of credit card application processing.

Automating Data Exchange with Partners

In general, all application-related message interactions and processing between the contracting parties are fully automated. Contracting sales channels such as the remitting bank forward their credit card application forms to SwisscardNet automatically. The signed paper forms are sent to the Document Management Center, another contracting party, for scanning, while at the same time, customer information is forwarded independently to SwisscardNet from the remitting bank's internal front-office application. Managing the asynchronous messages from these heterogeneous external systems clearly requires business and conversation rules that are able to act appropriately depending on the actual situation.

Optimizing internal Message Processing

Software agents, wrapping the functionality needed of more than 200 different applications running as services or functions on the legacy, make it possible to automate internal message processing as much as possible. Human users will be involved only when the business rules demand it. The majority of the credit card applications can be processed fully automatically based on rules. This even includes embossing and sending credit cards by mail in the best case (lucky path) or sending rejection letters when declined. This automated processing approach boosted productivity and quality tremendously, thereby allowing us to focus employee capabilities on investigating risk-related issues and interacting with customers, which in turn improved data quality and customer service.

Initial Project Scope

It was important from the outset to integrate the internal processing platform (Legacy) with the new workflow platform and at the same time to eliminate manual data entry, i.e. the initial retyping of paper-based application forms. It is widely known that integration costs often exceed project budgets and are limiting factors for many good ideas. Nevertheless, we found an innovative way to empower existing host functionality; embed our contracting parties; set up the reflection of our organization including roles, competences and responsibilities; and coordinate all of this using software agents and the new electronic workflow platform as kind of a glue between people and machines. These were all prerequisites for success, and we completed the set-up within only three months. The initial project started in January 2008 and went live with the new credit card application processing for 30 different credit cards in April 2008. This included successfully integrating the host functionality needed for the different validation checks as well as document scanning and recognition, thus replacing manual data entry from the very beginning. Furthermore, we also integrated the call center and the in-house letter printing facility. Various organizational and people management processes were also developed in parallel, including new employee management, new organizational unit management, employee critical change management, organizational unit critical change management and, finally, user profile management.

Extended Project Scope

After setting up the new participant-to-participant (P2P) business-processing platform, new processes were implemented that focused on extending our processes to include our major contracting parties. Between May 2008 and April 2009, we developed and deployed a new process every two months, including any integration of legacy functionality that may have been required. This was the ultimate proof of the successful implementation of the new P2P-workflow system, coordinating people and machines uniformly as participants. One year after going live with the first process, the SwisscardNet workflow portfolio covers the following processes:

- ✓ Credit card applications for private and corporate customers
- ✓ Control accounts for corporate customers
- ✓ Detailed accounts for employees of corporate customers

- ✓ Applications for credit card bundles for private and corporate customers
- ✓ Employees and organizational units life cycle management
- ✓ Fraud and chargebacks

Expected Improvements for the Future

With the new workflow platform, existing and future host systems can be leveraged and integrated as active participants within the new workflows. Introducing the ActionWorks® "language of business" as the common protocol for all of the workflow participants, separates business from technology and will enable Swisscard to improve business and information technology in the future with minimum risk and dependency.

Needless to say, the new platform fulfills many business expectations for process optimization such as increasing productivity, increasing transparency and mitigating operational risks.

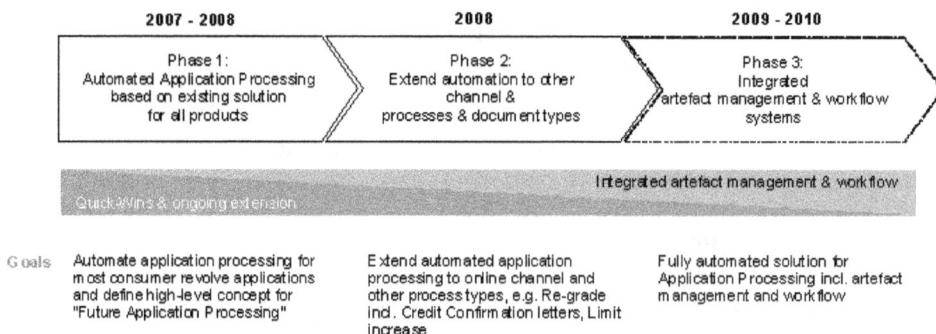

2007 - 2008	2008	2009 - 2010
Phase 1: Automated Application Processing based on existing solution for all products	Phase 2: Extend automation to other channel & processes & document types	Phase 3: Integrated artefact management & workflow systems

		Integrated artefact management & workflow
Quick Wins & ongoing extension		

| Goals | Automate application processing for most consumer revolve applications and define high-level concept for "Future Application Processing" | Extend automated application processing to online channel and other process types, e.g. Re-grade incl. Credit Confirmation letters, Limit increase | Fully automated solution for Application Processing incl. artefact management and workflow |

Figure 1: SwisscardNet road map

The major objective of **end-to-end automation** of the core application processes is achieved by the end of phase 2. The original plan was divided into three major steps: in the first phase, we concentrated on the functionality of existing systems; we then extended it to optimize the processing of new products in a second phase; and finally, we homogenized and introduced new services according to our business requirements in a third phase.

Thanks to the software agents, new systems can be introduced without affecting SwisscardNet's current case processing. A number of the plan's key steps are already complete, while phase 3 steps are still in progress.

THE KEY INNOVATIONS

We decided to purchase Action Technologies' Metro software as a people-to-people BPM system, which uses a closed-loop human interaction model to manage negotiations, agreements and customer satisfaction with work performed. The system also provides real-time monitoring of every step of every process, as well as the status of work within every commitment. Action Solutions and Systems Integration Center AG added inventions to this underlying system that dramatically reduced the integration time of third-party systems, which was key to extending process boundaries to our contracting parties. The patented interaction model from Action Technologies has been adopted as the communication language for the software action agents, which use a wrapping approach that enables them to deal with legacy software. In essence, we injected code into the legacy interface programs to allow them to collaborate in the business processes like any human actor. The SwisscardNet's software agent infrastructure helps to offload repetitive tasks from end users and guarantees compliance with our business policies. This resulted in what we call the participant-to-participant workflow system.

4.1 Business

The SwisscardNet innovation was driven by a combination of market expansion as the strategic business goal and service excellence as the essential competitive differentiation, with constantly increasing cost-efficiency requirements always in the background. Solutions to the challenges of growth, service and cost reduction often move in a direction that runs counter to much of the financial services industry, as these people-intensive services are very expensive to provide. "Straight-through processing" aims to shift the "people focus" away from repetitive work and onto value-added risk and customer service activities by automating as many business rules for processing as practical. Our strategy uses technology to augment people.

Paradox of Job enrichment thru Job enlargement

SwisscardNet improves the award-winning ServiceNet concept from Credit Suisse, the "case approach," by providing a unified platform for internal and external participants, such as the people and agents involved, to fulfill customer requests through distributed case management. Cases can be created by humans (manually) or by agents (automatically). Case processing, closing and archiving is structured by business rules and performed by humans and software agents cooperatively. The look and feel of the generic case user interface puts users' business models into terms they understand. This resulted in an average training time of two hours, and in several instances users adopted the system on their own initiative with no training. Management was thus able to introduce job enrichment for the human users (generalization instead of specialization) and delegate the burden of work to the agents (job enlargement).

Federated Business-to-Business (B2B) Platform

SwisscardNet actively incorporates contracting parties, e.g. remitting banks, into the case processing through both agents and automated data exchange. Relationship managers at the remitting bank can request credit cards without even recognizing that the processing is done by SwisscardNet. They are fully bound into the credit card processing but technically still loosely coupled and thus not highly dependent on the SwisscardNet's availability as vice versa.

Semi structured Information System

SwisscardNet ensures accountability, coordination, "visibility," end-to-end tracking and feedback – all of which are critical to delivering superior, swift service with reduced costs. One important benefit is that unstructured information – like free-text documents or images (e.g. scanned paper forms) – as well as structured data, such as recognized content from scanned paper forms represented in electronic forms by field/value pairs, are all visualized in a powerful and easy-to-use graphical interface. It is thus possible for users to visibly verify that the scanned and recognized data conforms to the original document with a single mouse-click.

Users can easily process structured and unstructured information in formal, pre-defined or not formally specified ways.

Communication and Interaction Whiteboard

SwisscardNet also accommodates the existence of unexpected and unstructured information by providing a whiteboard system that allows agents and human users to share the results of their efforts in the form of instructions and comments. When a human user opens a case, he or she immediately sees if an agent or another user has reported any instructions or comments concerning the problem-solving state, e.g. while scanning and using handprint recognition the ZIP code did not match the location, or while validating using the legacy application the cardholder's solvency or credit worthiness was not sufficient. Human users' and agents' communication and interaction during case processing takes place solely through the instruction/comment whiteboard.

Visible reasoning

Another important aspect of SwisscardNet is that the reasoning of the current state of a case or business object is visible through the audit trail, which monitors all actions, both human and non-human. In fact, the user can even see which condition was fulfilled as a part of which rule on which business object – and has thus led to the current state of the business object or case.

4.2 Process

Previously, processing at Swisscard was time consuming and inefficient. There were various tools to support execution within each of the processing steps, but most had to be operated manually and were not integrated, or even capable of being integrated with each other. Before SwisscardNet, users needed to know and use several systems. During the course of their daily work, they would have to log in several times to several systems and copy/paste data between systems. Feedback from external systems needed to be copied back and forth in order to proceed with process execution. Users had to know the relevant rules governing each credit card's application process. Updating the rule handbook required significant amounts of time. Today, software agents take care of these issues and only relatively few people (line managers) have to know about the legacy systems in detail.

When activities on behalf of external systems are required as part of process execution in SwisscardNet, the software agent takes care of them. As soon as the external system comes back with an answer, the software agent acts on the content of the response and according to the rules defined. The burden of knowing all of the rules is now delegated to the software agents.

The following subsections discuss the results of implementing people-to-people BPM principles in service-oriented architecture with action software agents.

Morphing People-to-People and System-to-System Approaches

Extending process boundaries to third-party companies and automating the burden of work and complexity in such a way that only exceptional or decision-making tasks need to be processed by human users requires the two extremes of people-to-people and system-to-system workflow paradigms to be brought together. When morphing these approaches, we first generalized the terminology used to describe the two players involved, people and systems, henceforth calling them "participants." Participants in our new workflow paradigm should communicate with each other as linguistic equals, sharing data where necessary and yielding processing control to whichever participant requires data for manipulation at a particular point in time.

In information technology, software agents have been proposed as one way to help people better cope with the increasing volume and complexity of information and computing resources. Using the patented interaction model from Action Technologies as the common interaction protocol for our participants allowed us to both *systematize* the way in which people interact on the one hand, and *socialize* systems interaction behavior on the other.

Because people already used this underlying model to interact with each other in the SwisscardNet workflow application, the major effort was to leverage the different systems involved to make use of this. Instead of implementing this for every system involved and ending up in a never-ending integration story, we introduced software agents: we wrapped third-party systems functionality where needed, aligned them with business activities and adapted Action Technologies' interaction model as the default core speech-act-based agent-to-agent protocol shared among all software agents ("action agents"). Action agents now use the same protocol as human agents, and the communication between participants takes place through the use of semantic messages in the context of business conversations via an event channel. Semantic messages represent more abstract, higher-level and business-process-related actions. They hide the clutter of proprietary application-specific details and provide business-like semantics. Semantic messages are exchanged through an event channel service, which supports different connectivity standards, provides different interfaces and enables synchronous and asynchronous message passing – thus realizing the advantages of loose coupling in complex cooperating systems.

Channeling Conversation between Participants

The event channel adopts the OMG's CORBA event service specification and extends it in such a way that its implementation provides semantic message brokering between participants. The service supports various available interface definition languages (IDL), such as web- or Microsoft Windows COM-services. Unlike most communication architectures, the event channel takes into account not only the individual message in isolation, but also the various sequences in which a particular message may occur. We believe that social interaction among participants is more accurately modeled by taking conversations – rather than isolated speech acts – as the primary unit of interaction.

As Winograd/Flores (1986) observes: "The relevant regularities are not in individual speech acts or in some kind of explicit agreement about meanings. They appear in the domain of conversations, in which successive speech acts are related to one another."

In the event channel, a conversation is defined as a sequence of messages between participants that takes place over an arbitrarily long period of time (long transactions), but which is still bound by certain termination conditions described in conversation policies as conditions of satisfaction. Conversations may give rise to other conversations as appropriate. As semantic messages come in, semantic events are triggered automatically. In contrast to method invocations, semantic events provide a form of messaging that the event channel service can use to dynamically request services and information from each of the parts contained in the message. Semantic messages use a common vocabulary of requestable business activities grouped in suites of related events and associated conditional actions. These business policies, combined with the conversation policies and the abstraction of people and systems as participants, form the building blocks of our new participant-to-participant workflow model.

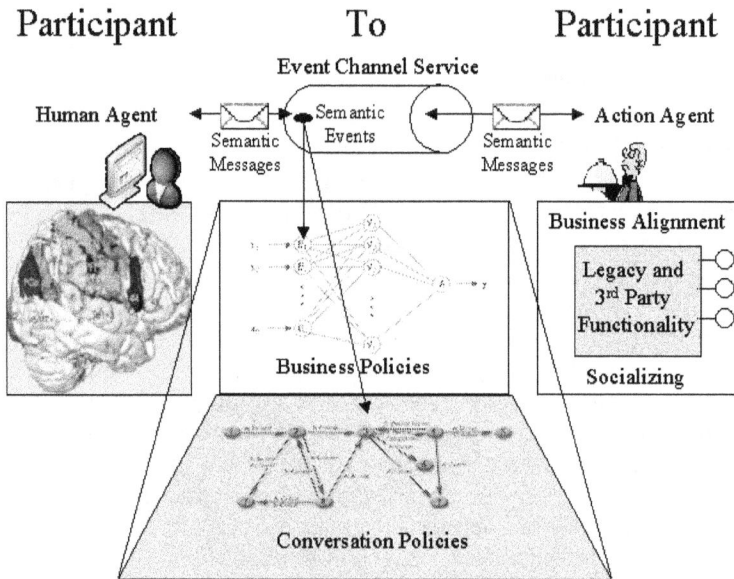

Figure 2: Participant-to-Participant (P2P) Communication Model

This federated system model is the architectural foundation for orchestrating the different participants in a uniform way. Specifically, this helps to overcome the limitations of passive artifact interface-based architectures in the following ways:

- *Scalability.* Agents are equipped with rule-based capabilities that run in the background to help people to perform case processing. They take into account the context of the person's tasks and situation as they present information and take action.
- *Scheduled or event-driven actions.* Agents are capable of executing tasks either at specific times or automatically in response to system-generated events.
- *Flexibility and opportunism.* Because they are instructed at the level of the business and conversation policies, they help to solve problems such as host system unavailability.
- *Abstraction and delegation.* Agents communicate with us, and we can delegate tasks to them. Rather than simply processing our commands, they share our goals and show us the state of work or what went wrong.

Participant-To-Participant (P2P) Workflow Model

SwisscardNet's participant-to-participant (P2P) workflow model deduces the reference model from the workflow management coalition group (WfMC) as described below. The lack of the process definition and activities building blocks from the WfMC reference model in our workflow model is because we integrated the modeling into the execution component (see also Jablonski and Bussler, Workflow Management: Modeling, Concepts, Architecture and Implementation, 1996). As a result, SwisscardNet process definitions will be composed dynamically at runtime and just before their usage (see also Kammer/Bolcer, Technique for Supporting Dynamic and Adaptive Workflows, 2000). This approach is also called "just in time" execution. For quality management purposes, this definition's agility can be further formalized using meta-cases, which take care of change management activities like testing, accepting and deploying new and existing definitions.

Business Process

| is managed by

Workflow Management System

| via

Process Instance

| include one or more

Activity Instance

| assigned via

Work Item

is — stored in — to

Case   Work Participant ◄— contains one
        List   or more

         is   is   is

MetaCase Person Agent Role

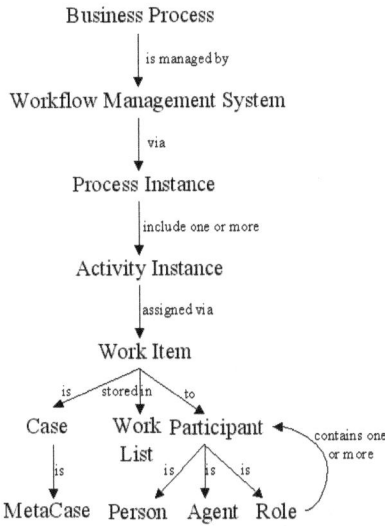

Figure 3: P2P Workflow Model

What makes SwisscardNet both simple and effective is the core concept that lies behind the design of the system: every work item becomes a *case*. Thus a case is the general unit of work, rather than individual messages, tasks, transactions or assignments. In order to define cases in advance, meta-cases are used. They do not simply define the details of the case, rather they guarantee testing, deployment and definition-versioning as well using a meta-data repository. Ad-hoc case definitions are part of every normal case and can be done by participants by entering processing instructions. The other important extension is that a workflow participant is a resource that performs the work represented by a case. This work normally involves taking one or more actions on information objects contained in a case and is assigned to the workflow participant via the work list. A participant is either a person, an agent or a role. A role is an abstract user containing one or more persons, agents or other roles. An agent is a virtual user, while a person is a human user.

Basic Characteristic of Action Agents

In the context of SwisscardNet, action agents can be thought of as virtual users. They respond appropriately to a basic set of speech acts (e.g. request, decline) and in a way that is consistent with certain desirable conventions of human interaction, such as commitments. In SwisscardNet, the whole organization – consisting of organizational entities (OE) and people with their profiles (roles, rights and obligations) – is reflected in an underlying subsystem called "user administration." By default, every organizational entity has at least one virtual office. During case processing, tasks that are not assigned directly to a person can be sent to the virtual office of the organizational entity required. People who have access rights to this virtual office can now enter it to check out work and take ownership of further activities.

CSG-OEBASIS
KIOS-O
Filler
DIV9-BET
CSG-J
    Kielholz Walter B.
    New
    Agent office - Chairman Board of Directors
CSG-JG
CSG-JV

In addition, we have also added an action software agent for every organizational entity by default, which can act as a kind of virtual assistant for all people assigned to this organizational entity. These agents inherit all of the profiles of their organizational entities, including roles, rights, restrictions and obligations. They have their own workboxes, where all messages sent to them can be placed.

Figure 4: Agent-Workbox in OE Tree

Forwarding messages can be done manually by human users or automatically as part of the execution of a conditional activity. Agents are embedded into the organizational structure in a very natural way. They work in a virtual office, where human users with permission to enter can monitor the cases that the relevant agent is currently working on and what the state of the work is. Drill-down to the current case is possible, as is a summarized view of all cases assigned to the agent. As long as agents are working on the cases, the cases are blocked, i.e. read-only views are the only views available. Only administrators have the rights to manipulate the cases currently being processed by the action software agent, e.g. to change ownership or cancel the current activity.

Our assistant agents significantly reduce the workload for their human counterparts, respecting policies and processing rules at the same time.

Open Cases by Responsible: Agent office - Running Applications   Back..   Forward..

⬦ Task	⬦ Fallnummer			⬦ Priorität	⬦ Document Date	Document Type	Document State	⬦ Marketing Code
Status: En Route								
Case	SWC-10182682	⊕	🐾	Normal	01.04.2009 11:43:06	MasterCard	NEW_CHECKED_AUTO	
Case	SWC-10182686	⊕	🐾	Normal	01.04.2009 16:14:07	American Express	NEW_CHECKED_AUTO	
Case	SWC-10182687	⊕	🐾	Normal	01.04.2009 16:18:07	American Express	NEW_CHECKED_AUTO	
Case	SWC-10183346	⊕	🐾	Normal	18.06.2009 11:38:46	Visa	FINALIZING	

Page Size: 20 ▾

Figure 5: Agent's virtual office showing the current state-of-work

Building SwisscardNet Workflows

SwisscardNet provides a framework for managing the following:

- All different types of workflows, whether fuzzy and not-well-understood or deterministic and highly repetitive, using ***cases***.
- (Un-)structured data (forms, text, images) as ***information objects***.
- Data exchange, long transactions, third-party and legacy systems integration through ***agents***.
- The behavior of cases and business objects, two special types of information objects, with ***business and conversation policies***.

SwisscardNet is an enabling technology for the end user programming paradigm that views workflow applications as cases containing collections of information objects. These information objects can be tied together via business rules. The framework includes a semantic messaging facility that defines high-level messages used to communicate the requests. With semantic events, the participants, human users and agents can act not only on cases but also on the information objects they contain. Information objects can be simple structures, e.g. e-mail messages, or more complex ones such as compound forms containing lists, embedded objects, single-choices and fields. An information object's dynamic defines the operations that can be invoked via semantic events as part of a business rule using scripts. Scripts are programs executed by interpreters. The scripting language is able to translate human-readable scripts into semantic events and activities. This allows a business user to create scripts that fire semantic events, which result in collaborations among information objects and cases. Scripts combined with information objects are pure dynamite: they let business users assemble flexible information object combinations in record time, they provide tenfold productivity improvements over compiled languages and they allow non-programmers to automate all sorts of tasks. Scripts provide the basis for agent technology because agents "like" to be self-sufficient. It is for this reason that events and activities are made available to agents by default when setting up a SwisscardNet case, and as a result are fully automatable. The conditions in the business rules decide when and whether human users need to be involved. Furthermore, chaining event/act pairs allows case processing to be simulated without the involvement of human users.

Setting up a SwisscardNet case can be done in different ways. Ad-hoc case processing is done by human users in defining instructions at run-time and decides ad-hoc who will be involved in further processing and how. Pre-defined case processing requires the definition of policies (business and conversation rules), business objects involved with their dynamics (state-transition model) and the layout of the graphical user interface. All this is done using scripts for just in time execution or meta-cases, which generate the scripts as part of the case processing.

Managing Business Process Management (BPM) using Meta Cases

Separating business from technology has much justification and is one of the SOA principles we used at the process level, introducing the scripting approach to define cases. Nevertheless, this end-user dynamic requires close monitoring of the change management process for process definitions. To ensure the quality of delivery, meta-cases come into play. Meta-cases describe case definitions and can be used both to define new cases as well as to maintain existing ones. Because all of the major SwisscardNet building blocks (cases, information objects, policies and participants) can be defined using scripts, this can easily be done within a meta-case, too. A meta-case creates ad-hoc test plans, based on the condition definitions, for all of the business rules' alternative paths, including traces of test results. They ensure quality reviews, generate the necessary set-up packages, enforce visas for deployment, enforce feedback from the IT department of successful installation in the production environment and, last but not least, update software releases/meta-repository. Depending on the security, policies and environment, even the installation of the definitions package can be done automatically as part of the meta-case process. Because of the availability of data exchange functionality, such case definitions could be sent by e-mail, automatically triggering the corresponding change management meta-case.

This allows change management to be done in the same way as all other business processing, using the same techniques and bringing the same advantages.

4.3 Organization

In the past, interactions surrounding client requests were very paper-intensive and all coordinated via phone, e-mail, fax, mail and face-to-face meetings. Because clients normally interact with customer relationship managers from our contracting parties, the propensity for misunderstandings and miscommunication was very high. Moreover, there was no inter-company visibility into the process, no formal accountability on who had agreed to perform which tasks by when, and no consistent audit trail. Introducing the electronic participant-to-participant workflows was key to bridging and reorganizing the way people worked together across company boundaries. Of course, we cannot dictate the way our contracting parties process their clients' requests, nor the availability of their service infrastructures. We therefore introduced a federated case processing approach, where event communication was standardized and decoupled for the first time. At the same time, we reorganized the front office data exchange taking place in our contracting parties' branch offices all over the world, and also made it paperless. The SwisscardNet workflow system made it possible to channel all of the different media (phone, fax, paper, electronic documents and e-mail) and to use a case approach to streamline the business requests from the front offices to our middle and back offices. SwisscardNet's federated system approach maximizes our independence and the quality of service in terms of availability, flexibility and self-government, while at the same time optimizing the collaboration and cooperation with our contracting partners.

Standardizing the Information Supply Chain thru Cases

The availability of the right information – presented to the right participant at the right time and in the right format – is key to successfully coordinating process execution across companies, people and systems involved. The SwisscardNet workflow system design meshes system-to-system, system-to-people and people-to-people interfaces through the same interface, using software agents and the underlying patented interaction model from Action Technologies. The generic user interface implements the case concept from Credit Suisse's award winning ServiceNet application, which has been extended and modified such that agent interactions and notifications are embedded, the structured information from attached documents is made actively available in dynamic forms, and the rules which are responsible for the current state of work are made visible to human users.

This case view provides the information needed for both extremely efficient processing of standard service requests, such as credit card applications, and effective responses to non-routine requests, such as acts of fraud and chargebacks. A routine case is moved quickly and completely through the different processing steps (internally or externally), while non-routine cases are also moved quickly and completely through the approval and collaboration steps. The case is always kept in view and no type of interaction, including third-party system events or notifications, is ever left open. Every case has a complete process audit trail managed by the system and updated automatically. The audit trail shows all of the activities within a case and thus significantly reduces the operational risk of violating rules and/or regulatory policies.

Overall, this solves one of the single largest and most widespread problems in process coordination, the lack of "visibility" into the processes across the enterprises involved. In traditional workflow systems, no single person has an overall view of the system, but only sees his or her own part of the process. As a workflow moves through the network of interactions and interdependencies, it disappears from view. There is no direct and simple way to track statuses, reviewing which workflows are pending, completed, due or delayed. There is no overall history attached to the workflow as it moves through the complete process swamp, and no flexible feedback on it or its progress. In contrast to the individual tasks and operations carried out within a given workflow, the workflow itself has no built-in metrics showing the status of the process. Swisscard's workflow remedies all of this. It is in this sense a distributed management system. It ensures that the steps in the process and responsibilities for carrying them out are handled within the context of a distributed case, whereby all information is captured and managed centrally in SwisscardNet's case structure: in the right context, format and time, and visible only to the right participants.

Users and What Their Jobs Entail Now, Compared to Pre-Installation

Our middle office's direct "customer" is the front office – people like relationship managers and their assistants from third-party companies, our contracting partners. The external relationship manager acts on behalf of the bank client and initiates a request in the bank's own proprietary application environment, knowing nothing about the existence of SwisscardNet; the software agents together with their human colleagues from the middle and back office, our human agents, ensure that the request is honored. It sounds simple – but of course, being able to fire off a request externally and with the assurance that it will be fully handled internally is not at all simple.

Customer care has to be provided in a business context that is extremely complex, time-dependent, global, varied and demanding in terms of operation speed, quality and efficiency. For our human users in the middle and back office, the differences between working with the old, semi-manual system and the new workflow solution have radically transformed their jobs in several ways. First and foremost, repetitive and error-prone tasks like the massive amounts of data entry have been automated and delegated to a third party (scanning and handprint recognition). Time-consuming tasks such as printing documents, routing them for approval and monitoring the review process through e-mails and phone calls have been eliminated by automating and delegating them to software agents for normal processing. Today, only exceptional tasks require the intervention of human users. It is thus that individual job enrichment has become a way of life among our human user professionals. In addition, the codification of rules and procedures for processing the different business scenarios ensures that everyone, human and non-human agents alike, is acting within Group policy.

Agents that reduce Work

In essence, the use of software agent technology is the key to successfully implementing the major objective of end-to-end automation, involving people only when policies require doing so. Furthermore, because we are talking about bridging the gaps between organizations' electronic interfaces, the need for more socialized system-to-system interfaces is evident. We are not just exchanging data; rather the interfaces have to manage long transactions and thus "commitments" between the different partners in a conversation-like manner. This applies especially to effectively managing exceptions, e.g. interruptions, and to becoming a pleasant working partner, notifying human users only when appropriate due to service level agreements, which are reflected in the business and conversation policies. Today's action agents successfully manage repetitive tasks with respect to defined policies, and notify their human colleagues through the instruction/comment whiteboard (see Figure 6) about what went wrong and why.

This way human agents are always up-to-date and can manage exceptional situations extremely effectively and delegate further processing back to the action agents. Action agents periodically gather publicly available information from third-party companies over the Internet and update internal information accordingly, for example ZIP code data mapping, which is used to validate address information. They verify the result of the handprint recognition of the scanned credit card applications and act according to policies for further case processing. They forward data to external subsystems, wait for the answer from the processing and automatically take the next steps according to policy rules. Action agents prepare and export letters to be sent to applicants, including semantic wording (text blocks) in the required correspondence language and according to the specific context, e.g. reminders or rejection letters. Furthermore, action agents ensure that all of the asynchronously exchanged electronic messages for the next processing act are available as well as checking their structural consistency.

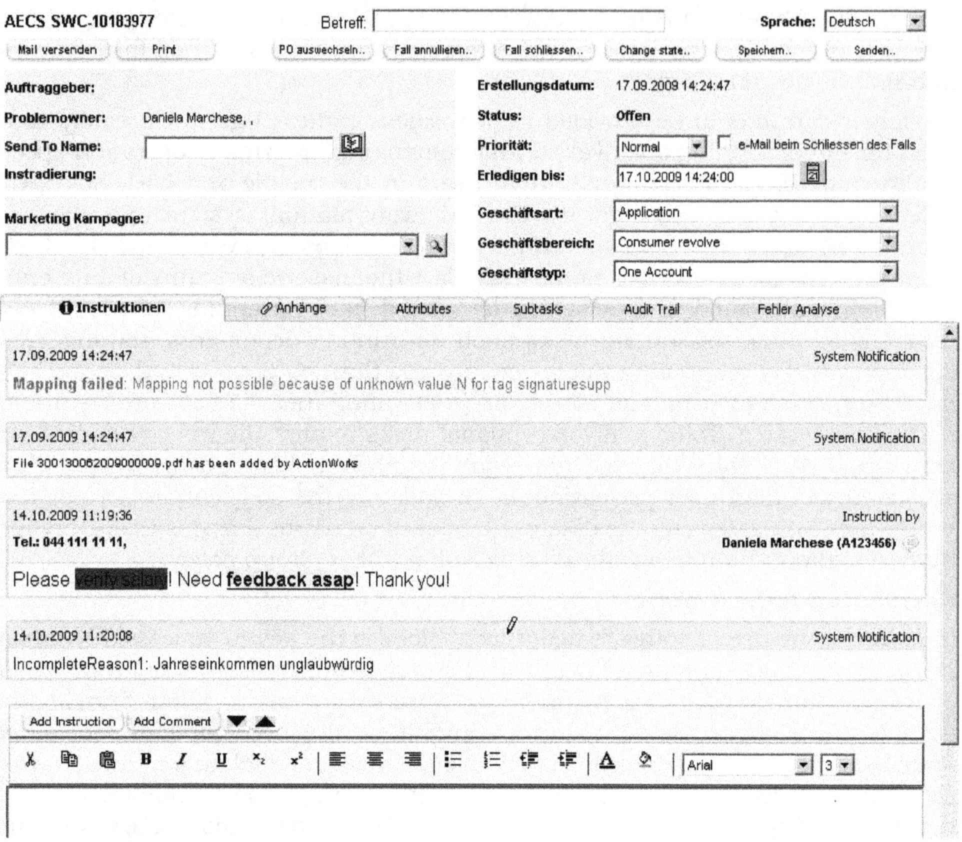

Figure 6: Whiteboard for Human and Action Agent's information exchange

This is what makes action agents a bit like digital butlers – the people at Swisscard successfully run their office life with the help of a gaggle of well-trained butlers.

The Implementation Team

The Swisscard core project team consisted of four people: a project manager, two business analysts and one IT professional (plus three developers from Systems Integration Center AG). Specialists from systems engineering and the data center also contributed to the project. Systems Integration Center AG and its adoption of Action Technologies' business interaction model as the common shared conversation protocol between participants were critical to the success of the project. Project launch was in January 2008 and the going live with the first workflow was on of April 1, 2008. This already included the integration of all the involved sub- and host systems. After the first launch, a new workflow has been deployed every two months, whereas the integration focus was more on integrating new functionality using the techniques already in place. All together, we delivered seven complex workflows in only 14 months, ending in March 2009.

HURDLES OVERCOME

5.1 Management

There were no big management hurdles – rather a member of the Swisscard executive board initiated the project. He knew about the success of the ServiceNet application (previous, award-winning solution) at Credit Suisse and enriched this solution with his own ideas – the outcome being that we have, in addition to ServiceNet (one generic process), one generic business language for both people and machines, who are treated uniformly as participants in business processing and respect the same conversation and business policies. The members of the SwisscardNet project team were charged with finding new ways of improving the middle and back offices' effectiveness and efficiency. The reorganization to introduce automation started in 2007; the automation was extended and external contracting parties embedded in the business process automation between 2008 and now; and finally, newer and more powerful back-end systems will be introduced and optimized by 2010 in order to service and leverage the middle and back office agents.

It was evident that for the successful implementation of all of these new processes, an innovative and unique workflow system was required that could not only service people in their daily work but also understand how people interact when carrying out their work. One prerequisite for automating business with external parties is closely monitoring the fulfillment of service level agreements and thus quality management. From the outset, it was evident to the management that automated quality management is an integral part of the new workflow platform, not only on a technical level but also specifically relating to business events. It is thus that cases are sent to specific quality assurance places by policies and that error analysis (good or bad) is included by default in SwisscardNet, as well as integrated reporting and statistical analysis. All this is critical for delivering superior, swift service with reduced costs.

5.2 Business

There was at the time a strong belief among Swisscard operations and IT people: what was needed was a "better" technology system. This led to problems that held up the deployment of the Swisscard concept of process and service, leading instead to a focus on replacing the technology platform rather than improving the process and service performance. In the end, these issues were resolved through a combination of the two: improving the process and service performance first, and afterwards starting to evaluate systems improvement.

The development of SwisscardNet started in January 2008. Only three months later, SwisscardNet was up and running. Systems Integration Center AG was able to build the first process quickly, including human agents as well as software agents, thanks to its use of the proven ActionWorks® business interaction model as the conversation protocol between people and systems. While setting up further processes, the major issue to overcome was that process design was surpassed by the speed of process implementation. This was primarily due to the software agent's generic approach: after implementing them once in the first workflow, we could simply tell them about new business and conversational polices. There was no need to extend them in any way, mainly because of the closed interaction loop of the underlying business interaction model from Action Technologies. To overcome this, we needed a way to improve process definition time without losing quality, which led us to the technique of defining case processing policies using cases known as meta-cases. This approach is extremely valuable because cases are defined in the same way as business cases are processed in SwisscardNet, just in a different context. Furthermore, change and version management came to be an issue because of time pressure. Prerequisites of releases, which had not yet been tested and thus not installed, were missing in production and were the reason for several support calls. All of these issues can now be managed and automated as an integral part of the meta-case processing, thus improving the quality of deliveries and guaranteeing change and version management.

5.3 Organization Adoption

The objective of the SwisscardNet initiative was end-to-end automation that would enrich human users' jobs and use automation to relieve them of the burden of certain types of work and needing to know all of the processing rules by heart. People were naturally looking forward to trying out such a new tool, yet it was not always easy to sell them on this approach, mainly for two reasons: First, the term "automate" almost invariably triggers fears of job loss. Secondly, nobody was really able to imagine what it would be like to collaborate with software agents. Responding to the first question is never easy, but most of us can understand that automation boosts corporate productivity and quality and thus, in the long term, guarantees jobs as well.

The other question wasn't as straightforward, because when people think about software agents, everybody has his or her own ideas and expectations. The most well-recognized software agent for people working in offices is probably Microsoft's Office animated paper clip. This guy is a fun novelty in the beginning, but after a while he always seems to appear at the wrong moment telling you something you already know, and thus most users sooner or later deactivate the feature. It must be said that in the beginning our own software agent was far from what it can do today, mainly because we have taken actual users' experiences with the agent as the inspiration for new features we hadn't thought to implement in the beginning.

One good example is that we initially had only one software agent in place, and because the agents are integrated into the organizational structure of Swisscard as virtual employees, the agents earn rights and obligations just like human employees do. This forced us to assign the agent to the highest level in the organizational hierarchy, thus giving it the right to see everything – but of course the agent's work then became invisible to most other people. This was intended by design, but after a while people started telling us that they were "surprised" by the agent's actions or that they don't understand why the agent "(re-)acted" in a particular way.

This led us to introduce the same user interface for software agents as for all human agents when it comes to ad-hoc instructions or comments: the instruction-comment view, where software agents notify human users about what happened and why. To overcome the obstacle that human agents could not see the workloads of their software counterparts, we created a software agent for every organizational entity (OE), thus endowing the local software agent with the corresponding OE-specific rights and obligations. From then on, human actors were able to check the workloads of their assistants using the virtual office views. This is extremely helpful for long transactions, when the agent waits for a reply message from an external partner or host system and the customer asks for the status of his or her credit card application entry. In fact, we developed the agent's user interface together with the human users, which provides a model of ideal collaboration between human users and their assistants. When users have the subjective sense that the application and live processes have a positive impact, then the application tends to be accepted and adopted very quickly. But the key to good acceptance was, in the end, improved functionality and performance.

As a result of this, teams at Swisscard could be reorganized such that individual teams now process all of the credit cards for specific cases. Previously, credit card applications were processed by several teams, but only for specific credit cards.

This was mainly because of the complex and card-dependent rules for processing applications. Today, thanks to the guidance and assistance of software agents, people can manage all of the credit cards/products within a given process. This is why management was able to introduce job enrichments for human agents and why it could even be said that it was the employees themselves who benefited the most from the introduction of SwisscardNet.

SwisscardNet Workflow Configuration

Hardware:

-1 dual CPU application Server
-1 dual CPU process manager
-2 quad CPU database servers
  configured in a fail over cluster
-1 dual CPU test server for unit and
  integration testing

Software:

-Microsoft Windows 2003 Server
-Microsoft SQL Server 2005
-Microsoft IIS Web Server
-ActionWorks® Metro 5.2
-ActionSolutions® Software Suite 2.0

BENEFITS

Until recently, it was not affordable for mid-size companies to implement process improvements across multiple companies and business areas. Nevertheless, even now the challenge is how to provide the impeccable financial services customers require on the one hand, and on the other hand how to keep pace with larger companies when it comes to enforcing compliance rules and fulfilling continuously increasing legal requirements, while simultaneously cutting costs. Many financial institutions have attempted to follow strategies that involve charging transaction fees or segmenting the market and reducing the level of service for particular client segments. Swisscard has bucked this trend by offering all of its customers the same level of service. Moreover, Swisscard provides services to its customers far faster than its competition, and at significantly reduced costs. *Mastering the information supply chain* was the key to improving business process excellence and to tremendously boosting both productivity and quality.

6.1 Cost Savings

Within the first fourteen months, seven different processes were deployed. The business case presented here focuses exclusively on the economic benefits of the first process, the *credit card application* process. This business case only takes into consideration the benefits resulting directly from the improved process design, i.e. cost savings from optimized process execution. Increased revenue or other earnings are not included, whereby initial investment costs for the software agent implementation are covered. All the other workflows were able to benefit from the existing software agency and thus have far exceeded the management's financial expectations. It is likely that as documentation of these additional business cases is completed, an additional white paper documenting the above-mentioned economic benefits will be submitted to the WfMC. The cost savings of the first year already amounts to over one million US dollars; the net present value (NPV) in 2009 nears the one million mark. The ROI of 338 percent fulfills the Swisscard management's expectation of having the business case in positive figures **within the first year**. Needless to say, the successful business cases of the other six workflows are grounded on this initial investment.

6.2 Time Reductions and Productivity Improvements

Reduced cycle time of 40%. Credit card application processing times could be improved by an unbelievable 40 percent through improved business and conversation policies. The availability of the right information, at the right time, in the right format and presented to the right (human or software) agent made these advances possible.

Increased productivity of 30%. The paradox of job enrichment through job enlargement has ended up with productivity increases of 30 percent. There were many critical when the SwisscardNet initiative was first announced. But now, one year later, the same number of employees can manage 30 percent more credit card applications and at the same time tremendously increase the quality of processing.

Increased quality of 10%. The number of withdrawals because of missing or incorrect information has been reduced by 10 percent thanks to the end-to-end automation paradigm, where human agents focus only on the activities which cannot be delegated to their counterparts, the action agents.

BEST PRACTICES, LEARNING POINTS AND PITFALLS

7.1 Best Practices and Learning Points

- ✓ Flexible design – Semiformal systems like SwisscardNet are most useful when we understand enough to formalize in a computer system some, but not all, of the knowledge relevant to acting in a given situation. We believe that this includes almost all real-world situations. The trick to designing semiformal systems, we believe, is to design flexible systems that allow us to exploit the patterns and knowledge we understand when they are useful, without getting in the way when they are not. And this is precisely the goal of the design principle used in SwisscardNet.

- ✓ Assistant Agents – Rule-based software agents perform active tasks for people without requiring the direct attention of their users. Agents can be triggered by events and act according to policies (rules). Agents assist users in different ways: they hide the complexity of difficult tasks, they perform tasks on the user's behalf, they help different users to collaborate and they monitor events and procedures. Agents work when you don't, and work where you aren't, and never get tired. Agents monitor events and always respect conversation and business policies when acting.

- ✓ Simplifying legacy integration – Requesting services through software agents at a higher level corresponds more to user *intentions* than to specific service *implementations*, thus providing a level of *encapsulation*, analogous to the encapsulation provided at the level of communications protocols. It is thus, that agents help to socialize existing system's functionality and in combination with a service-oriented architecture many of the standard services for distributed computing don't have to be reinvented.

7.2 Pitfalls

- ✗ Reliability – We should not assume that agents are infallible or perfect. They should be robust to inappropriate or malformed messages and should be able to support reasonable mechanisms for identifying and signalling errors and warnings.

- ✗ Visibility – Make everything relevant to agent's operation of a process (case) visible to people involved. When software agents do something, show the effects immediately. Otherwise people are confused and surprised at the results of actions.

- ✗ Responsibility – At every moment, human agents are in a position of authority and human actions affect the case's processing situation. If human agents just sit there for a time, letting software agent's activities go on in the direction they are going, that in itself constitutes an action, with effects that human agents may or may not want. At the end, human agents are solely responsible for the quality of process execution – this cannot be delegated.

COMPETITIVE ADVANTAGES

We have stepped ahead of our competition, both in terms of the technology, which is not available to any of our competitors, and in our combination of the business focus on a relationship management-centric strategy to embed external contracting parties in our business process execution. SwisscardNet provides the glue between external relationship managers and their clients, and between our internal middle and back offices. The technological edge is that we've modernized our IT people-to-people platform and applications ahead of our main competitors, thus enabling Swisscard to compete on financial service and specialization without incurring disadvantages faced by small and mid-scale organizations.

We have also reduced our operational risk by making sure that internal guidelines and external regulatory requirements are fulfilled. The integrated rule management in the new participant-to-participant platform allows us to adopt new requirements quickly, which in turn simplifies effective collaboration across enterprise boundaries. This is an advantage that should not be underestimated in the advent of stringent regulatory requirements, because the highest risk for companies today is rarely in routine operations; rather it is in informal, unstructured interactions among people working together. As a result, Swisscard is able to set the industry standard for service, grow our volumes and expand our client base without eroding our margins or cutting back on service. It will be very difficult indeed for most of our competitors to achieve the same results.

TECHNOLOGY

The SwisscardNet system consists of four basic building blocks: the SwisscardNet

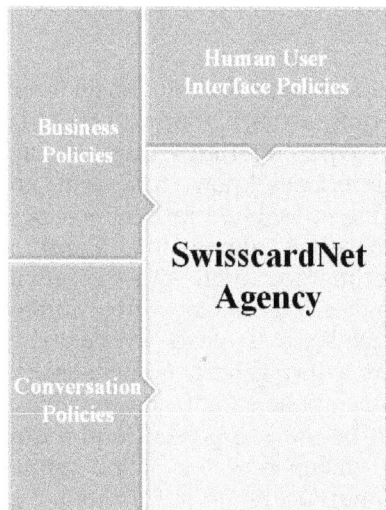

agency, the human user interface policy, the business policy and the conversation policy. All of these subsystems have been built on the foundation of the ActionWorks® process engine from Action Technologies Inc., using the Action Solutions Software Suite® from Action Solutions AG in Switzerland as the implementation framework. This framework consists of pre-built application parts and components for managing the various working styles in a generic, case-oriented manner, as well as a metadata repository for storing all of the relevant policy, definition and configuration information needed at run-time to process the cases within SwisscardNet.

Figure 7: SwiscardNet system overview

SwisscardNet Agency

SwisscardNet agency is the core building block for all agents working with Swiss-cardNet, including human and action agents. In a purely Aristotelian sense, an agent is one who takes action. In social and legal terms, an agent is one who is empowered to act on behalf of another. In our case, action agents exercise Swiss-cardNet agency – on behalf of the human Swisscard agents and in service of Swisscard. A key aspect here is that both the people and their agents use and modify the same information base of linked information objects. Although the initial focus of BPM was on the automation of mechanistic business processes, it has since been extended to integrate human-driven processes in which human interaction takes place in series or parallel with the mechanistic processes. Whereas human agents focus on tasks where human intervention or collaboration is required on an ad-hoc basis or according to policy, the action agents focus on automatable tasks and systems interaction.

For example, when performing certain individual steps in the business process requires sophisticated intuition or judgment, these steps are assigned to appropriate human agents within the organization. The agency creates a single integrated environment out of many different kinds of formal and informal information and many different applications, which allows people to use a simple and consistent interface for all workflow activities and applications to interact with each other. Thus, the action agent's major effort is toward leveraging the function call or message-oriented third-party interfaces in a way such that they follow the business policies as well as the conversation policies used in the agency.

The action agent's approach to dealing with legacy systems is to implement wrappers. The wrapper can directly examine the data structures of the legacy program and modify those data structures when necessary. At the host-side, existing entry forms are manipulated with screen scraping, views and the programmable mouse approach using the Rational Robotic System. This allows existing host functionality to be integrated without the need for low-level software integration, using a kind of manual input emulation.

Human User Interface Policies

SwisscardNet provides a direct manipulation, graphical and fully web-based interface to human users. Since direct manipulation requires information objects to be visible, users are constantly informed about the types of things they can act upon. Anyone with experience of iconic desktop interfaces knows that there are times when sequences of actions are better off being automated rather than performed directly by the user in overly simple and therefore tedious steps. Combining the expression of user intention through direct manipulation with the notion of an indirect management style of interaction makes it possible to free human users from the obligation to spell out each action explicitly. Instead, the flexibility and intelligence of the action agents allows humans to give general guidelines and forget about the details. These human user interface policies not only provide a general, dynamic graphical user interface that can be used to present and manipulate all kinds of information objects; they also define how the action agents have to react to system-generated events when human users are not present, e.g. *what went wrong and why* through the whiteboard, which is available by default in the generic case's GUI.

Business Policies

Rule-based systems implement a model of processing based on logical constructs called production rules. Production rules have two parts: the antecedent (often called the left-side or the *IF* component of the rule) and the consequent (the right-side or *THEN* component of the rule). The antecedent specifies some condition to be satisfied, and the consequent some action to be performed when the antecedent is true. In a rule-based system, the production rules are organized and collected in a structure called a knowledge base. As the conditions of given production rules in the knowledge base are satisfied, the rule is fired to produce actions that direct the behavior of the system. Scripts can be used to represent some consistent sequence of events. They must include a set of entry conditions that need to be satisfied before the script can be invoked, as well as a set of information objects with their corresponding actions representing the sequence of events themselves. All this information is managed through business policies.

Conversation Policies

One major issue when designing agent-oriented systems is how to implement policies governing conversational and other social behavior among agents. A conversation policy explicitly defines what sequences of which semantic messages are permissible between a given set of participating agents. Since the ActionWorks® business interaction model is well suited to all of the thinkable request scenarios that both action agents and human agents can make of each other, we've chosen to make use of the ActionWorks® business interaction model as the default core-speech-act model; it thus provides the common base for all of the interactions between agents, human and non-human, in SwisscardNet. The conversational state is represented by a simple finite state machine, which models the sequence of interactions that occur in the conversation. For each conversational state, the state machine has an action associated with every input event type. The finite conversational state machine of ActionWorks® coordinates commitments and interactions between individual agents or groups of agents. The conversation policy of SwisscardNet currently supports various conversational patterns, all of which are shared among the agents and based on the business interaction model of Action Technologies.

THE TECHNOLOGY AND SERVICE PROVIDERS

Action Technologies Inc., Alameda, www.actiontech.com

Action Technologies has delivered for more than 20 years award-winning Business Process Management (BPM) software that reduces the time and cost of decision-driven processes by 40-60% and typically generates returns of more than 300%. The ActionWorks® Suite enables leading global customers to analyze, redesign, implement and continuously improve their operations through a patented system for managing negotiations and commitments.

Action Solutions AG, Zug, www.actiontech.ch

Action Solutions has delivered the ActionSolutions® Software Suite, an application framework based on the ActionWorks® BPM suite. The ActionSolutions® Suite is a unique Business Activity Software Suite consisting of different frameworks reflecting the way people work together. These frameworks and it's unique way of assembling workflows using generic work-style patterns were the base for the successful, rapid development and deployment at Swisscard.

Systems Integration Center AG, Zurich, www.sicenter.com

Systems Integration Center was the IT-Implementation partner for this project. They implemented the Action Agents and adopted the patented ActionWorks® Business Interaction Model as the universal language of business between the participants of the SwisscardNet P2P-Workflow in just 3 months. This was only possible due to the patented ActionWorks® Business Interaction Model that acts as a universal translator between the language of business and the language of technology.

Section 2

Middle East-Africa

Abu Dhabi Commercial Bank, United Arab Emirates

Finalist, Middle East-Africa
Nominated by Newgen Software Technologies Ltd., India

1. EXECUTIVE SUMMARY / ABSTRACT

Newgen provided the bank with a BPM-enabled workflow platform, which not only helped bank to automate its processes, but also allowed seamless integration of the BPM solution with its existing applications.

2. OVERVIEW

Abu Dhabi Commercial Bank (ADCB), with a strong presence in Consumer and Corporate is a leading provider of technology-enabled services. In its objective towards complete automation of processes, the bank was in urgent need for a solution that would enable end-to-end automation of their key business processes and also provide integration with its existing applications. Newgen provided the bank with a BPM-enabled workflow platform, which not only helped bank to automate its processes, but also allowed seamless integration of the BPM solution with its existing applications.

Some of the **key benefits** are:
- Reduced TATs, processing time and servicing time
- Customer Service Quality & Satisfaction for both existing and new customers
- Avoid dependency on the physical documents
- Large volumes of transactions handled on daily basis

Some of the key challenges are:
- Processing delays and low productivity
- Dependency on physical movement of documents between branches and departments
- Difficulty in verification process and error identification due to unavailability of documents
- Difficulty in tracking and monitoring of processes
- Major challenges in incorporating process change requirements using the existing application

3. BUSINESS CONTEXT

Starting its operations in 1985, ADCB has established itself as the bank of choice for a large number of customers in the UAE. The bank has been making steady investments in its IT infrastructure and business automation solutions. Along with a core system, the bank also uses a card management system for debit and credit cards, a courier system for dispatch and tracking of customer documents, and a Short Messaging System (SMS) application for customer communications. However, most of these applications and processes were operating without any integration between each other. The bank needed a solution which would provide the platform for complete automation and integration between processes and existing legacy system. This requirement was also in line with the bank's commitment towards technology adaptation for restructuring programme aimed at becoming the most preferred bank for both external and internal customers.

4. THE KEY INNOVATIONS

4.2 Business

The following section describes the impact of the project on the overall business scenario.

Benefits accrued to the bank were both direct and indirect. Reduction in operating costs, travel and communication expenses, office stationary and infrastructure usage were some of the benefits achieved by centralization and implementation of the BPM solution. The bank also achieved other benefits like increase in productivity and reduction in IT infrastructure costs through better utilization of the resources.

- Unified interface for all the underlying applications providing business users with enhanced ease of usage and perform multiple tasks through single system access.
- Enhanced performance was observed in terms of tracking of the business users, process and overall TAT.
- Extended availability by providing secured access to the bank's Direct Selling Agents.
- Scaling up of operational activities, enabling the bank to keep pace with business growth and demands.

4.3 Process

The following section describes the impact of the project on the processes involved in improving the overall system.

- Real time integration with the bank's core system and other applications.
- Reduced TAT for Account opening and other processes.
- Removal of work duplication, by restricting data entry at the branch operations only.
- Unified interface for all the underlying applications providing business users with enhanced ease of usage and perform multiple tasks through single system access.
- Identification of discrepancies at an earlier stage and their faster resolution through checking and validation utilities while doing data entry at the branch level.

4.4 Organization

The following section describes the impact of the project at the organizational level.

- Improved productivity and efficiency of employees with reduction in non-core activities, branch executives are able to cross sell other products.
- Improved customer satisfaction through quicker and better servicing, reduction in the requirement of physical forms, and reduced customer response timelines.
- Scalable solution that enables faster rollout of initiatives and handle increasing business volumes.
- Flexible solution, in terms of incorporating changes in short durations in accordance with business requirements.

5. HURDLES OVERCOME

Based on the bank's requirements, Newgen developed a customized solution, consisting of the following products:

- OmniFlowTM - workflow solution
- OmniDocsTM - document management solution
- OmniScanTM (OmniCapture) - image capture and indexing solution

In the initial phase, Newgen helped the bank automate one its most critical process, the Account opening process. Integrated with the bank's existing core application, the solution provides easier and faster data exchange across systems. Buoyed by the results achieved within a short time of deployment, the bank also implemented and automated a number of other key processes such as Customer and Account Maintenance, Term Deposit Initiation and Maintenance on the BPM platform. At present, the solution has been implemented across 43 branches of the bank and supports 706 users. Every month, more than 61,000 documents are scanned and imported into the workflow for processing. For Account Opening, the system processes approximately 245 applications every day, which can be easily scaled up to meet any future requirement of the bank.

The new system allows users to capture relevant information and customer sign-off at the branches itself before the case files move to the Central Processing Department (CPD). Instead of customers having to submit complex forms, the system automatically generates the required forms. The branches update these forms online and take customer signoff before uploading in the system. On completion of the mandatory branch level activities, the files move to the CPD immediately for further processing. Through real-time integration with the core system, CPD users directly initiate the Account Opening process from the workflow solution. Through integration with the SMS system, the solution enabled the team to communicate to customers within 10-15 minutes of their account becoming operational. The solution also generates the welcome letter within 30 minutes of account activation. Post account activation, CPD is able to track and monitor the dispatch of the welcome kits to customers through the courier system, which has also been integrated with the workflow solution.

6. BENEFITS

6.1 Cost Savings

Benefits accrued to the bank were both direct and indirect. Reduction in operating costs, travel and communication expenses, office stationary and infrastructure usage were some of the benefits achieved by centralization and implementation of the BPM solution. The bank also achieved other benefits like increase in productivity and reduction in IT infrastructure costs through better utilization of the resources.

6.2 Time Reductions

Reduced TAT for Account opening and other processes.

6.3 Increased Revenues

Return on Investment of 230 percent.

7. BEST PRACTICES, LEARNING POINTS AND PITFALLS

7.1 Best Practices and Learning Points

✓ *Consistently tracking prospects opens new opportunities for cross-selling and up-selling*

✓ *Greater customer satisfaction, which demands immediate and informed response to their queries, is effectively implemented using a BPM solution*

✓ *A BPM solution establishes explicit and specific responsibilities with the stakeholders, thereby ensuring greater drive to accomplish work at their end.*

8. COMPETITIVE ADVANTAGES

- Scaling up of operational activities enabling the bank to keep pace with business growth and demands
- Compliance and Audit with easy KYC Process
- Incorporation of Islamic banking norms in very short duration due to Flexibility and improvisation of Processes

9. TECHNOLOGY

Opening of an account is the customer's first interaction with a bank. Newgen provided the bank with a BPM-enabled workflow platform for implementing an automated Account Opening process. The solution streamlined the overly complicated process. The customer approaches a Customer Relationship Officer or vice versa for opening an account. The officer captures the customer's details, verifies if the customer already exists, accordingly makes changes, captures the application form image along with the supporting documents and introduces it into the workflow.

Next, the officer submits the information to Customer Operations Manager for authorization. Once authorized, all the details arrive at the Central Processing Department (CPD), where the checks such as reviewing of customer and account information, verifying supporting documents, etc., are done. If cleared, the customer data is automatically pushed into the core system, else it is sent back to the branch for exception clearing. Information such as Account Information, Customer information including signatures, Cheque Book Request, Account Customer relationship, Account memo, etc., is pushed to the core system. Any new information is updated. CPD also generates a file for courier company for the welcome kits to be delivered.

Finally, a Welcome-kit letter along with other documents is generated and sent for dispatching through courier. Once, the kit is delivered, all documents related to the account opened are archived. If a kit is not delivered till a specified date, it is hand it over to branch for delivery to customer.

The BPM solution from Newgen has been integrated with the bank's Core Banking system, SMS system and Card Management system. The solution also enables generation of complete audit trail to view history of events taken place for any record.

The solution has been currently implemented at 43 branches of the bank, and is being used by 50 concurrent and 125 named users.

10. THE TECHNOLOGY AND SERVICE PROVIDERS

Other than Newgen no vendors were directly involved in the process except for the part where integration with the core banking system was done.

Other system interfaces to be exposed to the SMS gateway and Cheque Book System were developed by Newgen's delivery team. No external consultants were involved.

NAFITH Logistics PSC, Jordan

Silver Award, Middle East and Africa
Nominated by TraxAware Software LLC, Jordan

1. EXECUTIVE SUMMARY

Nafith Logistics Services is a company that delivers logistics support and trade facilitation services on a national and regional level, and one of the main branches of the company within Jordan is NAFITH-Aqaba.

NAFITH-Aqaba is a 250 employee organization spread over 39 remote locations working on a 24/7 shift structure to manage and control all trucks going in and out of the city of Aqaba. The NAFITH Truck Control System (TCS) is a public-private partnership project with a 10 year concession from the Aqaba Special Economic Zone Authority with the primary objectives of eliminating congestion, pollution, and increasing road safety. The purpose of this document is to layout the overall success elements of implementing the NAFITH Online Intranet Portal (NOIP) for the Nafith-Aqaba operation.

The following sections will clarify the innovations accomplished on various levels, the challenges overcome and the competitive advantages NOIP has added to NAFITH as the end user organization, as well as the vendor's experience. The document will also illustrate how NOIP was able to assist NAFITH in realizing its objectives. Finally, the paper will be discussing the future plans to enhance the NOIP.

The following terms are used throughout the document:

- **ASEZA**- Aqaba Special Economic Zone Authority
- **NOIP**- NAFITH Online Intranet Portal
- **TX** - TraxAware Software LLC
- **TCS**- Truck Control System

2. OVERVIEW

Upon being awarded the contract for a 10yr operation of the TCS, one of the key objectives for NAFITH was to "enhance the organization culture, through the creation of transparent HR processes", "Transform the public-sector mentality to a corporate one", and "create well defined business processes catering to all aspects of day-to-day work and procedures". These objectives were met through the development of the NIOP.

Working in the southern part of Jordan, with 250 previous public sector employees that come from a semi-tribal society that is based of favouritism, created several challenges for NAFITH. It imposed complexities for the future expansion of the company in other countries in the region, as well as imposed challenges in creating TCS Aqaba as the model operation for its marketing efforts worldwide. In addition, the competitive advantage of NAFITH business model was to ensure cost reductions and a 24hr seamless operation.

The project team consisted of the following departments:

- NAFITH Management
- NAFITH Administration and HR Departments (this includes the Purchasing and Warehousing)
- NAFITH Operations Department
- NAFITH Yards Department

- TX Technical Team

2.1 Implementation Process & Methodology Advantages

NOIP Application was built in compliance with TraxAware Software methodology which is by itself based on ISO 12207 and PMI standards for project management. Meeting these standards had a great effect on the flow of the project within its several phases.

Also, the application was built using Extreme Programming "XP Programming" concepts which allowed for the following factors to contribute to the success of the project:

- The fast delivery of the end product
- The direct involvement of TX software development team with different NAFITH departments
- The early identification of any contention points
- The creation of a harmonious team which was focused on studying and automating the business process maps.
- Setting up the project blueprints early-on and studying each process individually allowed the development team to understand how to automate the process, make the necessary modifications to them, and impact the speed and ease of implementing subsequent phases.

3. BUSINESS CONTEXT

3.1 Manual work at TCS before NOIP

Before NOIP was installed, existing operations were manually run against "what seemed to be" a predetermined set of instructions and procedures. Mapping out the processes and digging further into the details uncovered that most processes had an ad-hoc approach to their completion depending primarily on the person in charge at that time frame. Furthermore, all documents (personnel files, memos, announcements, etc) were physically stored in a filing storage room that had piles of files and continuously needed more space; searching for a document was a treacherous task, not to mention the unnecessary delays faced in certain processes and the lack of contingency plans if certain roles were not present. Branch and local management had little or no visibility on the different operations performed resulting in lack of visibility on personnel performance that led to an inability to perform strategic decisions in a timely manner. And finally, the privacy and security of personnel data and the complaint process were highly vulnerable.

The filling and distribution of different forms and announcements was done manually and through multiple communication channels which caused a huge waste of resources. Communicating homogeneously with the 39 locations 24/7 was a tedious task, whereby announcements would be copied and hung on bulletin boards at all locations for employees to see. There was no log to confirm that the announcement was read, causing all sorts of administrative and operational problems, some of which violate Jordanian Labour Law and breach contractual agreements.

3.2 Why NAFITH needed a workflow application?

The main objective behind implementing NOIP was derived directly from the objectives of NAFITH when it assumed the operations of TCS; to create a greater level of efficiency and productivity by providing each employee with the applications they need to do their jobs through a versatile portal. NAFITH management also realized early on that a web-based workflow engine would serve as a catalyst to introduce a corporate organizational culture within the NAFITH Aqaba branch.

Having everyone work on the application was a huge leap towards creating a standardized systematic method that governs the numerous internal operations of the company. Furthermore, it became a tool for building confidence between the employees and their new management, as favouritism was almost eradicated as a result of the automation. NAFITH management were aware that before they could look outside for new opportunities they needed to invest in cleaning their house first and to build a solid base whereby additional work can be added in a cost-efficient manner.

4. THE KEY INNOVATIONS

4.1 Business

4.1.1 NOIP Business Requirements

The NOIP main users or clients are NAFITH personnel at all levels of the organization, and thus all the services that were developed catered for them.

The following is the list of the system objectives which were implemented in the delivered solution:

- Reengineering of current manual internal processes at NAFITH to eliminate waste and modify them to be effectively automated. In addition to reduce paperwork and physical filing.
- Development of standard business rules that serve the processes at NAFITH while allowing for a certain level of flexibility with the application to cope with changing business rules.
- Present NAFITH Employees with complete web based cycles for all their needed activities, along with statuses of their applications.
- Having a central organization information hub between NAFITH HQ and NAFITH Aqaba Branch, making the information readily available.
- Assist NAFITH's different managerial levels to do the necessary audits and controls necessary for the daily operation.
- The system should have high security procedures in place allowing the privacy of communication between organizational hierarchies and guarding the private data of the employees.
- The system should improve efficiency and should assist the Administration and HR Department to better manage the personnel related process. It should reduce manual processes and paperwork, as well as eliminate redundancies.
- The system should allow for an automated internal communication, with read logs.
- The system should enable the staff to process different procedures according to predefined set of internal instructions and procedures set by NAFITH's regulations.
- The system should maintain an accurate up-to-date electronic record of all HR, administrative, and financial information, as well as be used as a central database to integrate all relevant information.
- The system should track the status of all applications, thus enhance personnel management activities and increase their satisfaction levels.
- The system should enable the assignment of processes/procedures to the correct staff/role responsible to carry out the tasks of these specific procedures.
- The system should generate statistical reports related to all automated activities from one comprehensive system/database.

- The system should offer statistical information in accordance with the needs of each user.
- Integration with FDfolio, NAFITH main TCS operations application, to allow single sign-on. As well as integrating with JAMSHEED, HQ accounting application for payroll purposes.
- The system should allow NAFITH to implement the Just-in-Time concept in the purchasing process and therefore maintain the optimal amount of stock of each of the company's consumables.

4.1.2 NOIP Functional Modules

Following are the core business components of the Nafith Portal:

- Human Resource Management System HRMS.
- Content Management System CMS.
- Warehouse Management System WMS

Human Resource Management System

The NAFITH NOIP HR module is able to track existing employee data and electronically automate all the HR related processes.

The HRMS includes services that fully integrate human resources, compensation and benefits administration, attendance, recruiting, training management and payroll.

- Payroll Management System: The HRMS helps the HR manager and staff to handle the employee's accounts more efficiently by integrating with accounting and financial application used by NAFITH, JAMSHEED, and gives the employees the ability to access and review their pay-slip record.
- Training Module: The Training Module allows for the creation of a separate profile for each employee that includes the training requirements for that employee. This module also allows for the training courses to be managed without creating conflict between staff schedules.
- Recruitment: The process of recruitment is consuming much time by the NAFITH HR department; the HRMS collect the applications and easily short lists the candidates in accordance with the position.
- Administration: the NAFITH NOIP provides many administrative services, such as:
  1. Managing Leaves: This module allows each employee to submit and get an approval on a leaves form from his/her manager electronically. The leave request workflow is managed by predefined rules in the workflow system.
  2. Employee Profile: Summary & detailed information about each employee to help NAFITH managers with decisions that are related to promotions, commissions, and awards are now readily available.

Content Management System

NOIP has a CMS or DMS (Document Management System) that is used to manage the work flow needed to collaboratively create, edit, review, index, search, publish and archive various kinds of electronic text. Such as announcements, news, emails, maintenance applications, leave applications, complaints and inquiries.

Nafith Portal CMS provides the following:

- An easily accessible repository of documents.
- A secure and easy to use filing and archiving tool.

- Activity log.

Warehouse Management System (WMS)

WMS tracks all supplies and provides real time information on their quantities with an escalation mechanism in case quantities drop below a pre-specified threshold.

4.1.3 NOIP Business Impact

- **Going Green:** the NOIP allowed NAFITH to achieve a milestone in its "going green" strategy. This was mainly achieved through the huge savings in paper and ink consumption.
- **Transparency:** the NOIP provides service modules with a clear set of predefined procedures for all staff members to follow and for management and external parties to audit. The NOIP insures that NAFITH is abiding by all Ministry of Labor laws, and that it is honoring all it contractual commitments. Furthermore, the NOIP has eliminated all forms of favoritism among the NAFITH managerial staff.
- **Less Waste:** the NOIP reduces errors and productivity loss associated with inputting and analyzing the same information in multiple systems. For example, the HR function has become more productive and effective, spending less time dealing with administrative tasks and more time focusing on HR initiatives, such as recruiting, employee retention and benefits analysis
- **Cross Organizational Communication:** the NOIP keeps employees informed & connected by allowing NAFITH to leverage its best practices, and deliver the information to the employees who need it the most. The NOIP has become an excellent way to create a consistent use of company policies and procedures, and motivate employees with company press releases and up-coming events.
- **Document Archiving:** the NOIP allows NAFITH to efficiently and effectively archive all the documents and forms that are processed by the system. One of the most important impacts associated with this function is the use of less physical storage space to store files.
- **Availability of Data:** the NOIP stores data in an easily accessible manner and makes it available in a readable and manageable format so that it can be exploited for statistical purposes. Furthermore, the NOIP allows the data to be tracked, eliminating data being misplaced in data storage cabinets.
- **Data Security:** NAFITH is able to maintain maximum security of sensitive data with user-defined, encrypted passwords. They can track logins with the use of a login activity report to see which employees are using the service.

4.2 Process

Prior to NOIP the organization's processes were defined as follows:

- Not documented
- Ad-hoc
- Non-standard
- Redundant and full of waste
- No time constraints associated

During the implementation of NOIP, all processes were mapped, documented, and distributed to relevant parties. A sample process is portrayed below.

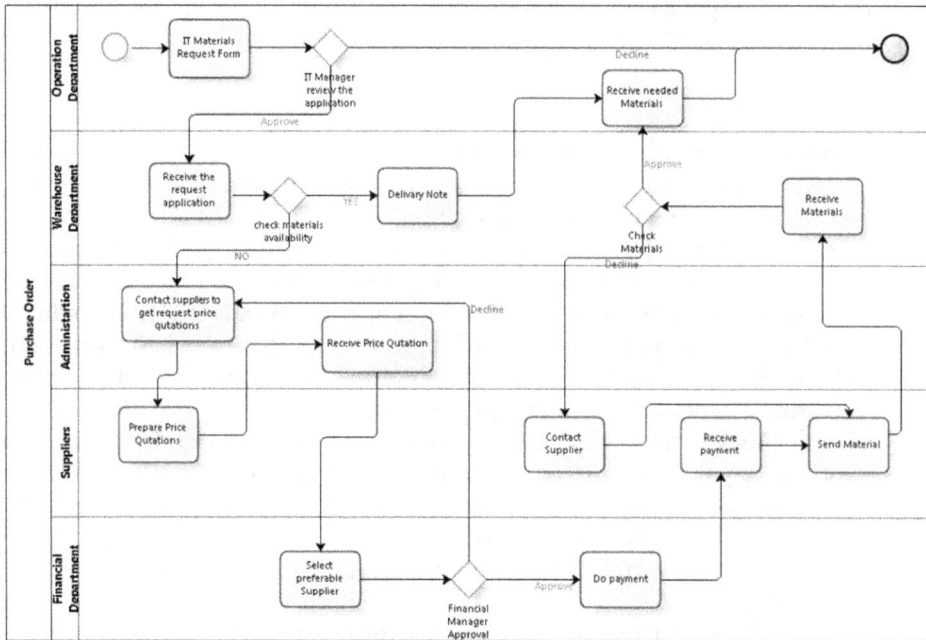

4.3 Organization

The application had a profound effect on the daily work of the employees; it had transformed their manual, paper-centric work into an advanced high tech automation. The following is a list of aspects of the organization was affected:

Booth Operators: no longer need to memorize procedures or miss announcements, or worry about the timely delivery of their vacation submissions. Now from the convenience of their office/booth they are able to stay connected with their organization. Furthermore, they are able to submit any complaint and voice opinions or suggestions privately to the designated party within the organization.

Middle Management: through the decentralization, they are able to lead their teams effectively, responding to requests throughout the day. This has been a factor in helping the organization shape its future leaders.

HR Department: the quality of their work has been elevated as they are no longer completely swamped with filing and issuing statistical reports, but are now more focused on core HR issues of HR development and training, organization structure and job descriptions.

Warehouse Department: with an automated WMS module, tied to an automated purchasing module, the warehouse has become more efficient with all the necessary notification to systemize their work, and making sure no items are out of stock.

Aqaba Branch Management: was able to focus on operations and business opportunities as opposed to the routine tedious tasks of organizational work.

Headquarters: the application was a bliss for all HQ departments, as now through a click of a button, they can monitor and audit the Aqaba branch and its departments, whether HR, Financial, or Administrative.

5. Hurdles Overcome

	NOIP Project Challenges	*NOIP Challenges Addressed*
Managerial Level	Tight delivery schedule & Budget. Clearly defining the security level of privileges on a role-based security scale. Time commitment of managers to design the system with their already swamped work schedules.	Weekly status meeting to review milestones and implement any needed corrective actions. Designed a set of interactive workshop and short interviews with managers as not to interrupt their schedules for a long time.
Business Level	Mapping out the process for all the procedures and documentation of different scenarios. Having the system reflect the legislations of the Jordanian Labour Law. Migrating manual data into an electronic one.	Prioritized procedures according to their importance and maturity level and then started by those that are more mature to establish the framework. Had a part time HR consultant on board to review the relevant module. Created technical scripts when possible to do the migration from excel sheets to limit the effect of that daunting task.
Organization Adoption	**Training** the staff to embrace the system and use it proactively in their daily work. **Resistance** of some roles due to the narrow perspective they had on their job description and thus assumed that with the automation their jobs are rendered redundant esp HR and Warehouse Employees. **Transition** process was complex due to the number of employees involved, the sensitivity of the procedures involved and continuity.	Early on, the direct involvement of the NAFITH team according to the relevant department was identified as a necessity for the success of the portal. The strategy on which NOIP was built was divided into a set of manageable modules, whereby the relevant team was involved from design to QA. After all comments are received and fixed, the operation department was selected for the first rolled out to first. This department served as the training centre for the remainder of the employees. So we had two kind of roll-out per module then per location. HR was integrated as part of the design team, they were also sent to HR workshop to understand the wide perspective of their job and plan accordingly.

6. BENEFITS

6.1 Cost Savings

The direct cost savings items realized immediately were as follows:

- **Paper consumption**: With the new application the paper cost has dropped by approximately 45% including other indirect cost such as recycling, printer and ink consumption. **The 45% savings in paper translates directly into 1.4 MT of paper**.
- **Fuel consumption:** in order to collect original copies of applications, a designated employee used to go to all the destinations to collect and distribute the originals applications. This used to be done 3 times a week. Upon implementation of the application, this was no longer needed as the original application is the electronic copy; this had a direct effect on the fuel consumption of around 5%.
- **Employees**: in their 2009 HR plan, NAFITH was planning to hire three additional administrative staff to cater for the work and collect/distribute the internal mail. This plan was cancelled after the implementation of the application, which saved the company around USD 26,300 in salaries.
- **Car**: in their 2009 budgets, NAFITH have budgeted to buy an additional car to increase the number of rounds necessary to collect and distribute the internal mail, this idea was cancelled after the NOIP implementation as it was deemed unnecessary, saving the company USD 19,000 in the cost of the car and an additional USD 3,000 annually in vehicle related costs.

6.2 Time Reductions

Time reductions were the main motivation behind building NOIP, this can be categorised into two categories:

Elimination of wasted work time: different employee levels seemed to be consumed in non business related activities instead of focusing on value added revenue generating ones, although no formal measurement has been conducted, this is expected to be as follows per organizational function:

- Top Management – 50% less time in conducting administrative activities
- HR – 60% less time on noncore related activities
- Employee Time – 20% less time on filling and submitting forms, and on following up on responses
- Headquarters – 60% less time accumulating branch related reports, and about 50% less time on- taking decisions on branch requests

Process Duration: this was significantly reduced across all the implemented modules. To give an example, the process of approving an annual vacation used to take in average 3-5 days; currently this has been reduced to an average of 3hrs. Similarly, the purchasing process used to take 4-6 days to be completed; currently it takes 2-3 days.

6.3 Increased Revenues

Top-line growth: NOIP had no direct effect on increased revenue as it was an internal project directed towards enhancing the internal organizational operation.

6.4 Productivity Improvements

Productivity improvements were realized through the time savings explained above. The application created a seamless environment for handling the "must to do" internal organization work, leaving more time to focus on business oriented activities.

In addition, it has been noticed that through improving the communication channel, employee participation in value added ideas has increased, 20 employee generated ideas have been reported six months after NOIP implementation as opposed to four in the six months before. This suggests that the environment created encourages employee participation.

7. BEST PRACTICES, LEARNING POINTS AND PITFALLS

7.1 Best Practices and Learning Points

- ✓ *Engage client team of all levels in building the application, especially if it directly affects their work.*
- ✓ *Transition phase is extremely sensitive, it needs to be carefully planned to ensure success as first impressions count.*
- ✓ *Explain clearly the objectives of application so as not to face easily avoided resistance.*
- ✓ *Use a well tested methodology in developing complex applications.*
- ✓ *Always simplify, create a friendly user interface and discuss processes in a language the client understands.*
- ✓ *Manage risks and create solid plans to mitigate them.*
- ✓ *Communication, communication, communication – all through the project.*

7.2 Pitfalls

- ✗ *Although it is achievable now, however, it would have been much easier to design the portal from the beginning to be a multi-lingual portal had the development team known that it may be utilized in non-Arabic speaking countries as NAFITH expanded beyond the Arabic speaking world.*
- ✗ *Avoid getting caught into cross departmental conflicts.*
- ✗ *After the implementation it was realized that now two roles may work on a process simultaneously. Allowing two roles to view and act on a request/report simultaneously is also achievable now, but it would have been much easier to design it at the beginning.*

8. COMPETITIVE ADVANTAGES

NAFITH has a 10 year concession contract to run TCS, and thus does not have any real competition. Moreover, NOIP is currently an internal application whose main derivatives had no competitive advantages behind them. Having said that, cost savings are always necessary in the volatile market which NAFITH operates in.

Long Term Plans: The next step in developing NOIP is to go external, to build on top of it a CRM module that automates the daily operational work between NAFITH clients "Trucking Companies" and the operations department. The CRM module will contain the following, to name a few:

- Announcement Module
- Permit Cancellation
- Permit Editing
- Online Violation Application

The CRM module is expected to increase the competitive advantage of NAFITH, as through the automation of that part of the operation, it is expected that the response time to client requests to increase thus creating more customer satisfaction.

9. TECHNOLOGY

9.1 New System Configuration

Client workstations running MS Windows XP access the system through SSL connection using MS IE 6 or higher, or Mozilla Firefox.

The following are all of-the-shelf software products which the system utilizes:

- Adobe ColdFusion 8 as application server
- Apache 2.2 with SSL as web server
- Oracle 10g as database server
- MS Windows 2008 server as servers operating system
- Ms Windows XP as client PC's operation system

9.2 Configuration View

The following diagram displays the current system configuration:

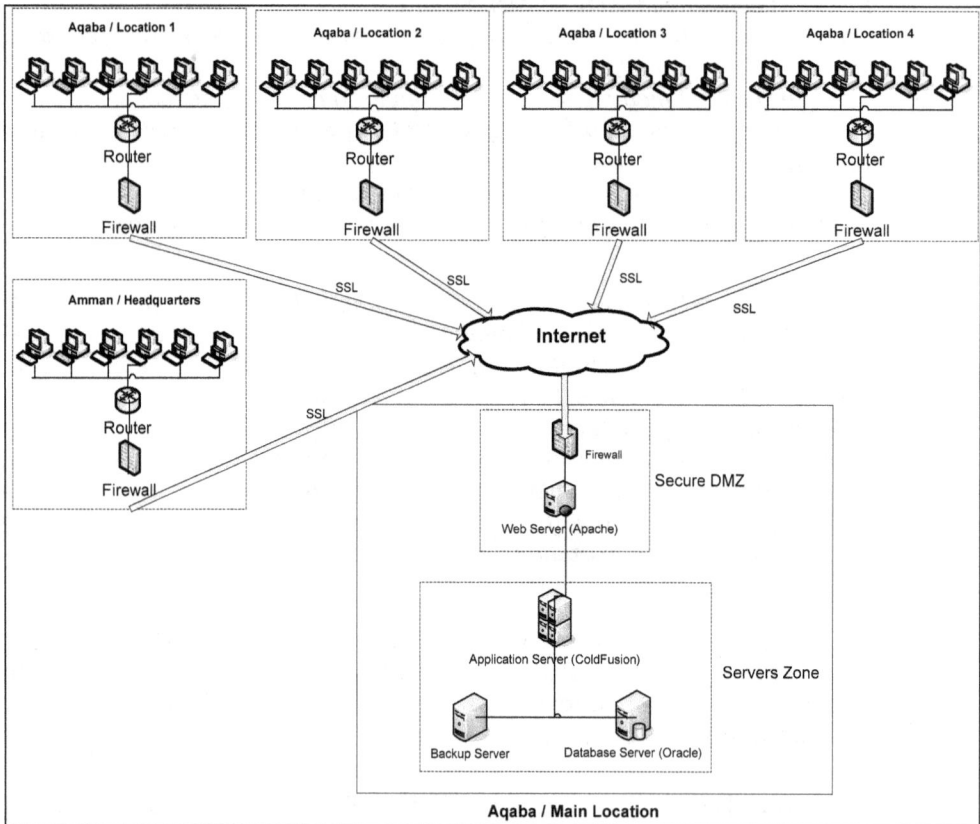

10. THE TECHNOLOGY AND SERVICE PROVIDERS

10.1 NOIP Workflow Engine

NOIP Workflow Engine was developed based on Adobe ColdFusion 8 to be a human-centric workflow. Human-centric, as opposed to process-centric, requires a high level of interactivity between the person and the solution in order to feed the correct information into the activity a person is responsible for, which facilitates processing any of the services a person is in charge of to feed the next set of activities and so forth.

The workflow engine manages and executes modelled business processes and binds all of the components in order to create a single instance.

From the figure below, you can see how other workflow components (Process definition, Process Management and web-based UI) interact with workflow engine (Process execution).

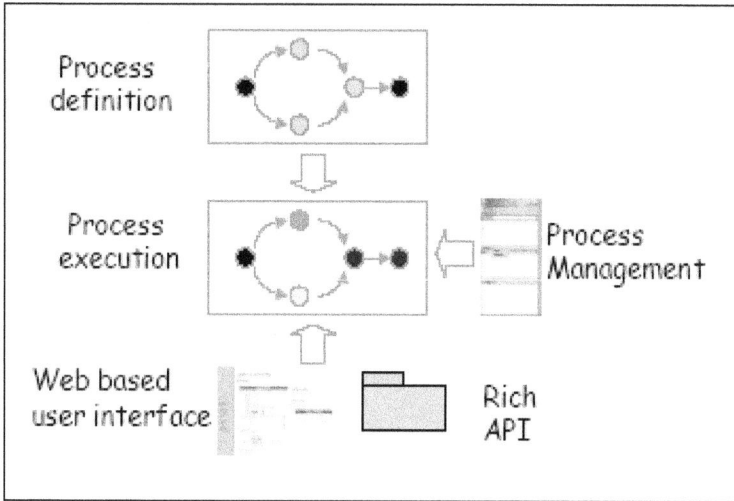

The diagram below demonstrates how NOIP Workflow binds the system components:

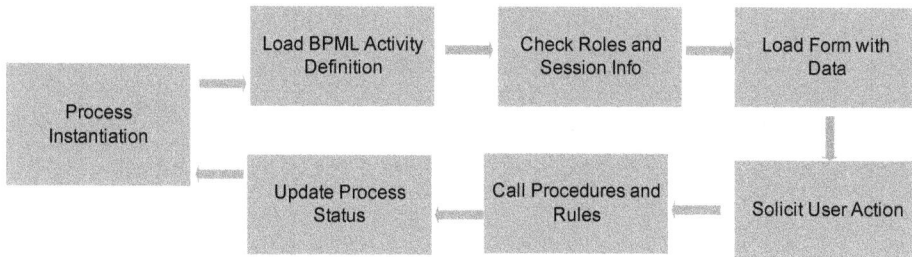

11. REFERENCES:

NAFITH Logistics PSC: www.nafith.com

TraxAware Software LLC: www.TraxAware.com

Nokia Siemens Networks, UAE

Gold Award, Middle East and Africa
Nominated by Appian, USA

1. EXECUTIVE SUMMARY / ABSTRACT

Nokia Siemens Networks was created in 2007 through the merger of the former Networks Business Group of Nokia and the carrier-related businesses of Siemens. Today, NSN is one of the world's largest network communications companies – with 60,000 employees, a leading position in all key markets across the world, and total sales of more than €15 billion a year. The Consulting and Systems Integration (CSI) unit within NSN is an organization of 4,000 staff, with sales of over €500 million a year.

CSI's particular business is an unusual mixture of high-volume/low-revenue engagements (i.e., consulting projects) and low-volume/high-revenue projects (i.e., major value-added service rollouts within large network implementations). The "mish-mash" tools landscape resulting from the NSN merger fundamentally did not meet the needs of CSI's dynamic business requirements. In addition, NSN's formation from two companies with, in many respects, polar opposite corporate environments created friction in operational execution. CSI desperately needed to get an established set of processes in place very quickly because without end-to-end visibility, fast and effective decision-making to drive the business was hampered, if not impossible. CSI looked to BPM technology to drive quick, highly-configurable, higher-value/lower cost process solutions to meet its business goals.

2. OVERVIEW

Nick Deacon assumed leadership of CSI's Business Process Management team when NSN was founded. Since that time, he has been responsible for the creation and implementation of the CSI process framework and the development of effective business process management suite technology use within CSI. Through previous professional experience, Nick has dealt first-hand with working environments that lacked robust processes and tools aligned to a process framework. His mission within CSI is to create a working environment that speaks one common process language, utilizing a business process management suite to manage the business effectively and support growth. From the start, this mission has been driven by Nick's vision to use BPM to transform the way NSN operates as an organization.

The basic tenet of this vision is that a competitive, industry-leading business needs to have full visibility into its fundamental business components (Sales, Delivery and Resources), as well as the ability to drive and maximize its business performance through effective portfolio management, knowledge management, remote capability and overall business management. This data needs to be accessible in a holistic environment that supports not only business management but also Consultant's, Engineers, Project Managers, and other employees.

Due to NSN/CSI's heterogeneous technological landscape, the end-to-end business could not be viewed at any stage. NSN's infrastructure housed large enterprise systems such as ERP from SAP, and other rigid and disconnected sales workflow, resource and knowledge management applications. These tools, designed for large (and largely inflexible) enterprise needs left CSI to manage its dynamic business by spreadsheet. This resulted in the inability to conduct real-time business management, limitations on Future Planning capability, inaccuracy of data both within CSI and the wider NSN, and significant overhead wasted on reporting, training and data entry. CSI desperately needed to get an established set of processes in place very quickly because without end-to-end visibility, fast and effective decision-making to drive the business was hampered, if not impossible.

CSI set a very aggressive timetable for success in its BPM program. Through a modular delivery approach, CSI targeted initial BPMS services rollout in 4-6 months, and complete end-to-end business operational management within one year. As Nick had expected with such a grand vision and journey ahead of him, there were minor set-backs and hurdles to be crossed along the way, but the resulting BPM solution, named "ZEUS" after the Greek God of Control, achieved pan-CSI rollout and effectiveness a mere 90 days behind schedule.

The results of ZEUS have been staggering. For a €1.8 million investment, CSI has calculated a €12 million annual productivity savings through the system. This impressive and transformational Return-On-Investment has been carefully benchmarked. For each principal role or function, CSI used 15 specific measures to compare time spent before and after the delivery of ZEUS. These benefits span all levels of CSI employees (Global and Regional Management, Consultants, Project Managers, Technical Support Managers, Solution Architects, etc.), the business as a whole, and across the value chain to customers.

3. BUSINESS CONTEXT

NSN inherited an array of inflexible and disconnected tools – SAP for logistics, a workflow solution for Sales, COTS solutions for Resource Management and Financial functions, and primarily local hard drives for knowledge management. Areas such as Delivery, Technical Support, and Reporting had no systems support at all. CSI was forced to use EXCEL to off-set the limitations of the enterprise systems, and to fill the large gaps. In addition, CSI had limited ownership of data entry and was reliant on others to populate CSI's needs. This left CSI with poor visibility into its Sales Funnel, Projects Delivery, forecasted Revenue, Cost and Margin and Demand and Supply Planning. CSI did develop and actively communicate a strong Process Framework, but with no holistic underpinning technology platform, it was difficult to manage and enforce. Additionally, that Framework was inherently dynamic, constantly changing and updating to reflect new business needs and new personnel/contractors joining the organization. The lack of embedded process created an inability to govern effectively, and poor visibility of business data led to inaccurate decision making and planning.

The "work" to be addressed by the ZEUS BPM solution covered CSI's entire business, from highly human-centric functions across sales, technical support, delivery, etc., to back-end system-to-system processes. This meant that all CSI employees were potential users of the system, necessitating an intuitive and flexible technology approach that would enable business-level user adoption.

4. THE KEY INNOVATIONS

Customers:

ZEUS is a comprehensive BPM Program encompassing multiple process solutions targeted to all three core elements of CSI's business: Sales, Delivery and Resources. CSI's customers have been directly and positively impacted by the ZEUS rollout. By allowing CSI employees to focus on what they do best, and giving management the real-time data to make better decisions, ZEUS ensures that customers receive the highest possible service from their CSI team.

Process:

CSI achieved complete end-to-end business visibility in 15 months, with periodic modular deployments of ZEUS application solutions for Service Delivery, Resource/Competency Management, Sales Management, Technical Support, Product & Portfolio Management, and Remote Delivery & Offshoring. Just two examples of ZEUS process transformation are:

The Resource & Competency Management application allows Resource Managers (RMs) to understand, for the first time, the skill sets of all employees, forecast accurate project close dates, and identify the required resources. All employees now rate themselves against the NSN portfolio of service products and general skills. A custom interface allows RMs to search this user store, filtering by skill sets and other criteria. Extended user profiles and reports give RMs a 360-degree view of resources and competencies, and detailed SQL Reporting delivers insight into current and predicted staffing needs, staff availability, and allocation ratios segmented by regions and sub-regions.

The Sales Management application enables Solutions Consultants to track and manage all of their sales opportunities throughout a well-defined series of sales phases. The application tracks the weighted value of each opportunity, enabling the business to accurately forecast potential and future revenue from sales across operational regions and lines of business. During the Sales process, resource needs anticipated for potential new projects are requested in the **Resource Management application**, with secured deals transitioning into the **Project Delivery application**.

ZEUS will continue over the next 6-12 months with the optimization of each of the modules to 'mould' ZEUS to the exact needs of the business. This optimization is greatly enabled by real-time process architecture and "on-the-fly" process modification capabilities of the Appian BPM Suite, upon which Zeus is built. Real-time data visibility on process performance and bottlenecks can be used to modify process models in-flight, with the changes deployed in real-time into the production application.

Appian's 100 percent web-based software and Service Oriented Architecture are also important factors in achieving NSN's BPM vision. Both significantly ease the integration challenges posed by such a large-scale BPM program. Appian's "Smart Services" also make SOA a useful tool outside of IT, giving end users drag-and-drop simplicity in employing web service components within their composite applications and mash-up portals.

Organization:

The solution touches all functional areas within CSI, as well as suppliers and customers.

- Projects Module: 400 users, Live since Sep 08, 2000 projects
- Technical Support Module: 150 users, Live since Jan 09, 600 contracts
- Socio-Business Networking: 2,400 users, Live since Feb 09, 800 pages
- Resource Management: 2,400 users, Live since Mar 09, training
- Competence Management: 2,400 users, Live since Mar 2009, 47% completion
- Sales Management: 500 users, Live since May 09, training
- Solution Management: 500 users, Live since May 09, training

- Business Management: 300 users, Live since Jun 09, training
- Remote Delivery/Offshoring: 1500 users, Live since Jun 09, training

The system receives an average of 240 log-ins per day at present from a 'real' user base of approx 1,500 users. As training is completed on the final modules it is expected that these needs will increase dramatically. All CSI employees now benefit from the efficiencies and lowered learning curve of standardized and repeatable workflow processes, managed by exception. CSI management also now has improved its business-critical decision making based on real-time data.

5. HURDLES OVERCOME

CSI faced the dual challenge of moving NSN towards a process-centric approach to business, while also developing and deploying ZEUS without generating negative attention from IT (with its entrenched reliance on enterprise systems such as SAP) and other business units in the company.

For these reasons, CSI chose to stay "under the radar" in communicating about ZEUS until it was up-and-running with a proven success. With its success benchmarked, CSI began intense, but selective, "selling" of its BPM story to other NSN business units at the management level. Since then, myZEUS portals and Zeus Regional Champions (ZRCs) have succeeded in building a highly-visible "ZEUS community" that has positively influenced senior NSN management to embrace the system and support improvements to service delivery. Technical implementation challenges have also been par for the course, but Appian's SOA support has greatly eased those expected issues.

Success Strategy to Overcome Challenges:

Quarterly ZEUS Champions Workshops bring together program champions from each of the seven regions and four Lines of Business and Practices to conduct planning, communications, and brainstorming activities. This is particularly important to achieve user buy-in and ensure alignment of the program across the complete business. **Monthly**, there is the Steering Board / Change Management Review involving Directors and VPs from across the business. A **fortnightly** communications session with the complete ZEUS Champions Community keeps them updated on program progress. Program teams hold **weekly** reviews. **Daily** project review meetings and Functional lead meetings maintain progress and address issues to keep the program on track.

A key to success has been creating the complete ZEUS Champions Community which covers the regions and Lines of Business/Practices. It has also been vital to get senior buy-in from the business unit leadership teams – 'convincing' them of the benefits of the program to them in order to get their full support. That said, having the 100% support of the Head of the Business Unit, is an absolute 'must have'.

Governance routines are operationalized through repeated communication sessions, the employment of the Champions Community (which is embedded throughout the business), and from having the 100% support of senior management.

CSI intends to use the Process Enterprise and Maturity Model (PEMM) to measure process maturity and to drive process improvement across the business. Significant agility is required as NSN and CSI are still just over 2 years old and there are constant changes and improvements that need to happen in order to drive progress and improvements. This has been difficult to achieve with only a small centralized team and requires the full support of the business which is a constant effort to maintain. Communication campaigns are important to try and keep this support, improving awareness and understanding at all stages.

6. BENEFITS

The measurable benefits of ZEUS include:
- Improved repeatability and reusability of solutions
- Improved business-critical decision making based on real-time data
- Maximized productivity for current business, and to drive/support future growth

These objectives are all being realized. Senior Management now has end-to-end visibility into the state of the business. Real-time reporting provides details on profitability, project status, and actuals versus forecast on margins and more.

Based on the above, the system is delivering **repeated productivity savings of €12 million a year**, which have all been benchmarked. For each principal role or function, CSI used 15 specific measures to compare time spent before and after the delivery of ZEUS. These benefits span all levels of CSI employees (Global and Regional Management, Consultants, Project Managers, Technical Support Managers, Solution Architects, etc.), the business as a whole, and across the value chain to customers. These benefits can be summarized as:

Benefits for Management
- On-line, 'Real-time' visibility of the business
- End-to-end control
- Portfolio and Product management
- Governance of processes

Benefits for Users
- A satisfying 'user experience'
- Enhanced inter-working between functions
- Clear visibility of responsibilities and status
- Re-usability and repeatability of Knowledge

Benefits for Customers
- Real-time Visibility of Project Status
- Improved CSI response time to bids and projects
- Benefit from CSI's global experience and knowledge

Benefits for the Business
- Cost reduction against reporting
- Cost reduction in data entry
- Cost reduction in bid preparation
- Optimization of processes
- Improved utilization
- Measurement of this value as a driver of top-line revenue has not been done.

7. BEST PRACTICES, LEARNING POINTS AND PITFALLS

The most valuable lessons learned through CSI's BPM program include:
- ✓ *Invest at the start in a Project Manager with a track record of successful BPMS Delivery*
- ✓ *Create sufficient branding for the solution so that future users can relate / refer to it easily (this enables more effective selling / marketing of the solution)*

✓ *Build a BPM community right out of the gate, and leverage it to influence senior management as the program evolves*

✓ *Leverage an experienced technology partner that emphasizes comprehensive, but easy-to-use BPM Suite technology*

✗ *The biggest pitfall to avoid is in how you get started with BPM and the initial process selection. Although the conventional wisdom has been "Think Big, Start Small," if you don't start with something meaty for the business (high enough value to make an impact, with enough risk associated to keep management engaged) your efforts are not likely to blossom into a full and successful BPM program.*

8. COMPETITIVE ADVANTAGES

ZEUS has allowed the CSI division of NSN to significantly drive competitive advantage and alter the playing field. It allowed CSI, early in its existence, to establish a common process language that enabled it to quickly ratchet up skills and delivery capacity to be more competitive in the market it had entered. It has also armed CSI management with a level of visibility and real-time control over all mission-critical business aspects and resources that surpasses the industry standard. ZEUS acts as CSI's system for operational business management, and the ongoing optimization/continuous process improvement inherent in the ZEUS program will support continued market advantage.

9. TECHNOLOGY

The Appian BPM Suite acts as the foundational platform for all of ZEUS. CSI selected Appian after a thorough vendor evaluation. In addition to technology strength, Appian won because of its commitment to a true partnership with CSI.

Nick knew that CSI was not exactly sure how to solve its end-to-end visibility and control problem, and that its BPM experience would be a journey of discovery. To ensure success on that journey, and to deal effectively with the inevitable unexpected detours, CSI needed its BPM vendor to be as much a business partner as a technology provider, helping to guide solution development and facilitate knowledge-transfer to move the organization towards BPM self-sufficiency.

Appian satisfied CSI's technical criteria based on the comprehensive features of natively integrated process, analytics, content and collaboration capabilities; Appian's extreme ease-of-use (including tailored user interfaces, personalized portals and information targeting, drag-and-drop process modeling, and ease of user and group administration); and Appian's flexible architecture (100% web-based with zero client-side downloads, service-oriented architecture and ease of integration). Appian's expertise in the human-centric side of BPM was an essential qualifier as collaboration and knowledge management play a central role in effective operations for CSI. The Appian platform acts as the single point of management for processes, process artifacts, stored documents and other electronic content (reports, task lists, images, video), plus associated metadata. Appian allows for the collaborative creation of all process artifacts and electronic data, as well as effective distribution, archiving, and protection. Features such as Single Sign-On throughout the entire system, and native search enhanced by integration with Google Search Appliance further extend the ease-of-use. Users interact with a rule- and role-based portal that facilitates CSI's need to capture, share and disseminate information in a flexible yet secure environment.

10. THE TECHNOLOGY AND SERVICE PROVIDERS

Appian is the global innovator in enterprise and on-demand business process management (BPM). Appian provides the fastest way to deploy robust processes, collapsing time to value for new process initiatives. Businesses and governments worldwide use Appian to accelerate process improvement and drive business performance. Appian empowers more than 2.5 million users from large Fortune 100 companies, to the mid-market and small businesses worldwide. Appian is head-quartered in the Washington, D.C. region, with professional services and partners around the globe. For more information, visit www.appian.com.

South African Post Office

Silver Award, Middle East and Africa
Nominated by Pétanque Consultancy, South Africa

Executive Summary / Abstract

Business is about engaging Strategy, People, Process and IT/Systems to achieve the vision.

The focus of this submission is on Excellence in BPM, with an element of workflow included, achieved through an innovative application of BPM. The case study is about how key business processes were mapped to deliver on strategy, embracing the elements of strategy, people, process and IT, within the framework of innovation.

The South African Post Office (SAPO) needed change on a number of levels: a fresh strategy agreed to in 2007 resulted in a new business model. This strategy was driven by the need for the South African Post Office to respond to changing markets and re-position itself as a major player in the region. This required SAPO to become more accessible, more customer-focused, more innovative in generating revenue and finding new and better ways of providing services to the urban and rural communities it services. The new model needed the right processes and people to eventually deliver on strategy. Through VizPro®, an innovative approach to process documentation and improvement, a number of challenges were overcome and resulted in benefits ranging from enterprise wide buy-in through transparency and participation, role clarity on who needs to do what to bring about the changes needed, along with capturing immense volumes of corporate knowledge in process maps that reflect the *business* view of the step by step activities needed to ensure achievement of strategic goals in storyboard format process maps that are easy to use and easy to follow.

The key innovation is that BPM was applied, and continues to be applied, in a low IT focus, high people impact formula that is delivering results.

Overview

Innovation in this case study was about doing things differently. What was done differently?

Firstly, instead of using Organisational Development approaches to create a fresh, powerful organizational structure that would effectively apply the new business model in order to achieve challenging strategic goals, the enterprise used process to first establish WHAT needed to be done, prior to defining WHO should be doing these activities.

Secondly, the approach was innovative on a number of levels: instead of launching process mapping from an IT perspective, which is the norm and uses BPMNotation or expensive BPM software, the enterprise

- Used the opportunity to capture immense volumes of corporate know-how from enterprise staff through facilitated, high energy, fun work-sessions, brown-paper style, but paperless, real-time, on-screen using MS Visio® to map processes in storyboard format, applying easy to follow, easy to use icons to tell the story of each process and to tell the story of how each process supported the attainment of strategic goals.

- Created an environment for teamwork and buy-in at all levels, focusing on transparency, collaboration and interdepartmental exchange of current and best practice processes.
- Ensured that by linking the process mapping to the corporate Road Map, there was a clear link between each process and strategy, measurable per process via KPI's that would feed into the corporate scorecard that reflects performance in terms of People, Profit and Planet.

Innovation elements, which translated to benefits, included:

- Provision for strategic alignment
- Cross pollination of ideas and how processes worked and should work
- Enterprise wide participation, collaboration and clarification of roles and improved practices, focusing on areas of risk, gaps and role clarification
- Making business fun, resulting in innovation (doing things better)
- Not using expensive BPM tools and software, but applying low-cost, highly effective technology to capture, record and reproduce information
- Using process maps that reflected how business regards their business, as opposed to how IT regards business
- Allowing for measurement of progress, through metrics and performance indicators being agreed on in each process and for the program as a whole
- Providing a process to funnel the knowledge and ideas of a wide range of staff into improved practice processes, creating non threatening platforms for change and most importantly, support for change.

No project or program is without challenges, which translate to lessons learnt. Although the words "change management" were hardly ever used, this project was about exactly that: changing the way people did what they were doing in a sustainable manner not only to bring about better performance, but to link into strategic goals. The key challenge was to ensure bottom-up participation, enthusiasm and benefits from the changes by enabling as many as possible relevant people to find time to attend work sessions *and* contribute meaningful *and* experience the benefits. This challenge was overcome by strong pressure from top management for teams to participate and deliver, linked to excellent logistical management of, at times, four streams of process work-sessions per day for a period of seven months by the Project Coordinator. Top management in turn was directly accountable to the CEO via the Strategy Team for performance and results, to the extent that no new staff appointments were approved by the CEO unless it was clear what role the incumbent would play in which processes! The lesson learnt: "if there is no *pull from the very top*, and if this pull is not *supported by those that need to execute and those that need to participate*, it ain't gonna happen". In short, there has to be a display of commitment at the top of the enterprise, filtering to the middle and the lower levels.

Users and application of the process maps that resulted from the project

- The first application of the process maps was to develop new company wide organograms based on what the processes defined needed to be done and what roles were needed to perform those functions.
- The second application was and continues to be that processes were and are adjusted, improved and / or developed to support the roll out of the new business model.

- The third area of application is in the induction of new employees where both unit specific and company processes are used to fast track newcomers into productivity.
- The fourth area of common application is in Internal Audit, where the process maps form the basis of all audits.
- The fifth area of application is in risk management, where risk areas are highlighted and can be monitored, managed and reported on quickly and effectively.
- The sixth area of application is in creating a performance culture that flows through the enterprise as each process has a set of KPIs that link to the Profit, People, Planet, KPAs of the Corporate Balanced Scorecard.
- The seventh area of application is in IT where the information is used for Enterprise Architecture, systems development and data management.
- The eighth application is in the communication of processes to external consultants, for example for the development of IT disaster recovery and business continuity as every process step indicates what system supports both for inputs and outputs.

BUSINESS CONTEXT

Initial State of the South African Post Office

The first Post Office in South Africa was opened in the Castle in Cape Town in 1792, but it was in the year 1501 that Pedro D'Ataide, the captain of a Portuguese ship, first placed a letter in a milkwood tree in Mossel Bay. The letter contained a message about the disaster that had struck his fleet. Today, on a daily basis the Post Office delivers almost 6.5 million letters to 10 million addresses in South Africa. It has more than 2 500 outlets covering the length and breadth of South Africa.

The principal function of the Post Office is to provide postal services inside and outside South Africa. With a Post Office or Post Office outlet in almost every South African town or hamlet, the Post Office is an integral part of South Africa

The turnaround of the South African Post Office is characterized by its first financial breakeven in 2004. In 2007 it became clear that the total business needed to lower the focus on cost cutting and instead bring about growth based on new products, services, markets and customer needs through innovation and creativity. This required an enterprise wide drive with buy-in from all levels of operation

During 2007 a new Business Model was developed with a focus on the following principles:
- Income generation while embracing triple bottom line sustainability
- Innovation to drive business growth needed to be enhanced
- Increased support of and alignment to the USO
- Each Business Unit to define, own and focus on their respective unique products, services and customers
- Each Business Unit to operate within the framework of a holistic view of all SAPO customers
- The respective Business Units would therefore need to adapt to focused marketing and needed to be supported by the Shared Services

The following Business Units were decided on: Mail Business, Logistics Business, Financial Services, Information Communication Technology, Property, Consumer Services, Corporate Services, Business Support and Transport Services.

Driving motivation for initiating the change program

The driving motivation for initiating the change program was to establish the "what" needed to be done to effect the business model in context of strategic goals and structure the activities, per business unit into "who" needed to do what at all levels in the enterprise.

In addition, once the business model was decided on, an effective structure (organogram) needed to be designed for the roll-out of the business model throughout the enterprise and it was clear that this was only possible if based on well defined processes per business unit where no process duplications or gaps occurred and where processes interfaced to support and align with strategy. There needed to be collaborative agreement on who needed to do what where in order to achieve strategic goals.

This required each Business Unit to define, own and focus on their respective unique products, services and customers, to operate within the framework of a holistic view, in others words align to strategy, to adapt to focused marketing for each respective unit, and to be supported by the Shared Services (Corporate and Business Support), whilst also preparing for possible deregulation and corporatisation.

THE KEY INNOVATIONS

The South African Post Office addressed this requirement with an innovative, comprehensive, inclusive, and company-wide approach in partnership with Pétanque Consultancy. Pétanque project managed the program and facilitated the over 500 work sessions that produced more than 230 detailed, storyboard format processes over a period of one year, engaging with over 300 key staff and many more enterprise wide staff, to identify what must be done to achieve strategic goals (execute strategy) and which roles are required for the implementation. This was achieved through the application of VizPro®, an interactive approach to process mapping through workshop facilitation.

This fresh approach resulted in thorough review of the organisation: instead of asking 'who needs to do what?' the question was 'what needs to be done by each business area in order to innovate and improve performance in support of corporate strategic goals and who needs to do this?'. This question, which was addressed through collaboration in workshops using process as the point of focus, resulted in improving the organisation inside-out.

At a high level, the approach was as follows:

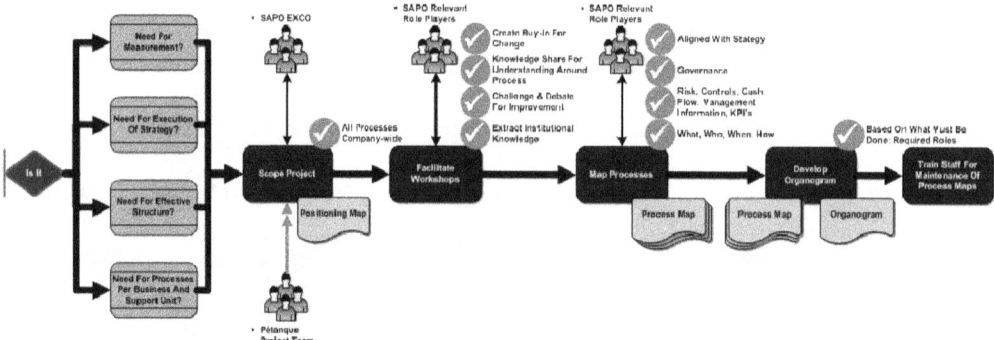

Figure 1 High level approach to address SAPO's requirements

The process approach included
- Development of a positioning map per business area, defining all those processes needed to support strategy
- Documentation of all the key processes that were defined in the positioning map
- Review of all processes to bring about innovation, improved practices and alignment with strategic outcomes
- Sharing and capturing of knowledge via an inclusive, collaborative and transparent process of work shopping and real time data capture on screen with MS Visio – refer visual 1

Visual 1 Interactive Workshops with real time data capture on screen with MS Visio®

- Using the information-rich process maps to derive the enterprise organogram that would provide the appropriate structure for successful roll out of the business model and attaining strategic goals, refer visual 2 and 3

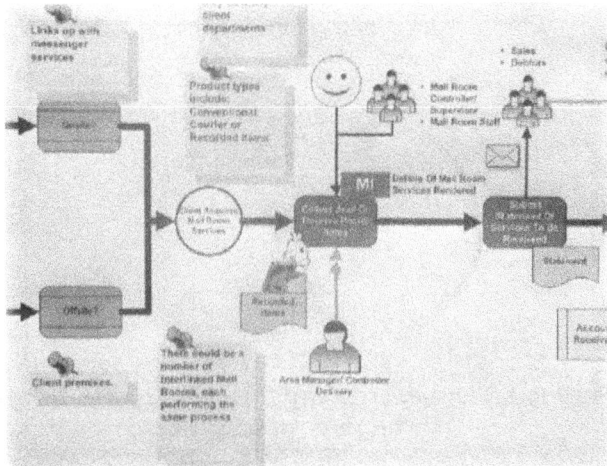

Visual 2: Close up of information-rich process maps

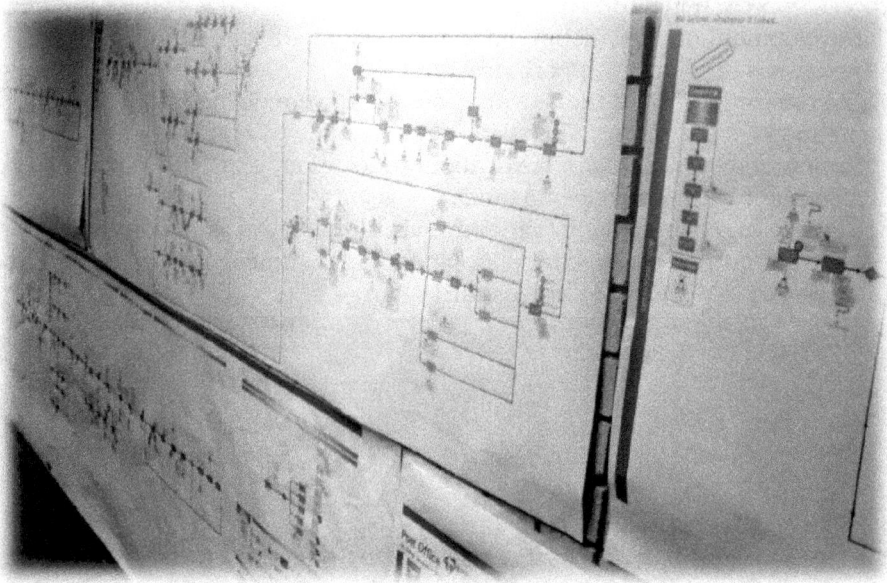

Visual 3: Information-rich process maps, using MS Visio® and printed in-house as A0 sized running maps displayed in the head office passages for all staff to view, challenge, comment and be informed on

The impact that resulted from the project:

Business

The impact of the project on the way the firm engages its key stakeholders, which include staff at all levels of the enterprise, customers, partners and suppliers and its shareholder, the South African Government.

Impact on Staff:

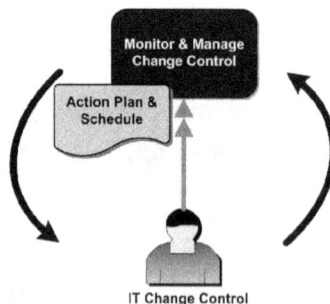

Mind Shift:
From "what must this person do"
To "what must be done – who needs to do it"

Monitor & Manage
Change Control

Action Plan &
Schedule

IT Change Control

Visual 4: Creating effective, strategy focused change in the enterprise through a mind shift

The impact is through the inside-out approach to improve service delivery in support of strategic goals. Easy to follow, storyboard format processes that speaks the language of business at all levels were mapped to develop the step by step of what activities are needed and then agreeing on the who or roles (who would be responsible, accountable, consulting and who gave or received information) to effectively attain strategic goals. The key element of the project was the creating a forum for knowledge share, challenge and clarification through facilitated work-shops. These engaged staff on all levels to align operations with management, to extract institutional knowledge, to capture staff's experience on operational level, to identify bottle necks, to bring about change, to collaboratively agree on risk areas and controls to manage risk, to agree on what performance needed to be measured where and through which metrics, provided by what system, process and people interfaces and to ensure that role players understand why change is critical so that there is buy-in for such change.

Impact on Customers/Clients, Partners and Suppliers

The Process maps hold a vast amount of information which has served the South African Post Office well in an array of applications. Relevant process maps are being used for pitching for new business, for alignment with partners and for clarifying supply chain processes, gaps and duplications with suppliers.

In offering new, innovative services to potential SAPO clients, the process of offering those solutions could be collaborated on, and agreed on with the new client. In other words, process solutions are explained to third parties by using the relevant map. This fast track understanding of what systems need to interface, how processes will link and what resources are needed per service delivery.

This has been used in the following successful new business ventures to date:
- Over the counter share trading to Vodacom, the largest cell phone service provider in South Africa
- New Retail Agent partnership with SPAR, a fast growing convenience store chain valued at R2 Million ($200 000) per year (for the first year)
- Registration of new social security beneficiaries. The, project commenced in January 2009 and beneficiaries have been registered and many Post-bank accounts opened

Through process enhancements,
- New products and solutions can be market ready more speedily. An example is the process improvements that were made in the "new product development" processes. There were three differing New Product Development processes in three different business units when the project started. These were standardized into one best practise process through collaboration between the three units and key role players and resulted in quicker approval and development time, providing for quicker " go to market" readiness.
- In rolling out capital projects via the Investment Management Process, end user customers at retail level has experienced the benefits of capital expenditure that has tripled and investment decision making that decreased from 6 month cycles to 1 month cycles.

The Business Units and their executives are internal SAPO partners, working alongside to achieve strategic goals. The following impact has been evident:
- By listing unaddressed process issues in the Action Lists, areas for improvement are actioned, assigning responsibility to an actioner with a due date. This includes assessing new solutions and systems. Refer Visual 5.
- Breaking silo mentalities as units see the process impact which their deliverable has on other Business Units and vice versa.
- Easily identifiable key performance areas and key performance indicators, along with what information needs to be captured where to provide the metrics for measurement, has been defined, collaborated and agreed on.

These are used in balanced scorecards and performance appraisals, linking into the corporate scorecard.

		achieved			
Effective business intelligence system	Develop a Knowledge Management Information System	KMIS	Yvonne	Review status on the 13 August 2008	In progress
Need formal Analysis forum with the GE Bu's		Corporate Alignment	Marietjie Lancaster	Review status on the 13 August 2008	In progress
Inconsistencies	Check if the SAPO Strategy and the information for use by business unit Is the same document	Consistent Terminologies used on all SAPO Maps	Justin	Concluded	
Acquisition process	Define an Acquisition Process	Acquisition Process	Marlize – content Pétanque - Mapping	Straw Man concluded. Detail to be populated. To develop an integrative process which will address	• Blue sky – to be developed (MB has information) • Include M&A processes

Visual 5: Action Lists, compiled, collaborated and agreed upon by workshop participants drive change, listing what needs to be done to change current practices to improved, strategy focused processes.

Impact on the Shareholder and the Enterprise

The impact on the shareholder is that the enterprise is re-positioning itself, moving towards a fit for purpose process and organogram implementation which ensures an enterprise that has the capability and capacity to provide the engine that will propel the enterprise into the strategic direction and outcomes SAPO aims for.

In terms of Structure / Organogram formulation
- Communication lines are identified, discussed and agreed to and implemented within the bigger picture of a strategically aligned enterprise.
- All structures are aligned to business needs and to the new business model.
- A fit for purpose organogram drives the enterprise.

In terms of Governance
- All elements that need to be complied with per process are identified and indicated on the maps and listed in the Action List for execution and ongoing implementation.
- The maps serve as Input into Internal Audit as all processes to be audited are defined, transparent and easy to audit. This brings about Time and resource savings for Internal Audit as processes and issues are defined.
- All processes are aligned to policies, charters, statutory and other compliances.

Process

The state of the process before and after the project

With regard to the state of the process of BPM and Workflow prior to the project, the following broad strokes paints the picture:

Prior to the project:
- Process was not regarded as a management element or as key to implementation of change.
- Processes were in the domain of the IT Department, and focused on an IT interpretation of business.

After the project:

- Processes focus on business' view of business, and provide IT with business requirement and business' understanding of their systems, people and IT requirements.
- Process features as a management and decision making element.

The program was rolled out as illustrated in Figure 1.

The project design principles

The overall process architecture and design principles focused on using easy to follow, easy to use, easy to maintain process mapping that is information rich and that would be understood by all stakeholders in order to bring about

- Documenting all those processes that support the new Business Model
- Identification of process improvement areas or where total process reengineering was needed - and continue to need to occur
- Identification and elimination of process duplications
- Identification of process gaps and closing those to positively impact on efficiency and cost
- Identification of interfacing processes and of end-to-end responsibilities, for example, how the Transport and Mail Delivery processes fit into and complement each other and where "handshakes" take place
- Business continuity, as the impact of risk factors are easily identifiable and mitigation, management or risk transfer is then built into the process
- The detail required for ISO accreditation by identifying which steps require what level and what specification of quality to comply to standards
- Input into Risk management as all risks are identified and marked on the step or stage where the risk occurs. Controls are defined and agreed to, ensuring that controls are assigned to role players and stakeholders agree on the "who is accountable for which risk and how those are managed"
- Performance measurement points that link to metrics. This means that role players are quite aware of what needs to be measured when, why and how and understand the link into the corporate scorecard
- Alignment of all processes with the company strategic objectives, deliverables and the corporate balance scorecard through the Change Controller, Key Performance Indicators and Key Performance Areas
- Linking all process KPIs with the company knowledge management system

The key consideration was buy-in and the approach was collaborative and transparent participation by SAPO employees.

Organization

Change can only be effective if staff doesn't resist, and SAPO managed to carry this out by engaging the entire organisation. This resulted in improved processes, developed by employees that are now responsible for execution to deliver improved service.

Further impact points include:

- Interactive, cross functional, fun and high energy workshops – people found up-skilling, knowledge sharing, transparency, clarification and collaboration value in attending workshops
- The workshops provided a forum for problem and issue discussion and resolution
  - All maps were made available to all staff members, which was and remains of particular benefit to those who did not take part in the

work sessions and to those who were invited (inclusion) to comment and provide input

- All roles are defined, discussed and clarified, and link to a strategic purpose
- Input into unit specific job profiles, allowing for inclusion and bottom up participation in organisation structures.
- The maps are used to train new employees: positioning maps provide for the "big picture" and the detailed process maps are effectively used for induction and quick understanding of roles
- Buy-in and a sense of participation in the creation of a new, improved enterprise.
- Centre of Excellence, its scope here and the challenges in creating the group and sustaining the change initiative.

The CoE concept will be considered in 2010 in all likelihood, however, the project was launched, coordinated and managed by Group Strategy who continues to manage version control and holds master data and maps.

Group Strategy oversees transferability as follows:

Availability

All maps are electronically available to all employees in the company.

Ownership

Every business unit head takes ownership of their respective maps, the accuracy there-off and Action Lists to continue the process of improvement and change.

Process facilitation, mapping and version control

- Resources from the Post Offices Group Strategy department has been trained in the methodology, process mapping and facilitation of the Viz-Pro® methodology
- They are also taking responsibility for version control.

HURDLES OVERCOME

Challenge 1: size of enterprise and high number of processes involved

SAPO divisions involve many processes. In order to create a clear picture of the processes involved, positioning map sessions for each division were facilitated to identify the core business priority processes that are needed to deliver the business requirements. During these sessions the role players that would be required for the workshops to map the processes were identified.

Challenge 2: scheduling of the work sessions

Engaging people in workshops was critical to the success of this project. Scheduling of the workshops was sometimes problematic. People were unavailable or couldn't get out of their offices for a day as they were the key to business continuity. To take these people out for a full day workshop was complicated. This problem was overcome by switching to half-day workshops in either the morning or afternoon, and some in the evening, which made it easier for role players to be available for the session.

Challenge 3: relevant participants in the work session

Another challenge was to have the right people in the workshop. The Project Coordinator and the Business Process Owners identified the key stakeholders of each process. This ensured effective use of resources' time. This was important because the timeframe to deliver the project outcomes was very limited.

Management

Management was supportive, assisted in scheduling and operational matters to ensure the best possible participation and participated where needed in most instances.

Business

The uptake form business was equally positive, at times the challenges around scheduling was indicative of the requirement of many business teams wanting to have their processes mapped and there were only four facilitation teams!

Organization Adoption

The strategies and experience driving organizational adoption is explained early on in this submission: staff appointment depend on a business need as defined and justified by process, risk plans apply processes to define and locate risk in the enterprise (at executive management level), performance is linked to process stages and steps, IT interfaces are related to processes, etc.

BENEFITS

The benefits are unlocked continuously as described under heading 4.

Due to the complexity of this enterprise, and for reasons of confidentiality, we reference a few qualitative benefits which must be interpreted in context with what has been presented up to this point.

Benefit	Examples of outcomes that bring about benefits	Quantitative and Qualitative Outcomes
Cost Savings	Role definition and alignment with process requirements	Reduction in staff and deploying staff into other areas, a focused organogram
	Addressing Duplications	The savings range across the business and include all those made through improved practises
	Managing Risk through quick identification and positioning of risks Business continuity is easier defined	Expensive reactionary roll-outs due to business breakdowns are managed
Time reductions (Reduced time-to-market, cycle time, etc.)	Reduced induction time for new employees	Days as opposed to weeks before being productive
	Reduced decision making time	1 month opposed to 6 months for project implementation in the Investment Manage
	Quicker delivery of services to customers Quicker turnaround for internal audit	Vodacom, SPAR brought on-line much faster A few days as opposed to weeks.

Benefit	Examples of outcomes that bring about benefits	Quantitative and Qualitative Outcomes
Increased Revenues (Top-line growth.)	More customers are serviced through improved processes	In a challenging economy, costs were saved that would otherwise have been incurred, thus, by managing inefficiencies and errors through process and people, margins are managed
	New clients are brought on board quicker	Go to Market to revenue realization cycles are improved.
Productivity Improvements	Role Clarity Duplications and unnecessary work are identified and actioned	Clear job descriptions Improved workflows
	Addressing Gaps	Managing risks and customer satisfaction
	Measuring performance per process and tying into corporate scorecards	Contributing to corporate strategic goals
	Structuring unstructured processes and including unstructured content into structured processes	Building an enterprise that operates in a new economy where entrepreneurship increasingly is required of staff and processes

BEST PRACTICES, LEARNING POINTS AND PITFALLS

Best Practices and Learning Points

- ✓ *Create a program or project that has extensive executive management support*
- ✓ *Ensure logistical capability*
- ✓ *Communicate points of departure, plans, progress, outcomes to all stakeholders at a level that makes sense to each individual*
- ✓ *Reward participation*
- ✓ *Show appreciation – up to the level of each individual*
- ✓ *Ensure a complete understanding of the process methodology*
- ✓ *Enable stakeholders to participate through effective facilitation and workshop management*
- ✓ *Use process maps that tell the story in depth*
- ✓ *Agree with participants and stakeholders in facilitated workshops:*
- ✓ *what governs processes and agree how it impacts the process*
- ✓ *how each process contributes to strategy and what must be achieved*
- ✓ *the purpose and outcome of each process*
- ✓ *the scope of each process*
- ✓ *the relevant, necessary, non waste, value add steps of each process*

- ✓ *the role players: those accountable, responsible, to be consulted and to be informed or who should consult and inform*
- ✓ *the in and output to each step*
- ✓ *the means of communication in each step*
- ✓ *steps where applications and IT systems are used*
- ✓ *the interfacing processes in each process*
- ✓ *the gates and options in each process*
- ✓ *timing elements in each process at various stages*
- ✓ *steps where there are risks and what controls or mitigations need be applied*
- ✓ *steps where metrics are generated for reporting and performance measurement*
- ✓ *steps where quality is checked*
- ✓ *steps where performance is measured and how this feeds into team, unit and corporate scorecards*
- ✓ *burning point steps*
- ✓ *steps, stages or groups of activities where change or innovation is needed or implemented*
- ✓ *Manage process integration: ensure that processes talk to one another, ensure effective cross referencing*
- ✓ *Track workshop participation: who was at which workshop: this ensure that the right role players are at the right process*
- ✓ *Run work session to integrate and cross reference processes and aspects of processes.*
- ✓ *Make output available in electronic and hard copy format as required*
- ✓ *Ensure cost effective printing of maps*
- ✓ *Create action lists that are easy to follow and monitor*
- ✓ *Tie action list management into weekly management meetings and to performance management*
- ✓ *Use storyboarding for position mapping and organograms to make information easy to understand and relevant.*
- ✓ *Push hard, very hard to conclude the project scope of work in the allocated time, going over time loses the momentum*
- ✓ *Celebrate the end result!*
- ✓ *Ensure effective close out.*
- × *The above ensure effective participation, alignment, buy-in and strategic focus.*

Pitfalls

- × *Manage workshop fatigue – it produces poor quality*
- × *Don't workshop if the right role players are not there*
- × *Quickly identify when politics enter discussions, affect process design and inhibit participation*
- × *Don't bring senior management into process workshops too soon, it inhibits participation at lower levels.*
- × *Be careful of going into too much detail, some people elaborate unnecessarily in order to justify roles or the scope of roles.*
- × *Manage anxieties*

These elements manage the risk of not attaining effective participation, alignment, buy-in and strategic focus.

COMPETITIVE ADVANTAGES

As a State Owned Enterprise, SAPO is not unlike other semi-government organisations that have profit taking as part of its strategic goals. In the Postal industry, it competes with privately owned, profit focused enterprises.

SAPO does not compete with other State Owned Enterprises (SOEs). However, it has proven that organisation wide change in SOEs can be effectively rolled out in a relatively short time, even though many of the benefits will take time to realise.

The SAPO strategy is to make it more competitive so that it can operate in the same space as competitors, and by embarking on this change program, it has taken the necessary steps to position itself competitively, even if the playing fields differs substantially.

The immediate plans to sustain the progress made is to continue process improvement actions that resulted from the program, to continue identifying those new areas that need improvement or innovation and apply the same approach as up to this stage. Process is an integral part of SAPO's sustainability approach, with the focus on people buy-in, interfacing with IT to remain current with competitors, and where feasible, gain the (short term) competitive edge.

TECHNOLOGY

- The underlying technology infrastructure, BPM or Workflow Suite used

The technology used was nothing other than laptops with MS Visio® 2007 and Windows. Images were projected with data projectors.

The BPM technique is VizPro®, a process modelling methodology that uses icon rich storyboard type process flows to capture information and provide for a platform to discuss, collaborate on and improve processes. Much like the old brown paper exercises, but only much slicker, using technology and working real time.

- Unique benefits delivered as a result of VizPro®, how that was implemented and the benefits that derived from that approach.

The benefits of the VizPro® methodology have been extensively referenced in this submission. Benefits are derived through the user-friendly story-board approach, the fact that it is business and not IT focused and the fact that the collaborative, inclusive approach through workshops, discussions and change management through detailed action lists makes it relevant for role players.

THE TECHNOLOGY AND SERVICE PROVIDERS

The consultants involved in the case study are Pétanque Consultancy, a consulting service focusing on process and project management to achieve strategic goals. They use the principles of the game Pétanque and visuals to link strategy to process and unlock savings through improved business performance.

They have successfully applied process to link outcomes and strategy: through people buy-in and the step by step of who needs to do what to achieve goals. They output workshop information real time in storyboard format, making it easy for role players to understand where they fit into the bigger picture.

- **For further information, go to www.petanque-c.com.**

Section 3

North America

AmerisourceBergen, USA

Silver Award, North America
Nominated by Metastorm, USA

1. EXECUTIVE SUMMARY / ABSTRACT

AmerisourceBergen is a global organization that has embraced BPM technology. As part of the competitive and complex pharmaceutical industry, the company was faced with critical challenges like maintaining high standards while managing growth, creating efficiencies, making better and faster decisions and ensuring regulatory and legal compliance. Company leaders recognized that BPM can help them meet these demands – while delivering extremely significant impact and ROI.

Today AmerisourceBergen has established a BPM Center of Excellence, having deployed and optimized nearly 200 processes throughout the enterprise with approximately 3,000 global users. Total annual benefits are in the tens of millions of dollars. This nomination will showcase AmerisourceBergen's enterprise-wide BPM success, with specific mention of one of its most innovative BPM implementations.

2. OVERVIEW

As a very large distributor in the pharmaceutical industry, AmerisourceBergen has numerous relationships with manufacturers, pharmacies, and hospitals. In addition, the company manages distribution of both brand-name and generic drugs.

AmerisourceBergen is challenged not only with physical distribution and inventory management, but also by the complexities of contract and relationship management with its many manufacturers and customers. Managing the contract and pricing details associated with each of these relationships is people-intensive and time-consuming – but it is also critical to the company's bottom-line profitability.

To address these challenges, BPM has been implemented enterprise-wide at AmerisourceBergen and to date, the company has over 3,000 users (including subsidiaries) and nearly 200 processes automated—and accomplished this with a small BPM implementation team of 4.

AmerisourceBergen uses BPM to enable processes such as contracts management and chargeback, AP vendor reconciliation, pro-generics competitive pricing and the quote to contract lifecycle. These and other implementations have enabled AmerisourceBergen to:

- Establish more efficient and accurate tracking capabilities
- Significantly reduce chargeback disputes
- Improve transaction transparency and improved supplier collaboration
- Realize millions of dollars in recurring cost savings
- Empower more process-centric thinking across multiple departments

AmerisourceBergen has also established a Process Center of Excellence – a panel of key business and IT people who assess processes, help with business case development, and oversee BPM projects to ensure they are successful.

3. BUSINESS CONTEXT

AmerisourceBergen is a comprehensive pharmaceutical services provider. To be successful in a highly competitive market, AmerisourceBergen needs to be constantly improving, changing and innovating.

To this end, AmerisourceBergen invests significantly and continuously in technology to extract strategic, financial, competitive and productivity dividends. BPM is an integral tool in the company's arsenal.

One area in which the company has benefitted from BPM innovations is contracts and chargebacks. This process drives the establishment of pricing and terms with each of the company's manufacturers and then controls compliance with pricing terms and payment of rebates from the manufacturer if the company is forced to sell at a lower price to compete. The process represents a cash flow of approximately $10 billion a year – and any disputes or inaccurate pricing data result in costly delays in getting the refunds the company is owed.

Due to frequently shifting business conditions, contract prices fluctuate. When they do, both the distributor and manufacturer need to analyze these changes and validate them against business rules. Traditionally in the industry, communications and record tracking required between manufacturers and distributors has been largely manual – with a heavy reliance on email, telephone, fax and postal mail – resulting in costly inefficiencies and inaccurate information.

AmerisourceBergen built a business case to justify implementing BPM – focusing on the hard dollar benefits the company would realize in the form of lower headcount, fewer disputes, and more accurate pricing information as well as soft benefits such as faster processing of price changes and better supplier and customer relationships. The company recognized that in addition to the initial pilot projects, many critical business processes would likely become BPM projects in the future. This made the business case for investing in BPM technology even stronger, as it would be a technology that could be leveraged across other areas of the business.

The contracts and chargebacks process was initially implemented approximately four years ago to enhance the data movement with providers, and it has been significantly updated within the last two years to enable further improvements. A major enhancement to the process was to address the mainframe legacy application for the process, which was redesigned to accommodate for all AmerisourceBergen's suppliers. Two critical new processes were added into the program. EBA (electronic business assurance) to Efile supports data coming through EDI (electronic data exchange) into a business process to manage and reconcile, and then sends it back to the legacy applications. The Efile process catered to all AmerisourceBergen's non EDI suppliers, who are now asked to transmit data in an electronic format such as email/Excel/text documents, etc. Those are then passed on to the business process.

4. THE KEY INNOVATIONS

With an implementation team of only 4, AmerisourceBergen has been able to implement nearly 200 processes and save the company millions of dollars each year.

4.2 Business

Prior to using BPM technology, processes at AmerisourceBergen were highly manual and involved significant amounts of paper, faxes, and emails—as is the tendency for this industry. With BPM technology, the company can automate processes and shift the business toward effective process management.

For example, in terms of the contract administration process, BPM provides greater visibility between AmerisourceBergen and its partner. This is a challenging process, with constantly changing conditions, and BPM gives both organizations a simplified method of seeing and understanding of the process. Within the process every new contract is scanned and audited properly before it is uploaded to the ordering systems. This solved the problems of price discrepancies caused by the previous manual contract loading process, and reduced losses and rebilling.

4.3 Process

The Center of Excellence team ensures that BPM is entrenched into the fabric of AmerisourceBergen. Nearly 200 processes have now been deployed enterprise-wide.

The implementation team uses a modified version of the Software Development Life-Cycle as its methodology. This enables them to categorize and prioritize projects, conduct iterative and rapid development, build reusable components, effectively involve the business and provide a 30-day warranty as a "cushion" for their implementations.

4.4 Organization

To date BPM has been extremely successful at AmerisourceBergen and delivers a high return on investment — thus building the foundation the company needs to continue expanding the use of BPM to other areas of the business.

AmerisourceBergen's Center of Excellence empowers more process-centric thinking across multiple departments and allows the organization to close the gaps between silos. Building the execution team was especially critical to this endeavour—people are the most important contributor to the success of BPM and the Center of Excellence at AmerisourceBergen.

5. HURDLES OVERCOME

While BPM enables significant innovations and improvements, new business, procedural and people issues brought about by the applications can change work practices and initially cause disturbances.

At AmerisourceBergen, any challenges are effectively met by the implementation team using the project management methodology and with the guidance of the Process Center of Excellence team. This sets the stage for a successful enterprise-wide BPM deployment.

5.1 Management

Executive sponsorship is integral to BPM at AmerisourceBergen and is department-driven. When executing a proof of concept for new implementations, executive sponsorship is provided by the department heads. For example, all processes built for the contracts and chargebacks were sponsored by the vice president of that area.

5.2 Business

In creating a business case for BPM and the Center of Excellence, the BPM team held multiple classroom and WebEx sessions to demonstrate benefits of BPM technology. Attendees were surveyed to identify business processes that would benefit from a BPM effort, then the team analyzed results to prioritize those that would generate the biggest and quickest return on investment.

5.3 Organization Adoption

BPM became a priority at AmerisourceBergen to improve internal productivity. The company saw the advantage of creating a Process Center of Excellence. It focused on the following business and IT drivers:

- Business Drivers
- BPM can deliver extremely efficient ROI if the business and IT organizations work together.
- Process capital residing in individual business unity can vary from company to company.
- IT Drivers
- Scalable and cost-effective server infrastructure.
- Create re-usable integration components and BPM libraries.
- Develop in-house product implementation expertise.

Managing the expectations of participants and accentuating the positives from change were also key factors in winning the business to BPM-driven change. Removing repetitive and tedious paper-based processes that suffered from high error and rework rates was seen as a positive improvement by staff.

6. BENEFITS

6.1 Cost Savings

As part of the business case for BPM at AmerisourceBergen, the company focused on hard dollar benefits in terms of:

- Lower headcount.
- Fewer disputes.
- More accurate pricing.

Now BPM delivers significant cost savings to AmerisourceBergen. Total benefits across the enterprise are tens of millions of dollars each year. Return on Investment (ROI) is achieved in as little as three months after each process going live.

6.2 Time Reductions

BPM provides AmerisourceBergen with:

- Faster turn-around times realization.
- More efficient and accurate record tracking.
- Contract changes are loaded in minutes, rather than hours.
- The ability to effectively balance resources.

6.3 Increased Revenues

BPM is enabling AmerisourceBergen to increase revenues in several areas. For example, automating the accounts payable process has improved reconciliations from 20% a month to 70% a month—thus driving significant revenue growth for that department.

6.4 Productivity Improvements

Examples of productivity improvements at AmerisourceBergen include:

- Greater transaction transparency.
- Greater management visibility into key performance indicators.
- An online audit trail of all activities.
- Improved accuracy.
- Increased accountability on the part of employees.
- Streamlined work allocations.

7. BEST PRACTICES, LEARNING POINTS AND PITFALLS

7.1 Best Practices and Learning Points

- ✓ Establish a COE team with adaptive individuals.
- ✓ Work in very agile and iterative mode.
- ✓ Build reusable components.
- ✓ Involve the business to ensure alignment.
- ✓ Take advantage of BPM technology.
- ✓ Categorize projects and look for quick wins.

7.2 Pitfalls

- ✗ Use BPM workflows for managing processes, not for transactional systems.

8. COMPETITIVE ADVANTAGES

To maintain competitive advantage and leadership in the pharmaceutical industry, AmerisourceBergen must contend with a rapidly changing environment. It continues to invest in innovative technology enabled business solutions.

Optimizing the supply chain, complying with regulations, managing risk and maximizing growth are all integral to the organization's success. By modeling, managing and monitoring processes using BPM technology, AmerisourceBergen understands its business and can rapidly and cost effectively adapt. It provides a smooth, simplified method for process building and on-going management, which enables the company to stay ahead of its competition. In addition, Amerisource-Bergen utilizes top talent for its implementation and Center of Excellence teams to provide the necessary intellectual capital and know-how.

As a result, the use of BPM has resulted in millions of dollars in recurring cost savings and a long-term competitive advantage for AmerisourceBergen.

9. TECHNOLOGY

AmerisourceBergen uses the Metastorm BPM Suite for its business process initiatives. The company selected Metastorm because the suite provides a platform for rapid development in an agile framework. With Metastorm, AmerisourceBergen has successfully adapted a strategy where new BPM implementations occur in less than 12 weeks.

AmerisourceBergen's BPM implementations are decentralized. Each business unit has its own BPM program, with its own application server and repository. Since the company is working in a decentralized manner it is important to have the implementations match this structure. The biggest advantage of this structure is ease in upgrading. This means that the BPM team does not need to affect all the departments when upgrading a process. Only the department that is being upgraded to a new release is impacted, while the rest of the departments can work normally.

All implementations run on Windows 2003 servers. They utilize:

- Eight VM servers
- One stand alone server
- Four database servers.

In addition, the product architecture is very effective at satisfying both business and information technology requirements for AmerisourceBergen.

Components used in the deployments include:

- Microsoft World
- Active PDF Server
- Rich Text Editing
- Spell check
- FTP .NET Assembly

This flexibility in components is important. For example, in many cases AmerisourceBergen needs to send claims documents to suppliers in non-editable PDF form. Whereas in other processes it is important to offer the option for users to edit matters using rich text editing.

10. THE TECHNOLOGY AND SERVICE PROVIDERS

Metastorm is the software and service provider for AmerisourceBergen. Its focus areas include enterprise and business architecture, business process analysis, business process management, and integration. Metastorm's software products are designed to help close the gaps and create a transparent, collaborative environment across even the largest organizations so they can ensure understanding, optimize execution, enable agility, and empower resources to deliver on goals at many levels of the organization .Metastorm Enterprise addresses these challenges with a unique set of interrelated, state of the art offerings that enable visibility across the enterprise and close the gaps between strategy and enterprise architecture, analysis, and execution. For more information, visit www.metastorm.com.

11. APPENDIX – PROCESS AND SCREENSHOTS

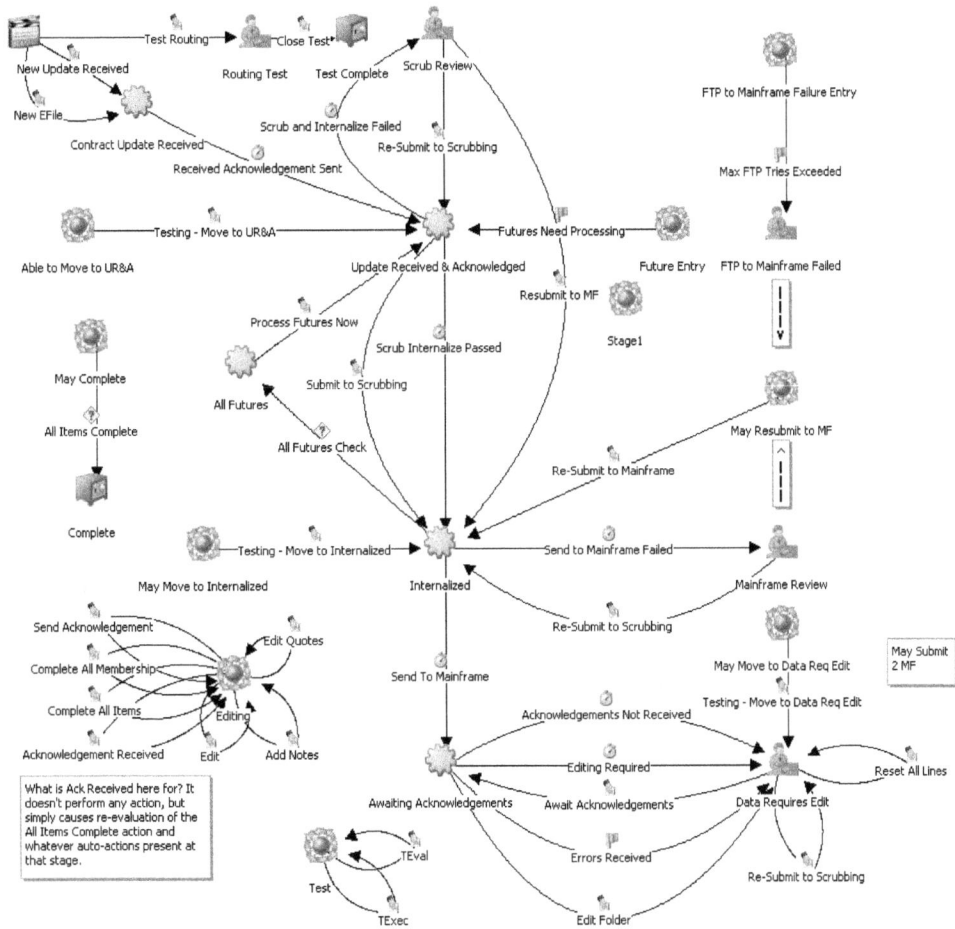

The Contracts and Charge Backs Process.

Watch List

Lincoln Trust Company, USA

Gold Award, North America
Nominated by Lincoln Trust Company, USA

1. EXECUTIVE SUMMARY / ABSTRACT

This paper describes the experiences of implementing an enterprise wide BPM program at Lincoln Trust Company. The program was constituted in early 2007 with an initial goal of managing core processes related to physical paperwork and an ultimate goal of using BPM technology to manage all strategic processes of the organization. When the program began the company was receiving over 100,000 client documents each month with limited to no control over these instructions. Initial, overwhelming success with an enterprise wide implementation of BPM technology to workflow-enable document centric processes led to the strong desire of company management to move quickly to our next goals of understanding, improving, and automating other strategic processes. By doing so we've been able to open our back office process for collaboration with a strategic outsourcing partner, drive processes to the web, reduce costs and risks, improve customer satisfaction, and completely turn around a damaged relationship between IT and the business.

2. OVERVIEW

Lincoln Trust Company (LTC) is a financial services custodian that provides individual retirement account (IRA) and employer sponsored retirement plan administration. Lincoln Trust differentiates itself among many of its competitors in that, as a custodian, in addition to offering traditional investments, the company specializes in offering administration of non-traditional assets such as private placements, promissory notes, offshore funds and residential and commercial real estate for investment in IRAs and other account types. LTC has approximately 350 employees and over $15 billion in assets under administration.

As the program started, the immediate challenge facing LTC were serious process problems related to customer instructions received via the mail. As mentioned previously, we were receiving over 100,000 customer documents each month. The gravity of the situation at this time cannot be overstated and we were quite literally sinking in our process problems. We had calculated the yearly weight of this incoming paperwork to be 18 tons and the weight of our filing cabinets was so much an issue that we had to continually relocate them throughout the building to keep the floor from sinking in spots. On top of all this each business unit had intensely manual, risk prone and costly paper-based workflow processes. The programs first priority had to be to "stop the bleeding" and implement a document workflow solution quickly. To accomplish this we choose to initially implement the workflow capabilities of a document management tool we already owned.

In early 2007, a roadmap was established with executive sponsors that identified 10 implementation phases to deliver document workflow to all business units. In order to move quickly across the enterprise a strategy was recommended that emphasized a common, standardized process approach and incremental 90 day deliverables.

The initial results were wildly successful. The BPM program was able to make a dramatic business impact that gained the attention of executives across the business and generated demand for higher-level process innovation. By mid-2008, after a series of phased rollouts, we were using workflow technology to electronically route and deliver nearly all incoming mail, faxes, checks, ACHs, and wires. Benefits of these initial implementations included, for the first time, being able to leverage an outsourcing partner and have portions of our back office processing performed offshore. Documents were not lost, we had full tracking of their business status, quality control rules were enforced, and analytics were provided to the business for use in staff level planning. In this first year and a half of the program we experienced a 90% reduction in customer complaints, decreased processing times by up to 75% in some areas, and calculated an ROI of 120%.

A challenge we faced early on was the businesses desire to perform higher level process automation (beyond document centric workflow) involving straight through processing with our core trust accounting system and integration with our customer portal. We understood that, in order to meet these process innovation demands, along with changing business models within our organization, we would need a more robust BPMS, and after an exhaustive vendor search, selected an industry leading BPMS along with a leading Business Intelligence platform for advanced analytics. Since mid-2008 we have utilized our BPMS to implement processes as varied as Mutual Fund Trading to general Service Requests.

To date, the BPM program at LTC has implemented 15 enterprise-wide business processes impacting 10 different operational business units with 5-120 employees each. Some of the business processes implemented have only 4 to 5 activities while others have more than 20 activities. This variety of processes and solutions demands a tremendous amount of agility not only from the BPMS and supporting applications but the teams that conduct BPM projects and implement the solutions. Listed below are the BPM processes deployed, with their respective production date up to 04/20/2009.

- Transfers In, New Accounts – 5/4/07
- Transfers Out – 5/4/07
- Institutional Front Office – 8/11/07
- Deposit Processing – 2/14/08
- Cashiering and Customer Credits – 2/14/08
- General Trading – 7/14/08
- Pricing and General Maintenance – 7/14/09
- Mutual Fund Trading – 7/14/08
- Service Requests – 1/20/09
- Distribution Rejection – 1/20/09
- Quick Trades – 1/20/09
- Distributions – 3/25/09
- Transfer Tracking – 7/6/09 (This deployment and below listed but not otherwise considered because of recent deployment dates and award rules.)
- Corporate Retirement Services – 9/14/09
- Online Distributions – in progress

3. BUSINESS CONTEXT

Lincoln Trust is a newly formed private company that was recently spun off from a larger parent organization, Fiserv, Inc. As a result of the divestiture the company went from 950 employees to its current size of 350 employees. In order to be successful as a smaller, private entity, it was imperative that the business model change and it was understood that the previous business model could not be sustained in a smaller company. The risk to reward dynamics had changed in our market place for a smaller company. Segments of the IRA business have historically been in decline and there would be no ongoing entity without this BPM effort. LTC had to fundamentally change how we provide services, and the supporting business vision needed to change how we identify, attract, interact with, and process work for our customers. In order to be successful and profitable, and position ourselves for future growth, we needed to change our business model and chose to embrace BPM as an enabling discipline. Our BPM program was initiated to enable change to the business model and enable an all new architecture.

Prior to the initiation of the BPM program the process landscape was extensively manual. Most processes were tracked using desktop tools such as Microsoft Excel, Access, and Outlook. There was no visibility into processes and it would often take multiple phone calls and research to resolve a client issue or simply to provide them status. Skill levels of individuals performing work varied and often senior level employees were spending significant portions of their day performing non value-add work either maintaining process status or providing follow-up to customers because of rework and inefficiencies earlier in the process.

Also at the time we began there was a seriously negative perception of IT. The business did not consider IT to be a strategic partner and relationships were strained. There had been two significant attempts under different IT leadership to implement a workflow solution in the years prior to 2007 and they both failed at much expense to the company. An executive over one business area had even declared that she "would fire all of IT if she could." As a result new leadership was brought in and the program was restarted with the immediate goal being to workflow enable our document processes and eliminate as much paper as possible from the business operations. The anticipated benefits were to move some processes to an offshore partner, speed processing times, eliminate lost documents, improve client service, reduce risk, and provide complete visibility into our processes and customer documents. Our longer term goals remained to leverage a more full feature BPMS and establish electronic forms on our customer portal (eliminate paper in the first place) and use a BPM approach to streamline and automate all our strategic business processes.

4. THE KEY INNOVATIONS

4.1 Business

Our first processes implemented in our "common shared process" model allowed us to work with our offshore partner, Fiserv Global Services, to take on business operations work that previously could not be outsourced due to our work being driven by paper rather than a workflow system supported by imaged documents.

Subsequent process implementations have allowed us to move away from paper transactions entirely in some cases. We can now engage our clients over our web portal for transactions that previously could only be requested by paper forms. However, we still have the flexibility to support paper form requests for client base that does not have access to or the desire to use a computer to submit requests.

We have integrated our process data with our VOIP telephone system such that, when we receive a phone call from our client and they have keyed their account number into the phone system, a "screen pop" will automatically appear for the Client Service Representative (CSR) that shows all completed and in progress process data, along with any images that are attached to a process, in addition to other information that is pertinent to the client relationship. This visibility allows the CSR to resolve many phone call requests from clients on the same call, requiring no call back on the part of the client or the CSR.

We are now integrating customer profitability scores into our processes so that our most profitable customers receive the highest levels of service. This allows us to turn our processes into a way to generate additional revenue by encouraging our clients to "upgrade" their accounts to receive enhanced service. Having customer profitability scores built into our process helps us ensure that we're consistently providing the highest level of service systematically and retaining our profitable customers.

4.2 Process

In January, 2007, we formed a small executive steering group and a small BPM team comprised of one project manager, one developer and one business analyst. We needed a cost effective strategy to implementing BPM very quickly across the organization. We came up with a two-tiered strategy. We would first use a "common shared process" model that could be rolled out quickly across the enterprise. This model would deliver imaged documents in a business process workflow and discontinue paper delivery. After a significant concentration of the business was "paperless", we would initiate the second tier of the strategy, to implement true, or "first order" business process models for our most strategic processes. While there would be customizable features for each implementation of the common shared process, in order to provide the necessary speed of implementation, the executive steering group committed to ensuring that their business units would not demand highly specialized features that would slow down the implementations. Below is a diagram that outlines the features of the common shared process:

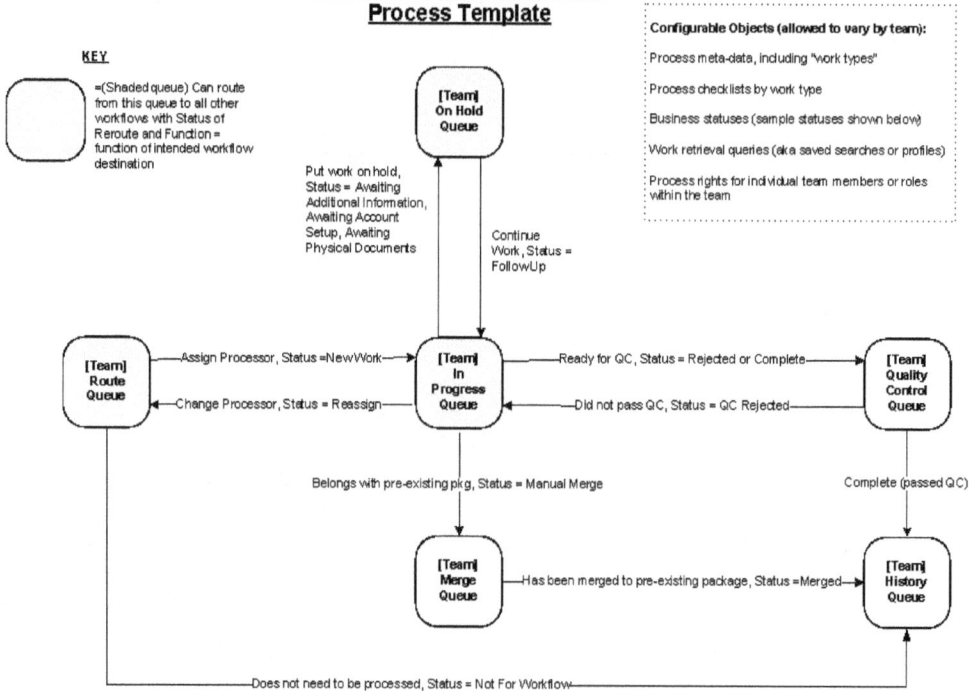

Overview of Common Shared Process Template

In February, 2007, we kicked off our first BPM project with the Transfers In and New Accounts business units and added several business unit employees to the project team as process owners and subject matter experts. In May, 2007, we implemented the New Accounts and Transfers In business processes using the "common shared process" model as the template. The project was a tremendous success and yielded many unexpected benefits.

By July, 2008, fifteen business units' business process documents, which initiated or supported over 145 business processes, were implemented using the "common shared process" to resolve the paper problem quickly.

As we implemented this process model across the business, we learned that adding new, seemingly simple or intuitive, features to the model was very difficult and required a good deal of custom software, which also added time on to our implementations. By extension, we were also learning that "first order" business process implementation and the analysis and automation it would require would definitely not be served by our existing workflow tool. After a good deal of research, we decided that we would be better served by acquiring a BPMS that we could integrate with our document management system (and any other line of business system) quickly and easily. Since we had demonstrated measurable benefits in our implementations since 2007, we were able to form the business case to justify the purchase of a BPMS (Lombardi Teamworks) in August, 2008.

Strategically significant business processes are now being carved out of the "common shared process" that hosted them previously and built into an individual business process model that manages all the activities of the process (not just those that are common to document workflow). As noted previously, this type of implementation is called a "first order business process" in our process architecture.

Both the common shared process and first order processes are now hosted in our BPMS and served with a shared set of document management web services that are integrated with our document management system, Oracle IPM.

As a principle in our process architecture, we make very limited modifications to our common shared process – only where required to prevent errors or reduce liability – limited improvements for efficiency and better visibility. We prefer to invest our limited IT budget in first order, strategic processes instead.

4.3 Organization

To help describe the impact of BPM and our implementations on the business, the following are a few direct quotes from managers:

- "We now have tools to map out, study and improve all our processes. They are user friendly and logical. I'm excited that we've embraced the BPM technology/culture that supports the way we want to manage our business." LaTeca Fields, Special Support Services Manager
- "We are able to use tools typically exclusive to IT. Amazing things have begun to emerge." Bonnie Lewis, Operations Vice President "The BPM Quick Trade component adds huge accountability to the trading process in that it requires one to route items timely and accurately." Brett Davis, Trading Manager
- "BPM has given us a way to dissect the manual cash reconciliation process, produce a plan to automate the reconciliation and report discrepancies." Cathy Maestas, Cash Services Manager

Evidence of BPM advancing as a discipline is literally written on the walls of the organization. Our BPM executive sponsors challenged their management teams to conduct BPM projects for at least five strategic business processes that operate within and across their business units. Many walls of the three floors of the building we occupy are now wall-papered with business process maps on long plotter sheets. Often you can find groups of employees standing around them and socializing about the processes. Many business units have invited all employees to scribble process problems and solutions feedback directly on to these maps by a certain date. These scribbles are later documented and used in BPM projects as inputs into sessions to identify process problems and solutions.

Another impact to the organization was that many employees now have the ability to telecommute. This became very important just recently during our business continuity planning and testing for the H1N1 flu pandemic. Without the implementations of the BPM program, our business continuity planning would have been extremely difficult, if not impossible.

As we mature our BPM program and framework, we are working towards a "practice center" model of organizing our program rather than a centralized business unit or single department ownership of BPM. When we discussed a "Center of Excellence", our organization struggled with the name and the idea that BPM might be "owned" by one area of the business. Our vision is very much to have BPM be a way of life in every business unit. The idea of the "practice center" resonated much better with our organization. The current evolution of the BPM Practice Center is a SharePoint site with links to our various project information, standards, articles, training materials, roadmap, etc.

5. HURDLES OVERCOME

5.1 Management

There have been many organizational challenges to implementation. At the time we began the program there were strained relationships between IT and the business that resulted in new IT leadership being brought in. The organization was going through a divestiture from our parent organization that resulted in a remaining workforce one fourth the initial size. Functional business teams were reorganized and consolidated as part of the divesture of business. Program credibility had to be established incrementally to get all business channels on board with the initiatives. Training and process mapping and analysis skills had to be provided to the business. We had also recently made the decision within IT that all development, configuration, and implementation for processes in our BPMS would be performed by an overseas outsourcing partner.

As would be expected, there have been technical implementation challenges as well. Internal standards and program framework were not in place when we started. There were learning curves for project staff on new technologies. Also, foundational architecture had to be established to allow for integration with Active Directory, SharePoint portal, the Oracle IPM document repository, and other host applications. Additionally, we did not have a well defined operational model for managing and supporting BPM technologies in production.

The biggest hurdle we had to overcome initially was an extremely poor relationship between IT and the business. This relationship was a hurdle for all projects requiring IT support. Resolving this issue was done primarily at a macro level outside of the BPM program, but the same principles were applied in BPM project implementations as well. These principles included taking to heart "the marketing of IT" as advocated by Forrester Research in (The Marketing of IT: A Core Element of Improving IT's Business Value by Laurie M. Orlov; delivering value as quickly as possible and working every day to build trust through using basic trust-building behavior keys.

The biggest management challenge we're facing now is BPM project prioritization. Demands for improvement are multiplied each time we implement a new process. Careful and thorough prioritization of small, medium and large BPM initiatives can get contentious. To resolve this, we apply BPM program governance in several contexts at Lincoln Trust Company. This governance is currently facilitated by the Business Process Automation team, which resides within IT. The program is led by Executive Sponsors that are all members of the company's senior executive team. The Business Process Automation team meets with this leadership group monthly to review the BPM Program Roadmap showing the major initiatives (1-3 month iterations) that are to be delivered during the year. The team also reviews a backlog, prioritized by the BPM Steering Group, of smaller process improvement solutions. The LTC BPM Steering Group is comprised of managers representing each business unit in the company. This Steering Group is also responsible for making key process implementation decisions, especially for processes that cross organizational boundaries, and for resolving organizational issues that arise during the implementation of a given process solution.

5.2 Business

As would be expected, the biggest hurdle we can encounter in the business is resistance to change. Change management practices are used extensively to manage this.

LTC's BPM program is fortunate in that our executive leadership has emphasized that nothing short of dramatic transformation, especially related to business processes, is expected of all levels of the organization. This is primarily due to being a new company, formed from the vestiges of an older company, with a desire to shed all baggage that might get in the way of achieving the new company's vision.

All employees are continually told through company meetings, phone mails, team meetings and their own leadership that they must continually challenge their business processes to create operational effectiveness. This direction and message is emphasized at the project kickoff and throughout a given BPM initiative.

Each BPM project team partners with a Human Resources representative that helps to assess the skills of the impacted employees. The representative also determines what will be changing as a result of the project and the requisite new skills and design and implement a training plan to help bridge the gap. Each business unit has a "super user" team that is responsible for ongoing assessment of the process and support of the employees on their team with respect to process questions and first line BPMS support.

Additionally, the BPM overall program and each BPM project conducted has a communication plan, identifying stakeholders, what they are interested in knowing, the best method for communicating this, how often they need to know it and who is responsible for communicating it. This keeps critical communications structured and effective.

5.3 Organization Adoption

Numerous strategies are employed on several fronts to drive organizational adoption of BPM. Central to this approach is communication about what the BPM program is, why it is being implemented and what is involved in conducting a

BPM project. We have many "lunch and learns" and similar communication events in which the participants in a BPM project (current or past) talk about what BPM is and what it's like to work on a BPM project. Additionally, executive sponsors of the BPM program speak at these sessions to share why BPM has been chosen to help the company achieve its goals and how important it is to participate.

We also work on building up motivators for getting involved in the BPM program. Only the organization's best employees are selected for participation in BPM projects. When selected, employees are told that they were selected for their skills and valued contribution to the organization. This brings a level of esteem to BPM program participation. The performance of an employee working on a BPM program initiative is recognized and rewarded in employee performance reviews. Executives attend many project meetings throughout the project, giving the employees opportunities for exposure to a level of the organizational management they may not interact with very frequently and reinforcing the importance of quality participation.

We work hard to create confidence and passion around the BPM program. Those involved with the BPM program have seen repeated successes with multiple solution implementations over the past two years, which have been widely communicated throughout all levels of the organization. This credibility gives participants the confidence that their efforts will be effective; they will be making an actual change in the organization, leaving their mark and making their lives and the lives of others better at work.

Finally, and most importantly, the BPM program is led by senior executives. These executives set directions and priorities for the BPM program roadmap, provide resources to BPM projects, make key process architecture decisions and resolve any conflicts needing resolution at their level. Their involvement also models behaviour for employees at other levels of the organization. We feel strongly that the importance of the senior executive participation in the BPM program cannot be overemphasized as a "make or break" element.

6. BENEFITS

6.1 Cost Savings

We have calculated a year one ROI of 120% and an overall cost savings of $2.2M.

6.2 Time Reductions

We have decreased process cycle times in some areas by up to 75%.

6.3 Increased Revenues

Increased revenues have been difficult for us to measure, but we've seen a positive impact in our ability to attract and retain profitable customers.

6.4 Productivity Improvements

The fact that LTC is able to process 75% of our process volumes prior to a divestiture with 25% of the original staff has been directly attributed to our BPM implementations.

Quality control processes, which are critical in our audit-intensive business, are standardized and enforced through automated decision rules in our processes so that we no longer need to fear whether or not we have properly followed our operational controls in place.

Our service level agreements (SLAs) with our internal and external clients are now built into the process so that business units now have the ability to reallocate work load volumes to ensure these important agreements are met.

7. BEST PRACTICES, LEARNING POINTS AND PITFALLS

7.1 Best Practices and Learning Points

✓ *A major component of LTC's BPM discipline that we consider to be a best practice is our project framework, which provides a structured, repeatable approach for project success. LTC's BPM project framework is tailored from a variety of different prominent industry methodologies, primarily the 7FE BPM Project Framework and the Lombardi Teamworks Implementation Framework (for iteratively executing process solutions in our BPMS). This framework is helpful because it is used not only to train the resources that administer the BPM program's projects, but it is shared with project stake-holders so they can understand how a given project will work.*

✓ *We have also had success with our project team composition. The Business Process Automation team coordinates the work of multiple BPM project teams. To ensure that the highest quality process solutions are delivered, several roles are involved in a BPM project depending on the types of solutions that are to be delivered in a given project. A typical core BPM project team consists of process owners and subject matter experts from the business units impacted by the project, a BPM Analyst, a Process Architect, a Data Analyst and a BPM Project Manager. All development and technical process implementation work in Teamworks is outsourced to an offshore partner for delivery.*

✓ *Each BPM project team conducts a weekly update meeting with the projects stakeholders to review project progress, make any needed process decisions and resolve any issues that have arisen during the week. All project teams working on BPM projects meet for a daily standup meeting to review progress on BPM projects and resolve any roadblocks.*

✓ *It's been very important to us to maintain a backlog of new process/projects and continuous improvement ideas prioritized by the business and continually manage these items.*

✓ *For more complex processes, we have used "story boarding" of the solution/user interface as a companion to the process map to help users visualize and agree upon process automation solutions.*

7.2 Pitfalls

✗ *At different points in our program, while we were learning how to mature our BPM program and project approach, we have had the opportunity to bring on site two different BPM consultants to help us conduct BPM projects. While these individuals were very professional and knowledgeable about BPM, they tended to be adamant about spending most of the contract time on the current state business process analysis/process mapping and relatively less time in the creation of the future state process, especially in our BPMS. The end result was that we ended up having to explain to our project sponsors why it took two months to document a current state process where, in other projects, we would have been performing QA testing on a process solution by that point. They key lesson learned for us was that, while we understand the value of getting a clear, detailed picture of the current state – our organization is best served by "time-boxing" this work into a previously agreed upon time frame.*

✗ *In our initial projects on our first workflow system, we did not involve a data architect in our process design. This made subsequent business intelligence deliveries of process data very challenging. We now integrate this role into every project, which has made process reporting much easier and less costly.*

✗ *The BA Myth: All of the vendors that we worked with early in our evaluation processes touted how a strong BA in the business could implement their own BPM system solutions. Our experience has been that business and IT partnership is critical to successful BPM efforts. Particularly when getting started, IT architecture and technical staff were critical to successful implementations, especially with respect to line of business system integration and data architecture.*

8. COMPETITIVE ADVANTAGES

The asset custody, trust and back office support for self directed retirement plans is very competitive. It is a business based on large volumes with low profit margins. Our profit margins have seen unprecedented pressures from the global financial crisis. In addition, competitors in our market niche have struggled to innovate with such a manually intensive, paper driven segment of the IRA industry.

Investment in our BPM program has enabled Lincoln Trust to differentiate itself as an industry leader in the alternative assets segment of the IRA industry and better respond to the global financial crisis. BPM has enabled us to impact the entire value chain from our partners to our customers in innovate ways that reduce costs, improve profit margins and ultimately retain and attract the best customers.

This investment at a critical time for Lincoln Trust will enable us to emerge from the global financial crisis a stronger more agile company that will be well positioned to grow organically or participate in a possible consolidation of the industry.

9. TECHNOLOGY

The BPM solution architecture has been implemented leveraging the following core vendor technologies:

- Lombardi Teamworks BPMS- used for simulation, optimization, process orchestration and integration, process automation, team performance and SLA tracking.
- Lombardi Blueprint- used for process discovery, mapping, and inventory
- Microsoft SharePoint- used for internal and external portals including dashboard and scorecard capabilities
- Microsoft SQL Server- used for BI capabilities including Reporting Services, Analysis Services, and Integration Services
- Cisco VOIP – used for integrated with portal screen pop of customer information including process details when a call is received from a customer
- Kofax Capture – used for document capture and indexing
- Oracle 10g RDBMS- used for operational data store and active data warehouse
- Oracle IPM- used for customer document imaging repository
- Top Down Systems, Client Letter – used for customer correspondence management and tracking

We have implemented a SOA and WOA architecture and Lombardi Teamworks is being used to enable process integration activity between multiple systems leveraging web services. Our BPMS is an architectural standard to orchestrate customer processes initiated from our external website.

All internal form development is done using Teamwork's coaches and external forms are built using .Net and presented on our portal.

Example of an internal process form:

In addition to, and in support of BPM process initiatives, LTC has developed an active data warehouse. The warehouse supports customer interaction and process initiatives in several ways. First, as processes are initiated in Teamworks the warehouse scores the customer based on customer profitability and value allowing everyone interacting with the process to be aware if the customer is a high-level Tier 1 client. Additionally some BPM processes have OLAP cubes designed within the warehouse that provide process analytics. Process data is loaded into a data warehouse using Microsoft's SQL Server Integration Services (SSIS) and the business now has business intelligence tools from Microsoft to analyze data using analytical cubes.

Information is delivered using a "My Workspace" concept through Microsoft SharePoint Portal, ProClarity, and SQL Server Reporting Services Reports (SSRS). Critical data regarding current staff workloads, overall processing volumes, and SLA management is obtained. In addition, through SSRS, all end users have the ability to run secure, Web-based, interactive reports, designed with multiple filtering and drill-down options to view all the imaging and process data needed to conduct their jobs and service clients.

We've also gotten a surprising amount of benefit from the Blueprint process mapping technology we've licensed. We have trained business staff members and they are initiating BPM projects by documenting their processes along with process problems, duration, and severities within the tool. The business then presents their findings to the BPM program team members, using the tool, for collaboration on solutions.

Here is an example of the Claims process as documented by a line of business manager.

10. THE TECHNOLOGY AND SERVICE PROVIDERS

Lombardi Professional Services were utilized to assist on installation and configuration of Teamworks BPMS in our environment. They were also utilized to assist us in implementing our first processes in Teamworks and with knowledge transfer to our internal BPM team members. www.lombardi.com

Twinstar Inc. professional services were used initial to assist with our imaging system setup and integration.

Pinellas County Clerk of the Circuit Court, Florida, USA

Finalist, North America
Nominated by Global 360, Inc. USA

1. EXECUTIVE SUMMARY / ABSTRACT

Supporting the most densely populated county in the state of Florida with a population of nearly one million residents, the Pinellas County Clerk of the Circuit Court office needed a process and document management solution for the Probate Division of the Clerk's office. This solution needed to not only make all court files and their supporting documents electronically available to all Pinellas County judges, lawyers, office staff, the public, and the entire County judicial system, but provide improved court file workflow and create an improved audit trail within the system. Moreover, the Clerk's office wanted to position itself to be in compliance with the state's legislative mandate requiring them to support e-filing and make records publicly available via the Internet.

In January 2009, the Pinellas County Clerk of the Circuit Court went live with Global 360's Case Management solution, Case360, to create a collaborative and team-centric environment to electronically access court files, documents, tasks, deadlines, and threaded discussions from within a single case folder, using an interface tailored to each individual's roles and privileges. The solution has revolutionized how works get done within the Clerk's office, increasing service levels to attorneys, the public and the court by being able to provide everything they need to do their work instantaneously while also providing a reliable platform for future growth.

2. OVERVIEW

The Pinellas County Clerk of the Circuit Court office is responsible for maintaining court records and pleadings, securing court evidence, collecting and disbursing court fines, and a variety of other functions within the County's judicial system.

By serving as the primary information collection department for the County's judicial system, the Clerk's office is instrumental in ensuring that the County courts efficiently serve its citizens. However, like many counties experiencing rapid growth, Pinellas County experienced process inefficiencies fuelled by millions of paper-based records that hampered its ability to effectively support and service the public, county judges and attorneys, the judiciary, and the state and county legal community as a whole. The system was plagued by inefficiencies due to the time required to sort, copy, distribute, file, secure, and store court file documents.

The Pinellas County Clerk of the Circuit Court needed a process and document management solution for the Probate Division of the Clerk's office to not only make all court files and their supporting documents electronically available to all Pinellas County judges, lawyers, office staff, the public, and the entire County judicial system, but provide improved court file workflow and create an improved audit trail within the system. Moreover, the Clerk's office wanted to position itself to be in compliance with the state's legislative mandate requiring them to support e-filing and make records publicly available via the Internet.

Transitioning from a paper-based workflow system to document imaging and a case management system presented the biggest challenge to an office culture that was steeped in two hundred years of a paper-based legal system. Other significant challenges involved integrating work processes and business processes between different agencies and making sure that the business needs of each agency and their individual users were fully understood and met.

The chief goals were to improve efficiency and productivity in Probate case files management by transitioning from paper files to electronic files through imaging, make all court files and their supporting documents electronically available to all Pinellas County judges, lawyers, office staff, the public, and the entire County judicial system, provide improved court file workflow and create an improved audit trail within the system, and position the Clerk's office to be in compliance with the state's legislative mandate requiring them to support e-filing and make records publicly available via the Internet.

Since moving to an electronic case management the Pinellas County court system has enjoyed the following benefits:

- Reduced costs and enhanced productivity by streamlining work processes between the Clerk's office and the Court
- Improved customer (Judiciary) satisfaction with ease of use
- Effectively managed compliance requirements
- Eliminated the need to handle, file, and route paper documents and court files
- Provide immediate access to electronic records without delays traditionally associated with transport of documents
- Search and retrieve functions
- Simultaneous online access to electronic records by multiple judges and/or judicial staff members
- Round-the-clock access to records from courthouse or secure, remote, Internet access
- Audit function with automatic tracking of user login and systems activities

3. BUSINESS CONTEXT

The Clerk's Probate office was very burdened working in a clerical type environment, especially given the huge amounts of paper coming into the office on a daily basis. Most of the office staff's time was spent dealing with the paper – either scanning it, processing individual pieces of paper or preparing the files, filing documents away, and then also pulling cases and sending them to other locations. They spent an enormous amount of time looking for missing pieces of paper or files. And if they were behind in maintaining current case files, this increased the volume of paperwork they would have to go through to locate requested documents and files. This often resulted in the very slow turnaround of documents critical to lawyer's cases or judge's rulings.

Delays in accessing required files impacted the entire spectrum of Probate customers. The staff, judges and magistrates who did not receive files in what they considered a timely fashion, the public, which needed to be able to view files, and attorneys, who might be waiting for closing documents critical to their cases. Compounding the problem was an inability to determine the priority of each request, resulting in less critical document requests sometimes being fulfilled ahead of more critical requests.

Since 1999, the Clerk's office had been scanning all new Probate cases as they entered the office, but a method for accessing and distributing those images to the court for review had never been developed and the internal staff had no way of leveraging those images for their own work as well. The staff grew as a result of this dual system by 25 – 30% and it became increasingly difficult to maintain it given budget considerations. In 2006, the Clerk's office began imaging everything that came in – not just new cases but all pleadings.

Since then, the Clerk's office has been looking for a way to create a bridge to this information that would enable them to get this information to the court for their review and interaction and back to the Clerk's office for review, access, and archiving.

The following were motivating factors that drove adoption of a new case management and workflow system for the Clerk's office:

- The Florida Supreme Court has adopted electronic access standards for a state wide Internet portal allowing attorneys and the public to access court records, make payments and electronically file documents. Court clerks in all 67 counties must begin implementation by October 1, 2009.
- The Clerk's office is dedicated to taking the necessary steps to reduce paper use to save trees and move towards more "Green" initiatives.
- Eliminate the nightmare of dealing with and managing paper case files and the slow time issues around retrieval.
- Judges, lawyers and the public demand online access to court files and records in near real-time from their offices, homes, and mobile devices.
- Law firms want to have instant access to the files.
- High cost of purchasing supplies in support of court case files.
- Storage costs are extremely high, especially given that a lot of records such as felony and probate records have retention periods that are 50 or 75 years. That is a long time to securely keep and store a record.
- Storage of records is very expensive. These records are very vulnerable in the state of Florida, as they are a coastal state and subject to hurricanes.
- Need to secure records in the best possible way.

4. THE KEY INNOVATIONS

4.2 Business

Service levels to attorneys, judges and the public have increased exponentially. The staff is able to provide requested case files or records almost instantaneously.

Judges, attorneys, legal firms, staff, and the public have all been positively impacted by the new system. They can all now view entire case files and court records and all their supporting documents 24/7/365 from any computer, enabling better customer service to the Judiciary and the public. They no longer have to waste time physically coming to the courthouse to view files. This also saves the staff time that was previously spent engaging and fulfilling the customer request.

Case files and records can now be viewed simultaneously by multiple stakeholders at multiple remote locations.

Clerk office staff is receiving fewer phone calls from attorneys and the public requesting case file or record request statuses as they now have online access. This has freed the staff to focus on more value-added activities within the office, eliminating time spent on clerical activities.

The ability to file a document with the Clerk's office and have it immediately processed and sent to the Judge for signature has been very well received by the Bar (attorneys). Attorneys have filed documents, anticipating a week's delay in needing to request a service before the document "posts" to the docket, only to find out that the document was processed and docketed within a day. These attorneys have now changed their procedures, requesting services much sooner after filing. One example of the solution changing "how work gets done" within the Clerk's office.

The Clerk's office is now able to directly email images to attorneys or whoever requests them.

The public, as well as attorneys' offices can now view a Judges docket and be able to see that, for example, a proposed "audit" has been submitted and forwarded to the court. They can then see when the docket code changes status, indicating it has been signed. This is very important to the public and to attorneys.

Judges conduct what they call "ex parte" where they meet with attorneys to discuss specific paperwork and provide help. Attorneys can now enter the office, have their paper work scanned into the system, visit with the judge, have the judge sign the paperwork electronically, and by the time the meeting is over, copies can be provided to the attorneys if they need them. This process can take less than half an hour. Previously it might have taken several days to complete.

The staff is able to ensure that the oldest work is processed first, ensuring better customer service to all requested services.

The entire system and the processes that drive it are more transparent to all of the Clerk's customers and stakeholders.

4.3 Process

State of the Process:

The Probate Department handles specifically estates, guardianships and mental health cases. The Clerk's office receives the cases, the estates or guardianships, from the public and attorneys and the cases are processed.

In the past, attorneys would take paperwork directly to the court for review and approval. This could potentially be delayed if the court was unavailable or at another location and unable to view the file. Once the court reviewed the files, these signed records might be taken home with the attorney and never come back to the court. Other times, a judicial assistant might bring it down to the Clerk's office, which may take a day or two resulting in several days passing before the paperwork was properly processed with the Clerk's office.

Now, the submitted paperwork is reviewed, scanned and then forwarded to the court electronically for action if necessary. Then the court electronically signs the papers, they come back from the judge, are prepared for distribution and copies are made as necessary. The case is also processed per any instructions handed done by the court.

Overall Process Architecture:

The Case360 implementation in the Probate Department at Pinellas County incorporates a simple workflow process that integrates with various components that were already in place. Paper documents are captured at the front-end, using the existing Execute360 system. The resulting images are then passed to the Case360 system where they are routed among four major groups of individuals: Intake, Audit, Magistrates, and Judges. The system allows Intake and Audit users to "prepare" cases for the Magistrates and Judges by identifying the key documents to be reviewed and acted upon, as well as the additional supporting documents that may be needed for proper handling of the case. When necessary, documents based on Microsoft Word templates can also be created and made part of a case. Finally, users also have the ability to apply their signatures to the images electronically.

Where appropriate, the Case360 system will pass information to and from the mainframe-based docketing system used by the County. This allows users to review the docket history on a case without having to exit Case360.

When document processing is complete, images are returned to the Execute360 system for permanent storage. A subset is also made available via an Official Records subsystem that allows for public viewing of documents.

The design was guided by the following principles:

- The overall goal was to convert the processing from one in which documents were processed as paper and then scanned at the back-end when complete, to one in which documents were scanned at the front-end and processed as electronic images.
- The workflow process assumed that the users knew their jobs and were capable of making processing decisions without much direction. Therefore the implementation provides little in the way of detailed task management, and instead simply allows for several queues from which to draw work, and just a few places to which work can be routed. Few pre-defined paths are used since the intention is to allow the users to decide on the appropriate destination for any given item of work.
- The design was intended to maximize flexibility by making the system as dynamic as possible. As a result, documents are loosely linked together based on a unique reference number that is applied to each document as an index. This approach allows new documents to be available in the casefolder as soon as they are indexed with that reference number. All users can therefore access all the documents in the case immediately, regardless of where they are in the process. In addition, the user interface is dynamic in that the data and options available change automatically depending on where one is in the process, and what one's role is. Thus, Intake workers and Judges will have different, persona-based views of a case.

Process Design Adaptation:

The workflow process in Case360 is fed by work arriving from Execute360, and returns work to Execute360 when it is complete. The design, however, will allow for the replacement of Execute360 with few changes to the Case360 process. The interfaces for receiving and sending the information to and from Execute360 will necessarily change, but the core workflow processing in Case360 will remain the same. A project to migrate from Execute360 to Case360 is, in fact, currently under way.

The absence of pre-defined workflow paths in the core workflow process means that in one sense the process has run-time adaptability. Users have the knowledge and authority to select the appropriate destination based upon the type of document and the processing required. They are not required to always route work to the same "next step."

Service Oriented Architecture:

The system relies upon the services of several components that are external to Case360.

The Execute360 system is accessed via the Service Broker provided by Global 360. This allows users to search for documents that reside in Execute360 (whether old ones that pre-date the Case360 implementation, or new ones that have been sent there after Case360 processing). The search capabilities allow users to locate both Execute360 and Case360 documents in a single query, and make them available to the user as a single result list. This capability is implemented in part by steps in the Case360 process that automatically update images and index information in the Execute360 route.

The mainframe-based docketing system used by Pinellas is automatically updated by a step running in the Case360 process. As documents are completed, this step accesses web services that add docket entries that correspond to the documents being processed. The user interface in Case360 also provides the ability for users to add docket entries, or to list existing ones, using similar web services.

5. 4.4 ORGANIZATION

The new solution and workflow has changed the way work gets done within the Clerk's office, making all the employees more efficient and effective at delivering data and services.

Natural hesitancy at first has given way to realization that new processes have improved all aspects of the organization's day-to-day activities.

Clerk office staff is receiving fewer phone calls from attorneys and the public requesting case file or record request statuses as they now have online access. This has freed the staff to focus on more value-added activities within the office, eliminating time spent on clerical activities.

The staff takes a tremendous amount of pride in providing excellent customer service and customer satisfaction. They pride themselves in processing work quickly and accurately and getting responses back to the attorneys or other people waiting for the data.

The staff no longer spends time looking for lost cases and pleadings, which took a tremendous toll on the staff morale when these incidents occurred. It is now very rare for a case file or supporting document to be lost.

The staff no longer has to spend time preparing files to be moved to other remote locations and tracking the movement and securing of those files.

Office staff's desks are no longer cluttered with files as they have gone almost completely paperless.

"It has revolutionized the office," said Diane Elliot, Manager of Probate Court Records.

The time saved on clerical duties has enabled the staff to cross-train on a lot of different functions. The staff employees have enjoyed the opportunity to learn new things and it has changed how everyone views the work conducted within the office. They now can engage in more constructive work within the case management system.

The employees are happier and they feel more motivated to do their work. They can constantly see the amount of work pending in their queue and are more concentrated on their work. They are no longer diverted by having to pull files, look for pleadings, and file cases back. Even assisting customers on the phone is easier.

Employees feel more confident with the information they are providing because they can see the documents, so if they say the case file or document is with the court, they can be confident the court has it.

They are able to monitor their work queues, which has really increased productivity a great deal. It has almost become a competition within the Probate department to see who can get their work done the quickest and keep their work queue empty.

6. HURDLES OVERCOME

Management

The Pinellas County management, from the Probate Department, through the Court and Operational Services, and on up to the Clerk himself were solidly behind this project. There was active participation from the key players, and they made sure that their team stayed active and involved throughout the entire process.

The organization of the County itself did pose some challenges, however. It is segmented in that there are, in addition to the Probate Department itself, a Clerk's Technology area and a Business Technical Services area that provide services to the various departments. In addition, on the Court side there are the Court Administration area (including the judges and magistrates) and a Court's IT area. It was sometimes difficult to coordinate all of these resources and to reach consensus, and the Court Administration and Court IT groups in particular were not always available during the initial phase of the project.

Because the Court Administration and IT groups were less comfortable with the initial system and their perceived lack of input into it, a second phase of the project was agreed to. This phase would have a short duration and would quickly result in the deployment of a version that would directly address many of the concerns of the Court. In addition, both Global 360 and Probate Department staff provided one-on-one training and assistance to the Court staff to ensure a successful implementation of this phase.

Business

In general the County was comfortable with the design goals of the system. They had no problem giving up paper and processing documents electronically. One hurdle was getting the judges and magistrates to approve the use of electronic signatures for signing image documents. There were two principal concerns initially:

The judges and magistrates were concerned about the security of the signature itself, and wanted to make sure that no unauthorized person could access and apply the signature. They needed to be accessible only by the individual judge or magistrate. This hurdle was overcome by demonstrating the approach that would be deployed, and assuring them that the signature was tied to the users' logon ID. As long as the ID was secure, the signature would be too.

They were also concerned about the general use of an electronic signature, rather than one signed in ink (preferably in a different color than black). Before agreeing to a solution the Court sought the opinion of higher courts and administrative bodies in the State of Florida to ensure that electronic signatures were acceptable.

Organization Adoption

The Probate Department was so committed to the new system that it was deployed rather smoothly. Train-the-trainer training was conducted, after which the end-users received training and had time to spend on the test system. Procedures were adopted by the department that eased the transition. Despite this, occasional design problems were discovered that resulted in changes in the next phase designed to plug some holes. At no time, however, was there anything other than enthusiastic support. The fact that the department was used to dealing with capturing documents and accessing images (albeit at the back-end), made this implementation a logical next step for the users. They also quickly saw the value in the system as the paper-shuffling and distribution was immediately minimized.

The Court Administration area experienced more frustration. While some judges became proficient quickly, others required more assistance. In addition, plans were put in place to quickly address some concerns in a second phase. For example, a process was created to convert Microsoft Word documents to images to make them easier to sign. In addition, queries were created to make it easier for the judicial and magistrate assistants to organize work going to and from the judges and magistrates. The increased attention received by these groups made them more comfortable with the system itself, as well as with their level of input to its design.

7. BENEFITS

6.1 Cost Savings

* Saving anywhere from $4,000 to $5,000 a year by not having to purchase supplies in support of court case files. Don't have to buy and order expensive case binders, labels, tabs, boxes, etc.
* Saving millions of dollars in storage costs for files that have retention periods of 50 and 75 years in some cases.
* Eliminated transportation costs associated with having to move documents between offices.
* Able to process higher volumes of court documents with fewer staff resources.

The implementation and the change in policy has expedited subscriptions to electronic subscriptions, creating additional revenue ($60 sign-up charge for 5 per month plus 100 clicks. Also translates to reduced labor costs.

6.2 Time Reductions

At the Clerk level, processing times have decreased. Previously, paperwork was received, sent to a judge where it might sit for a day or so, and then be returned to the Clerk's office for Probate processing. Could take up to 3 to 5 days. Now, incoming paperwork can be received, imaged, sent to the judge and returned signed to the Clerk's office in as little as 60 seconds.

At the Audit level, locating and pulling requested files could take up to one day. Now, requested files can be located for printing or electronic distribution almost instantaneously.

At the Judge level, Judges can help other judges from the location of their choice, whether from home, office or some other remote location. Judges can work weekends or any time that suits them. One Judge who was in court all week, was able to catch up with a queue that had reached 200 items

6.3 Increased Revenues

The implementation and the change in policy have expedited subscriptions to electronic subscriptions, creating additional revenue ($60 sign-up charge for 5 per month plus 100 clicks.

6.4 Productivity Improvements

- Reduced time to process court files from days to hours, sometimes minutes.
- Judges able to received documents for review within 24 hours of receipt in the Clerk's department.
- Typical case file work cycle reduced from 4 days to no more than 2 days.
- Fewer boxes to handle and move has reduced the chance of injury to couriers and reduced amount of time they spend in the Clerk's office.
- Management has full visibility into all Clerk's office work queues so the staff always knows exactly what work is pending and can escalate a case is the situation calls for it, making the office more responsive to emergent cases.
- Work can be managed even though it is being handled at more than one location.
- The audit trail provided by the system enables the management and the staff to know when items are processed and forwarded for other people to work on and the staff knows when they get it back.
- The workflow improvements have standardized all of the basic procedures for processing court files and documents, so training is easier and faster, and everyone can cross-train on different roles and responsibilities.
- Better customer service. They can access files on their own with anytime access

8. BEST PRACTICES, LEARNING POINTS AND PITFALLS

- ✓ *Start off with a small project as test case.*
- ✓ *Work closely with your vendor to ensure best practices are explained and begun at the beginning of the project.*
- ✓ *Ensure that all partners and stakeholders have a very clear understanding of the project's overall goal and the project milestones along the way.*
- ✓ *Ensure that you have cooperation from court staff and judges and whatever IT departments they have.*
- ✓ *Communicate, communicate, communicate, and train, train, train.*
- ✓ *Utilizing a solution that considers the end user first has made user adoption and acceptance considerably easier than forcing end users to learn a system not adapted to their role within the process.*

- ✗ *Don't view your project as having an end date, but treat it as an ongoing project. We have continued to make enhancements to the system even though we are extremely happy with it.*

9. COMPETITIVE ADVANTAGES

The biggest advantage to going paperless with the new case management system is that multiple people can be working on the files at the same time. Simultaneously, Clerk staff, judges, attorneys and the public are able to review and work on files from their remote location.

The other primary advantage to the Clerk's office is the improved workflow between the Clerk's office and the judge. The Clerk's office is able to have the judge apply his digital signature to the cases and send those files and orders back to the

Clerk's office electronically. This flow and efficiency in being able to turn work around quickly makes the Clerk's office very responsive and efficient.

It also enables judges to work when they want to and where they want to, giving them greater flexibility in getting their work done. During hearings, judges are able to pull up records and transcripts online faster than attorneys can produce hardcopies.

Going forward, the case management system will be deployed in support of the misdemeanour, criminal, juvenile, and civil areas of the county court in a continuing effort to convert all paper court files to an electronic format and make them accessible to all stakeholders and customers.

10. TECHNOLOGY

Overview:

Pinellas County is a long time Execute360 user. In the Probate Department, Execute360 was used for backend processing, capturing documents after they had been processed as paper. The addition of Case360-based imaging and workflow system enables the Department to process documents electronically. This provides a more secure environment, makes documents available to multiple users simultaneously, and facilitates retrieval.

Process:

- Documents are scanned and indexed in Execute360, then delivered to Case360.
- In the first Case360 route, documents are received by Intake or Audit via CaptureBroker, and routed among the various departments as needed. Microsoft Word documents may be added as well.
- When completed, documents are sent to a second Case360 route. Here they are validated, and docket entries are added to the mainframe via web services. Documents are then sent to Execute360 via Content Broker.
- Returned documents are archived for permanent storage. A subset of documents are recorded as public records. Attorneys and others can access documents on a public website.

Access to Work:

- All work is accessed via queries that result in list output, Queries may be used to find work in workflow queries, or may be file cabinet searches that locate work regardless of where it is in the system.

What the User Sees:

- This is a typical example of what a user will work with. This view combines index data from both the process instance (the workitem in workflow) and the case folder it contains. The tabbed interface conserves screen space while providing access to all documents, discussions, and custom functions. When selected, the tabs in the top section execute queries that dynamically list all documents for the case that are appropriate for the tab. If new documents are added to the system, they will automatically appear the next time the tab is selected. The specific tabs that a user sees depend on their security rights.

Process Instance fields

Casefolder fields

Dynamically built list of documents. Varies by tab.

Tabs for discussions, history, and custom functions

Dispatch buttons to route workitem

Document Preparation:

The Intake and Audit Department users must "prepare" cases for judges and magistrates. Typically this means identifying new documents that need review, as well as older ones that serve as supporting documentation.

Document Preparation tab lists new documents and allows user to select documents for review by judge or magistrate

Custom toolbar buttons allow users to move documents from one tab to another, to change their status, or to mark them for completion.

All Case Documents:

This tab is a dynamic file cabinet search of all documents for the case, regardless of whether they are Execute360 or Case360. Users can copy documents to the Document Preparation tab in order to include them when preparing cases for review.

The All Case Documents tab lists all documents for the case, regardless of age, status, or storage location. The *Imaged Documents* section lists documents in the Execute360 repository (accessed via **Content Broker**). The *In Progress Documents* section lists those in Case360.

Judges Tab:

The Judges tab only shows those documents that have been selected for Judicial Review or marked as Supporting Documents during case preparation. This enables Judges to quick access all the documents they need to process, rather than having to sift through the entire case. The Magistrate tab has similar functionality.

The Judge tab lists documents prepared for review. By Intake or Audit users, or by judicial assistants.

The All Case Documents tab is available should they require additional information.

Processing Details:

The tab shows the user who last touched the process instance in each area: Intake, Audit, Judge, and Magistrate. It also lists other process instances currently in workflow for the same case. Multiple process instances results when a case is at a different step, or has a different work category, than other instances.

Docket Tab:

Docket entries on the mainframe provide the official history of transactions that apply to the case. The Docket tab provides access to the mainframe system without having to switch to s different application. When the user selects the tab, a web service utilizing GT software is automatically called, and the entries are

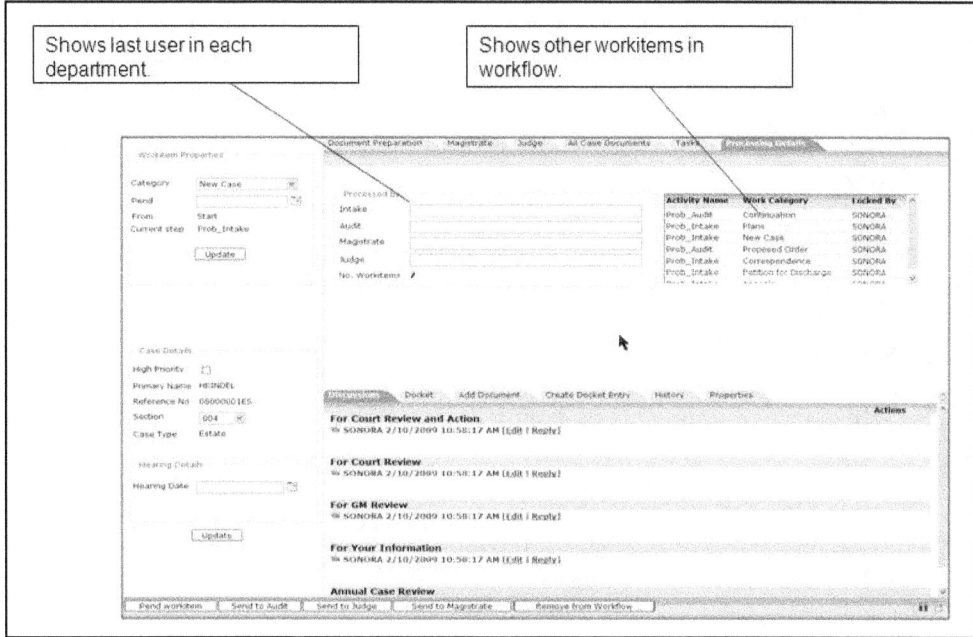

listed. Five role fields defined in Case360 contain for each user, the ID. Password, and other access information necessary to pass through the mainframe's ACF2 security. Password data is encrypted in the Case360 database for security purposes.

Date	Docket Entry	Activity Code	Ver
01122009	NOTICE TO CAVEATOR	NTCV	F
01122009	ORDER-CHECKLIST	ORCK	F
01092009		TEXT	N
01092009	CLERK'S SUMMARY WORKSLIP - INTAKE	CKWS	N
01092009		TEXT	N
01092009		TEXT	N
01092009		TEXT	N
01092009		TEXT	N
01092009		TEXT	N
01082009	AFFIDAVIT OF INDIGENCY	AFIN	N
12122008	ORDER TO FILE REQUIRED DOCUMENTS	OFRD	F
01062009		TEXT	N
12052008	ADDENDUM	ADUM	N
12012008	DISPOSED BEFORE A HEARING	DISB	N
11132008	TESTING DOCKET ENTRY	TEXT	N

Create Docket Entry Tab:

Authorized users can manually add docket entries to the mainframe when necessary. This tab allows them to search for a docket code to utilize, and to specify the docket date. GT Software-based web services are called to perform the function when the Create button is selected, using the same mainframe access parameters (stored in role fields), as the Docket tab.

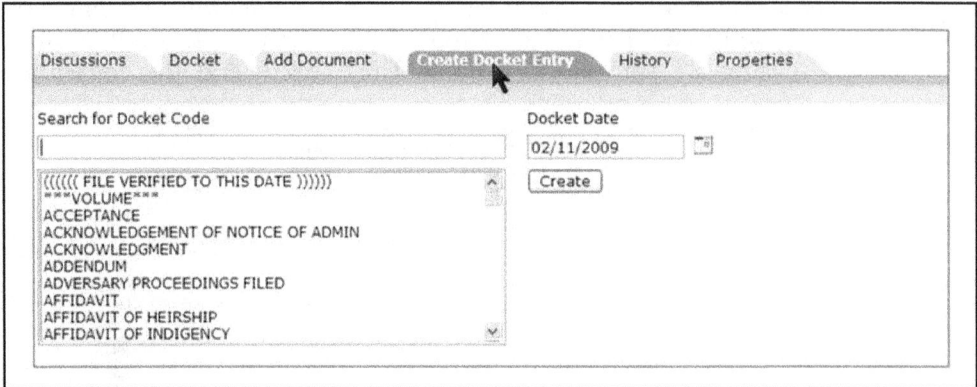

| Discussions | Docket | Add Document | **Create Docket Entry** | History | Properties |

Search for Docket Code

Docket Date
02/11/2009

((((((FILE VERIFIED TO THIS DATE))))))
VOLUME
ACCEPTANCE
ACKNOWLEDGEMENT OF NOTICE OF ADMIN
ACKNOWLEDGMENT
ADDENDUM
ADVERSARY PROCEEDINGS FILED
AFFIDAVIT
AFFIDAVIT OF HEIRSHIP
AFFIDAVIT OF INDIGENCY

[Create]

Add Document Tab:

Users have the ability to create new Microsoft Word documents based on pre-defined templates. This tab utilizes the Case360 AJAX interface and enables users to filter the list of templates by typing any portion of the template name. When a Create button is selected, the system creates a new Filestore object containing the Word template, and indexes it with the case number. The document is immediately available from other tabs, such as Document Preparation, because the query on the tabs searches based on the case number. Judges can use this function to create documents such as court orders while hearing a case.

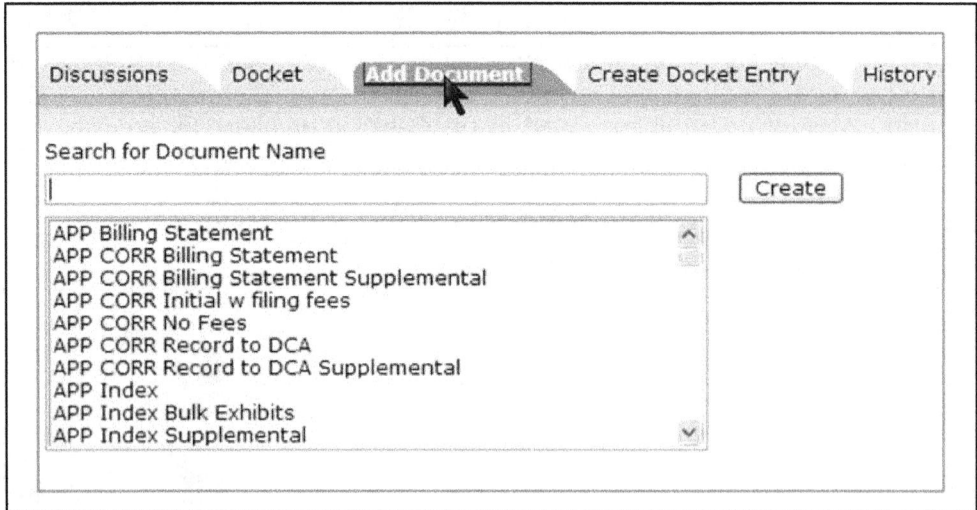

| Discussions | Docket | **Add Document** | Create Docket Entry | History |

Search for Document Name

[Create]

APP Billing Statement
APP CORR Billing Statement
APP CORR Billing Statement Supplemental
APP CORR Initial w filing fees
APP CORR No Fees
APP CORR Record to DCA
APP CORR Record to DCA Supplemental
APP Index
APP Index Bulk Exhibits
APP Index Supplemental

Imaging for the Web:

The Imaging for the Web application utilized by Case360 has been modified to include custom annotation capabilities. Authorized users, including Judges, can add an image of their signatures to electronically "sign" documents. The signatures are stored in a secure network directory and are accessed automatically when the Signature menu pick is selected. Users can also automatically affix the date, UCN number and reference (case) number to the document. Annotations can be made permanent, if desired.

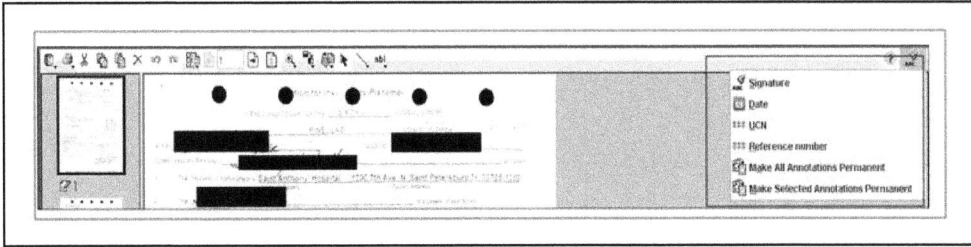

11. THE TECHNOLOGY AND SERVICE PROVIDERS

Global 360, Inc. was the sole process and document management vendor, integrator, and consultant for this project. (www.global360.com)

About Global 360

Global 360 helps organizations to better manage processes today and make improvements for tomorrow. Our market leading process and document management solutions improve business performance by maximizing the productivity of all participants in a process. To accomplish that, we address the unique requirements of all key roles that are critical to improving a process. Providing the industry's first persona-based BPMS and role-based interface, Global 360's viewPoint delivers an intuitive, configurable, and personable user experience, accelerating time-to-deployment while reducing the development costs typically associated with complex BPM user applications. And with real-time performance data, managers can find and fix problems before they impact customers and extend these efficiencies to customers and partners. Building on our strength in financial services, government, insurance, consumer packaged goods, manufacturing, and the retail sector, Global 360 has helped more than 2,000 customers in 134 countries reduce paper, automate processes, and empower individuals to truly change how work gets done. Global 360, Inc. is headquartered in Texas with operations in North America, Europe, and the Pacific Rim. For more information about Global 360's process and document management solutions, please call 1-214-520-1660 or visit the company web site at www.global360.com.

San Francisco Public Utilities Commission, USA

Finalist, North America
Nominated by Interfacing Technologies, Canada

1. EXECUTIVE SUMMARY / ABSTRACT

The retirement of baby boomer workforce is putting companies' productivity and readiness to the test. How quickly and efficiently companies rearrange their operations to the generational swap will set their competitive edge in the next years. Creativity and determination are crucial to overcome the challenge. The San Francisco Public Utilities Commission (SFPUC) implemented a business process management and workflow solution to drive change efforts across its organizations. The SFPUC deployed innovative ways to capture the baby boomers' knowledge and transmit it to the new generation; without missing a step in service efficiency and quality, the SFPUC prepared itself for major challenges such as environmental preservation.

2. OVERVIEW

The San Francisco Public Utilities Commission is a department of the City and County of San Francisco that provides water, wastewater, and municipal power services to San Francisco. The SFPUC has over 2000 employees and provides four distinct services: Regional Water, Local Water, Wastewater (collection, treatment and disposal), and Power to 2.4 million customers (1). Two great challenges faced the San Francisco Public Utilities Commission in 2009 to maintain its high level of operational competency. Stemming from the baby boomer retirement, the challenge of knowledge capture, knowledge management, and knowledge transfer were considerable. And secondly, the SFPUC encountered a reliability and accountability issue via the incorporation of a vast number of new generation utility workers in a short period of time.

The SFPUC implemented a business process management and workflow solution (Interfacing Enterprise Process Center® - EPC) to manage knowledge retention issues and establish new ways "to share information and collaborate across the organizations" (2). The SFPUC mapped out its processes with associated step-by-step procedures and made this information available for all utility employees to use on an on-demand basis as reference documentation and training material. Additionally, SFPUC launched a serious analysis of roles and responsibilities across departments in order to distribute process ownership and assign clear task accountability. Supported by a holistic perspective of the organization and a visual representation of tasks, utilities workers improved their sense of ownership and readiness which in turn enabled the SFPUC to extend its accountability beyond its organizations to reach end users.

As well as a challenge, the retirement of a significant portion of the workforce also created an opportunity to increase SFPUC overall process productivity and adopt latest technologies. With a new process-orientated vision of its organization and sustainable business architecture, SFPUC was able to establish a clear path towards process execution. Leveraging the EPC workflow engine, SFPUC was able to "replace" several human centric manual tasks with automated services and monitor the performance of these processes over time. The analytical data collected provides management with the business intelligence to uncover inefficiencies and strive to achieve a continuous process improvement culture within SFPUC.

3. BUSINESS CONTEXT

The baby boomer workforce retirement concern is often discussed within the media but most companies have not yet faced the reality of the situation. San Francisco baby boomers make up a slightly larger proportion of the (San Francisco's) total population as compared to the state and country. As of the 2000 Census, baby boomers made up 27.2% of the country's population, 26.9 percent of California's population, and 30.5 percent of San Francisco's population.

As they age, current projections indicate that San Francisco's baby boomers will cause a significant increase in the senior population that mirrors the national trend. The July 2007 (the California Department of Finance) projections estimate that the aging of the baby boomers by 2030 will swell the population age 65 to 85 from 10 to 16 percent in California and from 13 to 18 in San Francisco as compared to the 2000 Census figures. ("*San Francisco Baby Boomers—A Breed Apart?*" report, prepared by the *Advisory Council to the San Francisco Aging and Adult Services Commission* (2008).

Mirroring the baby boomers' national scenario, the San Francisco Public Utilities Commission estimated in December 2008 that a 20% of its workforce would to be retiring in 2009. Moreover, because of the technical nature of the SFPUC workforce, this challenge was exemplified. As a result, the SFPUC acknowledged the need to improve its practices to capture, retain, and transmit knowledge to respond efficiently to the generational swap that could jeopardize its operations.

4. THE KEY INNOVATIONS

4.2 Business

The SFPUC felt a necessity to shift from traditional practices of knowledge capture to methods that will improve SFPUC accountability and productivity in the new millennium. The SFPUC addressed the operational risk presented by the baby boomer retirement using an innovative manner. The SFPUC implemented a creative and ambitious business process management and workflow solution to address its knowledge issues and correct process inefficiencies across the organization.

The SFPUC provides water, wastewater, and municipal power services to 2.4 million customers(1), throughout a complex net of processes and procedures orchestrated in different schedules across the SFPUC departments; thus, effort coordination and collaboration among departments are essentials to provide quality work. The business process management approach facilitated the SFPUC to identify work crossovers by mapping processes and procedures from a process-centric perspective across departments, which increased visibility between departments and transformed a cluster of processes and procedures into a holistic process framework. Supported by its cross-functional flowcharts, the SFPUC was able to identify gaps in work handovers and tasks redundancies. Carrying on its BPM initiative, the SFPUC demolished silos, and initiated a change of culture across its departments.

In the event of losing a great number of its workforce and having to incorporate a junior workforce in record time, the SFPUC needed to maximize its resources to cope with the knowledge challenge, plus enhance the quality of its overall services (for example, obtaining ISO14000 certification). As a result, the SFPUC pushed the envelope higher and went beyond optimization of some of its processes to automate steps that were manual, costly and added no value to its citizens (e.g. travel reimbursement process). With this tactic, the SFPUC alleviated budget and employees' workload to transfer resources to where they were more needed; for instance, in the field, serving the citizens of San Francisco and surroundings.

The SFPUC BPM initiative gave employees vision into their processes and encouraged them to provide feedback into new ways to be efficient. The SFPUC did a great leap towards its competitive advantage incorporating technology to fill the gaps and correct inefficient handovers of work. This new visual-oriented solution, built to be more intuitive and error-proof (represented by business process management and video technology) established a new way to capture knowledge and transmit it within the SFPUC, which appeals to the next generation of tech savvy workers as well as caters the internet entry-level users (baby boomers).

4.3 Process

Like many government bodies, little incentive to share knowledge was given, resulting in a bureaucratic dynamic in which employees were hesitant to expose their underlying business processes. This lack of visibility created elevated operational risks with the baby boomers retiring from the organization. The SFPUC relies on utility employee's know-how and skills to deliver effective services. In addition to routine tasks, the SFPUC has inspection processes and procedures that due to their complex nature take about 45 days to complete, and are often not conducted on a regular basis (once every 5 – 15 years). Further emphasizing the need to properly document and manage each process as a means to eliminate the current knowledge transfer gaps. (2)

New employees rarely have all of the knowledge needed to operate or maintain a specific system, facility, or piece of equipment. Furthermore, in a world where government policies, regulations, technologies, infrastructures, and customer expectations are continually changing, there is no guarantee that experienced employees have received the information they need to perform reliable work. Even utilities that actively manage their physical infrastructure sometimes pair high-tech equipment with old-school approaches to information management -the shortcut for documentation is "Ask Fred"- (3).

SFPUC turned to business process management software to unite people, processes, and technology. For instance, the work order flow of the SFPUC's wastewater enterprise, as mapped using a BPM tool, provided step-by-step manual linking instructions on how to complete each task with the documents used to complete the task. The deliverable for this task cluster is a work order request that is accurate and complete before it is assigned to a maintenance planner and the field staff members who perform maintenance work. This system included processes with hand-offs to other city departments. (3)

Beyond knowledge management, a key driver for the San Francisco Public Utilities Commission BPM program was to minimize/remove tasks which were the source of employees' discontent. The intent of this strategy was twofold; decrease the turn-over rate of new employees entering SFPUC, and secondly, increasing the likelihood of the current workforce electing to delay their retirement. They selected the Travel Expense Reimbursement process as the first process to automate within the organization. The reimbursement process was prioritized as mission critical because of four primary reasons:
- Lengthy, costly, manual nature of the process.

- 80% percent of the workforce runs this process.
- Increasing the workforce job satisfaction.
- Process cost brings no added values to the citizens of San Francisco.
- Required compliance financial controls and audit trail.

Leveraging EPC workflow, the SFPUC reduced time and costs associated with a processes' development and implementation. For example, the standardized expense reimbursement process of the wastewater department asked employees to print out a form, complete it by hand, and attach to it the receipts. Then, employees had to physically walk the documents over to their supervisor workstation for approval. Supervisors were required to manually review and approve every expense item and then physically remit the expenses for 3 additional levels of approval before the controller was able to issue the reimbursement.

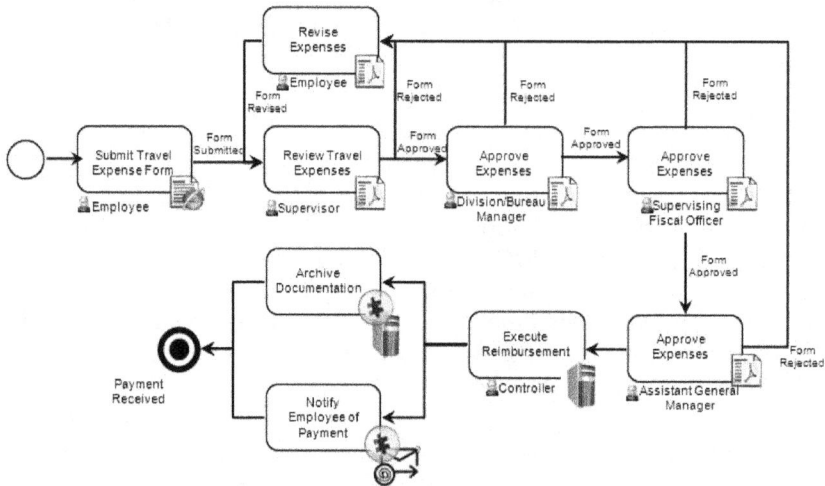

Figure 1. Automated Travel Expense Reimbursement Process

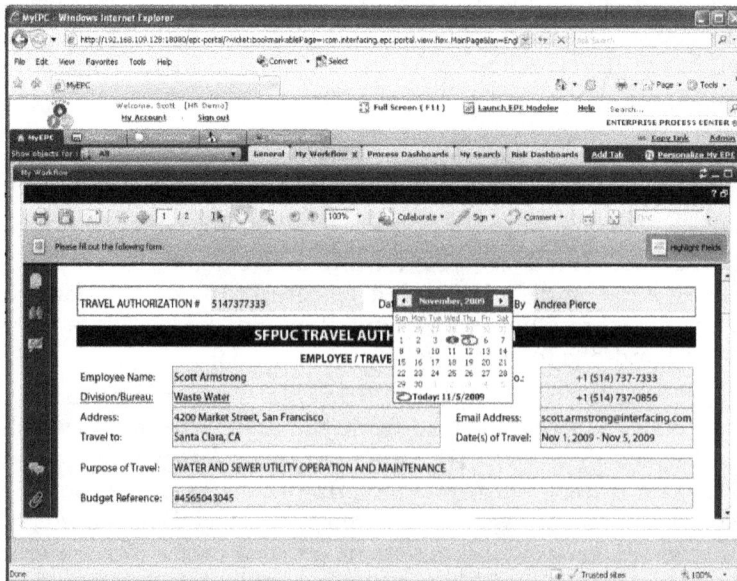

Figure 2. SFPUC Travel Authorization eForm (EPC Web Portal)

Using the travel reimbursement process as a successful proof of concept for the value of extending their business process management program beyond knowledge management and process optimization to include automation, SFPUC is in the midst of prioritizing and rolling out the workflow on other critical customer facing processes (eg. Energy Conservation Incentive Process)

4.4 Organization

The SFPUC started tackling the knowledge management problem using a wiki-tool to address employees' need for information sharing. Although valuable, the shortcoming of the wiki lied in the fact that documents lacked relevance. A document search query resulted in hundreds of entries found making it impossible to locate the proper required information, causing employees to return to the old "Ask Fred" approach.

The SFPUC is required to comply with regulatory permits for such diversified water and air quality standards group as CEQA, CEQ, NPDES, BAAQMD (4), and is currently also in the process of obtaining ISO14000 environmental management certification. As regulatory requirements constantly evolved, the SFPUC had difficulty with communicating new environmental regulations or permits required to staff. Thus, this lack of knowledge may result in employees in the field unintentionally violating a norm while performing work - a major liability risk for SFPUC.

The SFPUC mapped key processes, their steps, and for each step, visual maps displayed roles, responsibilities and deliverables using a business process management application. Each step was also linked to the documents (e.g., maps, forms, task videos, and permits) needed to perform the step. (3) Employees will refer to technology to fill in the gaps of information. The BPM application "took data and turned it into usable information" (2). The SFPUC employees became a "more engaged, highly performed workforce" and new employees showed a "shorter learning curve" (2). Business process management facilitated the SFPUC to implement and control specific business strategies (e.g. ISO 14000 certification).

5. HURDLES OVERCOME

Management

Although process mapping was nothing new to SFPUC, Business Process Management was an unknown concept which required validation for management to endorse an organizational-wide BPM initiative.

January 2009 SFPUC launched a 30 day proof of concept (POC) to deploy the Enterprise Process Center® BPM software within the IT group with the mandate to model and communicate the IBM Maximo asset management processes across organizational entities. These were flagged by management as critical to the organizational because SFPUC was in the midst of undergoing a major software upgrade from version 4.0 to 7.1; a major change that due to the number of touch points involved it was handled as a new implementation (2). Limited visibility of both the current and future Maximo processes posed a significant operational and change management threat to the organization.

The knowledge gained and shared, within such a short period of time, during the POC provided management with the justification required to move forward with the BPM program in support of its current largest organizational challenge—the end of the "baby-boomer" era.

Business

In March 2009, the SFPUC management team, led by the assistant general manager, held meetings to define and prioritize mission critical processes (extra weight was given to those processes with a prevalent number of retirees.) Process prioritization was the one of the greatest challenges that the SFPUC encountered because according to SFPUC union laws, organizations are not entitled to ask an employee their date of retirement; therefore, management lacked data to make well-informed decisions. With this setback, it took management approximately two months of analyses to reach a consensus on process priorities.

Another significant challenge encountered by SFPUC was to identify the Subject Matter Experts (SME) for the mission-critical processes. With then current process knowledge being ad-hoc as well as undefined process and task boundaries, overlapping responsibilities was common and accountability was resisted. Using the SIPOC methodology from Six Sigma, SFPUC overcame this hurdle by breaking out large-scale process knowledge into more manageable pieces (sub-processes) and associating ownership at different levels.

Organization Adoption

The greatest lesson learned by SFPUC was the importance to communicate clear and positive objectives to invitees of a process discovery workshop prior to commencement. During roll out, the first two days of workshops were unproductive because there was a vast amount of resistance from the attendees which posed immediate concerns for the overall BPM program. Analyzing the attendees' profound resistance to the initiative uncovered the root of the issue had been directly related to the workshop objectives phrasing. The messages circulated to the attendees provided no details of the objectives of the program as a whole and contained negative feedback phrases such as "this process is seriously broken". Groups entered the workshop sessions straight away on the defensive and were pre-prepared to prove they did in fact have process knowledge, obviously creating a hostile work environment.

All negative connotations were immediately removed from the communiqué and the overall objectives of the program (knowledge capture & retention, collaboration, process improvement) were also added. A simple change in message provided an instant transformation in attitude and overall workshop quality starting day 3 and going-forward. Attendees now view workshops as an opportunity to provide input into their operations and a forum for change requests and improvements.

6. BENEFITS

6.1 Cost Savings

"The cost of lost knowledge is hard to quantify—but the cost savings are evident" (2). The BPM and workflow initiative also supported SFPUC's ongoing paperless push to engage employees to be more environmentally responsible in their tasks. The benefits of paperless operations are: reduction in the real estate needed to store historical documentation, decreased printing costs, and less time to retrieve and distribute documents.

The addition of video technology to the process maps also led to cost reductions. For example, the Moulton Niguel Water District in Laguna Niguel, Calif., captured video of how its pumping and energy management practices were performed. Those videos were then reviewed by the staff members from departments ranging from maintenance and IT to engineers and electronic control technicians. Their observations were combines with additional data analysis, and the district was able to change its energy consumption practices in a way that resulted in dramatically reduced electrical cost (3).

6.2 Time Reductions

In July 2009, the wastewater department automated the travel expense reimbursement process and implemented electronic dynamic web forms with field validations -to reduce the number of key errors- that employees complete online and attach their corresponding scanned invoices for submission. The eform then moves though a multi-tiered approval phase where automatic e-mail notifications are sent as constant reminders and business rules enforce due dates with automated escalation actions. By automating the process, the throughput processing time from employee request to reimbursement is estimated (limited historical data) to be reduced by as much as 50%. Additionally, workers will now have the ability to track the status of their expense requests online – putting the knowledge into employees' hands instead of leaving them "in the dark" which causes aggravation and low morale.

6.3 Increased Revenues

As a public entity, increased revenues were not a critical success factor for SFPUC. The mission of the San Francisco Public Utilities Commission is to serve San Francisco and its Bay Area customers with reliable, high quality, and affordable water and wastewater treatment while maximizing benefits from power operations and responsibly managing the resources—human, physical, and natural—entrusted to its care.(6) The drive for the SFPUC to implement a BPM and workflow solution was to manage knowledge, correct inefficiencies and optimize processes to transfer resources to generate value to its citizens – all achieved throughout this program.

The SFPUC continues to be a technology leader within the public domain and is one of the few departments within the city of San Francisco to consistently close quarterly expenditures below allocated budget – viewed as a "profitable" department.

6.4 Productivity Improvements

The SFPUC centralized electronic knowledge base was used as a method to supplement job shadowing and overcome glitches due to lack of information which stall employees and threaten their performance in the field. Videos synthesize information by exemplifying the critical steps of processes and procedures; plus they can also be used to review by an employee who missed, were unclear on, or simply forgot a portion of a classroom or onsite training. Video procedures instill confidence in staff members that a procedure works, because they have actually seen it work. Finally, visual recording of the execution of an unusual process or procedure allows employees to watch a task that is rarely performed (e.g. a procedure that can only be performed in low-demand conditions). (3) The SFPUC strategy reduced employees' *downtime* due to insufficient access to data.

7. BEST PRACTICES, LEARNING POINTS AND PITFALLS

7.1 Best Practices and Learning Points

- ✓ The pre-built APQC Process Classification Framework within EPC provides a great benchmark for kick starting your BPM program.
- ✓ The pre-built ITIL process library provides great insight into best practice IT service management processes and controls.
- ✓ Workflow optimizes standardized processes by automating tasks that do not add value to processes and reduce the number of errors when executing a task.

✓ Business process management software facilitated SFPUC management staff to view the organization at different levels and process interaction and by clicking on the processes exposed more detailed information (e.g. documents, tasks).

✓ Being able to standardize and reuse processes across the organization, for example, an inspection video and an expense reimbursement process, reduces time and costs associated with development and implementation. Plus, practices across the organization are consistent.

✓ Video technology is an alternative for knowledge management that transmits consistent information across the organizations, and it can be used as a basis for reviewing and refining practices.

✓ Business Process Modeling Notation (BPMN) is an effective standard for business process management initiatives for both technical and business users by providing a notation that is intuitive to business users yet able to represent complex process semantics.

✓ Low level small-scale processes do not allow employees to understand their contribution to the whole organizational system and as a result, they feel less engaged in their work.

✓ BPM software can automatically generate end-to-end value stream maps optimizing the level of visibility within a process.

✓ Paperless operations cut costs associated with printing, paper storage and filing.

Pitfalls

✗ Avoid ambiguous communication and use simple messages in which goals are clearly stated

✗ Do not bite more than you chew—prioritize your processes then divide and conquer

✗ Do not try to run before you walk—first establish a sound business architecture before moving to process workflow automation

✗ Your business is not a light switch—you cannot flick a switch to turn all your processes into executables; select small scale processes to workflow/automate for quick wins to start and gain buy-in

8. COMPETITIVE ADVANTAGES

The changes that the SFPUC carried out across its organizations gave it a competitive edge over other government organisations and over those in the private sector, situating the SFPUC as a benchmark of its industry.

The SFPUC were invited by the Water Environment Federation to share their successful business improvement program at the 2009 Technical Exhibition and Conference (WEFTEC) in Orlando, FL. With the presentation entitled, "Tackling the Exodus of Knowledge as Utilities' Workforce Exits the Labor Market." The presentation outlined change efforts that are being implemented by Wastewater Enterprise. Two of the change efforts are content-centric focusing on IT tools and interfacing with technology. mIToolbox, a wiki software, used to capture, distribute and allow access to important data through a web portal that gives all staff access 24/7. And a Business process management software that allow SFPUC to capture its mission critical functions utilizing a mapping step-by-step process that will assign role responsibility to tasks and attach documents needed to do quality work. "This practice provides training for present and future workers and will streamline our process and help us become more operationally efficient. (5)

The American Water Works Association Journal published a feature story, entitled "Using IT, Part 2: Achieving comprehensive knowledge preparedness in your workforce" about SFPUC business management initiatives to overcome a knowledge management challenge (October 2009 101:10.) The article discussed the IT tools available to help with three vital components of knowledge preparedness: Knowledge capture, knowledge management, and knowledge transfer.

The SFPUC competitive advantage gives them an additional gain in the recruiting field presenting itself as a more appealing workplace, with greater chances to retain employees. The SFPUC is a more efficient and accountable organization, committed to offer better and competitive services for the citizens of San Francisco.

9. TECHNOLOGY

San Francisco Public Utilities Commission implemented the Interfacing Enterprise Process Center® business process management software in support of their innovative knowledge management program. Differing from conventional process repositories, EPC's 'smart' process repository allows users to manage all objects from one central location, view all object uses and process touch points, reuse objects across processes, create user defined attributes on all objects, conduct impact analyses, and much more. EPC enables users to effectively take a step back from their business processes and view all related process components, providing a blueprint of their business operations. Using EPC, SFPUC was able to build a sound business architecture and establish a clear path towards process standardization and execution.

Enterprise Process Center® "is easy to use requiring little or no training for rollout therefore lowering resistance especially by our non-tech employees. It also allows us to easily train new employees with the knowledge relevant to their roles and responsibilities. (Finally,) it (...) appeals to the millennial generation and their learning style, we hope this will help us to attract and retain them as well." (2)

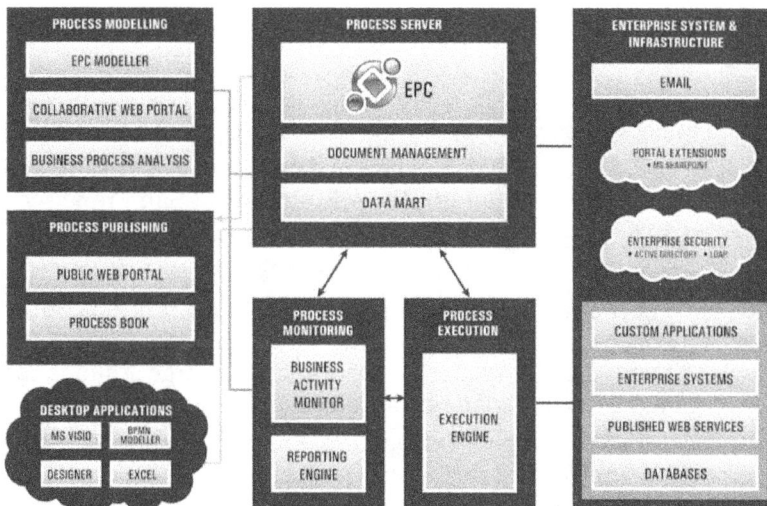

Figure 3: Interfacing Enterprise Process Center Architecture

EPC functionality allowed SFPUC to:
* Map processes graphically in the easily understood Business Process Modelling Notation (BPMN).

- Comprehensively document end-to-end processes, capturing critical job knowledge.
- View process related documents, resources, assets, risks, controls, and all process touch points.
- Conduct resource capacity planning, activity based costing, bottleneck identification, critical path analysis.
- Automate selected human-centric tasks using web forms and Adobe pdf eforms.
- Automate selected system-centric tasks and execute Service Oriented Architecture (SOA) business and agile development strategies by aligning process workflow using services to integrate with existing systems within your organization.
- Adapt process instances on-the-fly as well as create ad hoc process execution (rewind, skip steps, etc.) for complete flexibility.
- Leverage an integrated English syntax business Rules engine
- Track & monitor processes performance via the integrated OEM Cognos BI module

10. THE TECHNOLOGY AND SERVICE PROVIDERS

Interfacing Technologies Corporation (founded in 1983) is a leading international provider of Business Process Management (BPM) software that allows business users to manage the entire lifecycle of a process. Interfacing's software and consulting services span the entire process maturity model: from static process modeling in their Free BPMN Modeler for MS Visio®, to their multidimensional collaborative BPM suite the Interfacing Enterprise Process Center® (EPC). Interfacing EPC supports a range of process management initiatives; documentation, simulation, governance (Risk/ Control), deployment (SOA), and monitoring. Interfacing's solutions focus on motivating business users to create a sustainable process culture across the organization through the implementation of best practice quality frameworks and methodologies (APQC PCF, ITIL, eTOM, Six Sigma, SCOR, ISO). (www.interfacing.com).

11. REFERENCES:

1 -"San Francisco Public utilities Commission Delivers Easier-to-read Bills and Enhanced Customer Service."Pitney Bowes, Group 1 Software, Inc. 2007.

2 – Andrea Pierce, PMP, CRM ITS - Business Applications and Development San Francisco Public Utilities Commission City and County of San Francisco.

3 - "Using IT, Part 2: Achieving comprehensive knowledge preparedness in your workforce." American Water Works Association. 2009.

4 – Name of some of the regulatory permits that the San Francisco Public Utilities Commission supports: California Environmental Quality Act (CEQA), Council on Environmental Quality (CEQ), National Pollutant Discharge Elimination System (NPDES), Bay Area Air Quality Management District (BAAQMD)

5 – "SFPUC Delivers Workforce Development Presentation at WEFTEC Conference" Catherine Curtis, Wastewater Enterprise. October 2009.

6 – "SFPUC Water Enterprise Environmental Stewardship Policy". San Francisco Public utilities Commission. FINAL DRAFT June 27, 2006

County of San Joaquin, California

Silver Award, North America
Nominated by Oracle USA

1. EXECUTIVE SUMMARY / ABSTRACT

The County of San Joaquin Information Systems Division is the central IT organization serving the County of San Joaquin, which is a midsize California county with a population of more than 650,000. The county's information systems division supports its systems serving general government, human resources, law and justice, and health services. To better serve our county and support the California Administrative Office of Courts (AOC) modernization initiatives we initiated a modernization effort using Business Process Management (BPM) and Service Oriented Architecture (SOA) technologies.

In our first phase we have successfully added SOA, BPM/BPEL & BAM, an Application Development Framework (ADF), J2EE appserver/webserver, RAC and Databases to our Enterprise Architecture (EA). Furthermore, during this first 18 months we developed an application for local warrants which has 30 modules and local admin console integrated with LDAP, CUPS, ActiveX, CLETS, CJIS and CAD systems. The Law and Justice application for Warrants has been live for over 18 months and has accumulated 30 million transactions with the application supporting over 6,600 employees, 18 Law and Justice Agencies in County of San Joaquin and integration with CLETS and Police Mobile car units. This success has been recognized by the California AOC and is published as a best practice success on their website.

2. OVERVIEW

The County of San Joaquin Information Systems Division is the central IT organization serving the County of San Joaquin, which is a midsize California county with a population of more than 650,000. The county's information systems division supports its systems serving general government, human resources, law and justice, and health services. To better serve our county and support the California Administrative Office of Courts (AOC) modernization initiatives we initiated a modernization effort using Business Process Management (BPM) and Service Oriented Architecture (SOA) technologies.

As the 15th most populous county in California, San Joaquin County has responsibility for providing a wide and diverse range of programs and services to over 650,000 County residents. In order to accomplish this mission, the County is organized into 28 departments with more than 6,600 full and part-time employees. Although many of the County operations are concentrated in downtown Stockton, the County delivers services and has sites throughout a 1,448 square mile area.

San Joaquin County provides over 400 different programs and services for its constituents ranging from prenatal care by Public Health to senior services from the Department of Aging. The County provides protection under the law to its residents through the Sheriff's Patrol and Custody systems. The County also provides its constituents with health care services through San Joaquin General Hospital, as well as providing for their recreation through Community Centers and Park and Recreation programs. In addition to providing County services, the County is the provider of many state and federal mandated programs such as

WorkNet and CalWorks. These are just a few examples of the scope of work of San Joaquin County. The service spectrum is immense.

Of special interest was our Aging Criminal Justice Information System. The County's current Criminal Justice Information System (CJIS) was developed in 1986. The system is used on a daily basis by nearly every law enforcement entities within the County. The system faced two challenges. First, the Administrative Office of the Courts announced that all County Courts will migrate away from their existing County Justice Systems and move to a new State-developed system by fiscal year 2007-08. This departure of the Courts from the County system will impact the ability of the system to function and meet the needs of law and justice entities in the County. Second, the County's existing Criminal Justice Information System reached a point where the technologies it utilizes have become obsolete and difficult to maintain. A system outage caused by a failure of one of these older technologies would have a tremendous impact on the daily law enforcement operation in the County.

3. BUSINESS CONTEXT

The County is continually assessing its current business and computing environment, searching for opportunities to increase operational efficiency and improve the service it delivers. During this assessment, a number of issues ("Business Challenges") were identified. A summary of the Business Challenges are listed below:

Decreasing Budgets

Government budgets in California are being stretched and will continue to be stretched into the foreseeable future. San Joaquin County will have limited dollars available to invest in technology; those dollars must be invested for the greatest overall good to the County.

Growing County Population

San Joaquin County is one of the fastest growing counties in the nation. As the County's population grows, the demand for County services and the cost of delivering County services is likely to grow correspondingly.

Changing Demographics

As the population in San Joaquin County changes, so do the County's demographics. The number of households in San Joaquin County that have and use a computer is growing. County government faces the challenge of delivering cost effective solutions to constituents that will likely expect government services to be commensurate with the services they receive from private businesses – namely services that are available when it is convenient for the customer and available via their home computer.

Service Constrained by Organizational Structure / Process

In many cases today, it is very difficult for citizens and businesses to know who within County government provides the services they seek. In certain instances, multiple departments are involved in delivery of the service, requiring a citizen to travel around San Joaquin County, going from department to department, in order to complete the entire transaction.

Aging Criminal Justice Information System

The County's current Criminal Justice Information System (CJIS) was developed in 1986. The system is used on a daily basis by nearly every law enforcement entity within the County. The system faced two challenges. First, the Administrative Office of the Courts has announced that all County Courts will migrate away from their existing County Justice Systems and move to a new State-developed system by fiscal year 2007-08. This departure of the Courts from the County system will impact the ability of the system to function and meet the needs of law and justice entities in the County. Second, the County's existing Criminal Justice Information System reached a point where the technologies it utilizes have become obsolete and difficult to maintain. A system outage caused by a failure of one of these older technologies would have a tremendous impact on the daily law enforcement operation in the County.

Selection and Use of Technology

San Joaquin County spends millions of dollars annually on technology. The County's technology investments are often made with a departmental focus rather than with a broader countywide perspective. The inconsistent selection and use of technology can result in duplication and excess cost to the County as a whole. The inconsistent use of technology can also create barriers to data sharing and technology use that lead to higher cost of ownership and lower benefits from the technology investment. Our modernization initiative focused on these three aspects:

- Replace an outdated and difficult to maintain warrant system to improve the county's ability to manage making arrests, issuing warrants, and maintaining histories, and to transition to the new state court system
- Implement service-oriented architecture (SOA) to simplify integration between several county law and justice systems with diverse architectures and transfer law enforcement data to court system's mainframe
- Ensure the highest level of security for sensitive data

4. THE KEY INNOVATIONS

The modernization of our Integrated Justice Information System is a strategic initiative that started with setting our visions and goals in 2005 and laid out our road map until 2010. We set forth to develop interfaces and functions that continue to support the law and justice duties of the Sheriff's Office, Public Defender, District Attorney and Probation Department, as well as the needs of other local law enforcement entities. During the redevelopment effort, the County will focus on reducing unnecessary redundancy and consolidate like functions to decrease costs and improve overall system performance.

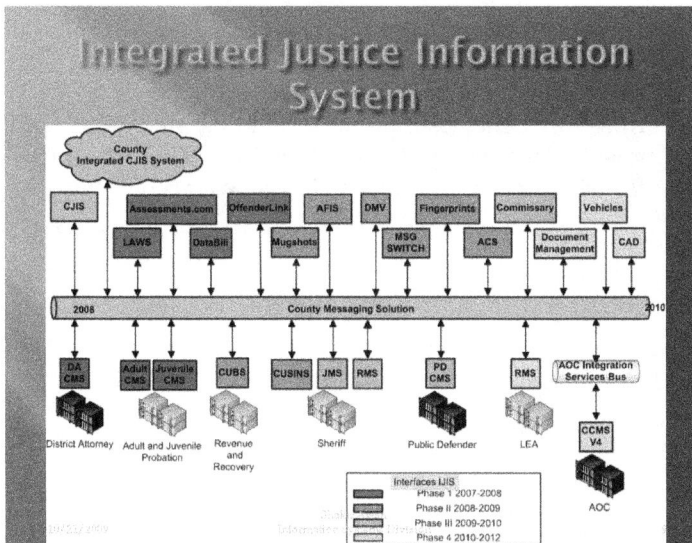

Figure 4.1: Phased Production Roll-Out of San Joaquin County IJIS

- Our choice to modernize IJIS using SOA and BPM technologies is both aligned with our strategic vision and met to lower our business risks by providing agility and a phased implementation roll-out:
- Think Big: We chose a BPM & SOA approach to meet our long-term EA modernization. It had to be robust, scalable, standards-based, and open to last and meet our long term vision
- Start Small: We chose to implement this in phases. Our first production system on was the Local Area Warrant System (LAWS) and has been in production for over 18 months.
- Move Fast: Now that we have a proven BPM & SOA platform in place we are building and rolling out new capabilities. For example our average Interface Development time was cut in half from 1 year to 6 months.

4.2 Business

Our IJIS modernization project has far reaching impact on the way we engage with our customers (the general public of San Joaquin and specifically Departments interfacing with CJIS) and Other Agencies (specifically California AOC).

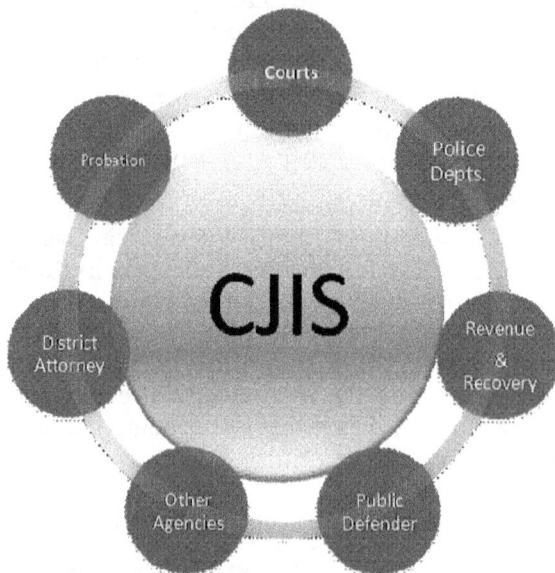

Figure 4.2: Stakeholders interacting with CJIS.

Prior to our modernization effort processes were integrated with point to point tightly coupled approach. This proved to be a high Total Cost of Ownership (TCO) and High Risk approach to running our business. We recognized that this was not sustainable.

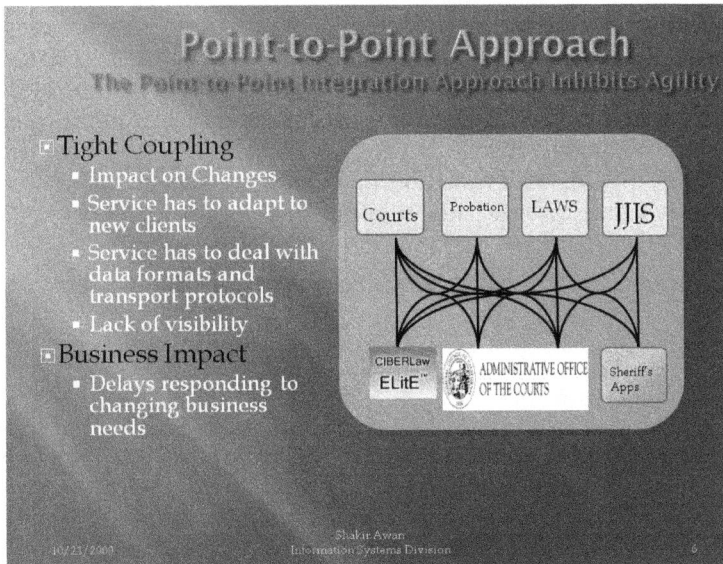

Figure 4.3: Historical As-Is Processes were Point to Point

To reduce our risks, costs and position us to meet our strategic vision; we chose a more Agile Service Enabled approach. This started us down the path of modernizing our EA using BPM and SOA technologies.

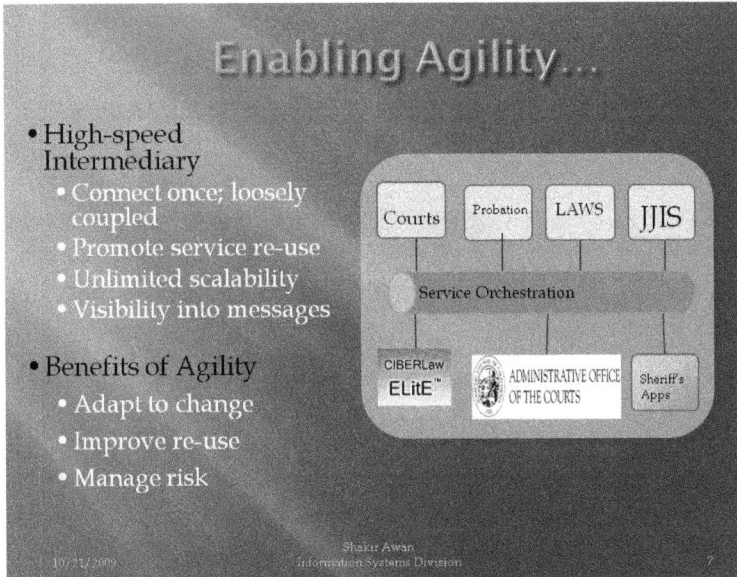

Figure 4.4: New Processes are now Service Enabled

Note that modernizing to a Service Enabled EA aligns with our Best Practice Strategy:

- San Joaquin County seeks to maximize the investment of each dollar spent on technology in order to improve overall business operation and service to the public. To accomplish this, the County will make appropriate investments in technology in order to:
- • Improve County Service Delivery
- • Expand County Services

- • • Realize Efficiencies

4.3 Process

As you can see from Figure 4.3 (above) our original processes used a lot of legacy systems with tightly coupled integration processes that were unsustainable from both a cost and risk perspective.

With our BPM and SOA modernization processes are now implemented with both the Orchestration and Service Bus Layers. This allows for better agility, re-use, and scalability.

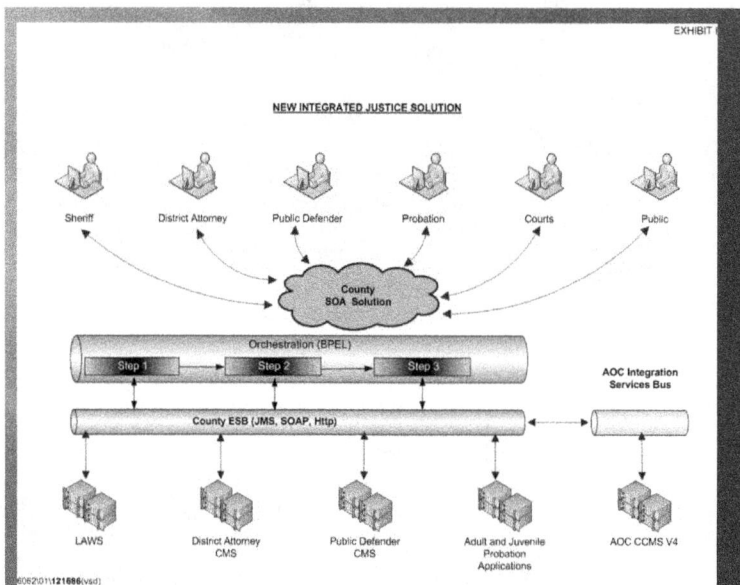

Figure 4.5a: New Integrated Justice Solution Process

Figure 4.5b: Process Monitoring of the BPEL Processes

The core principal behind our modernization is a phased approach to leveraging SOA Adaptation. We are evolving from a Monolithic Legacy based EA to a Service Oriented EA.

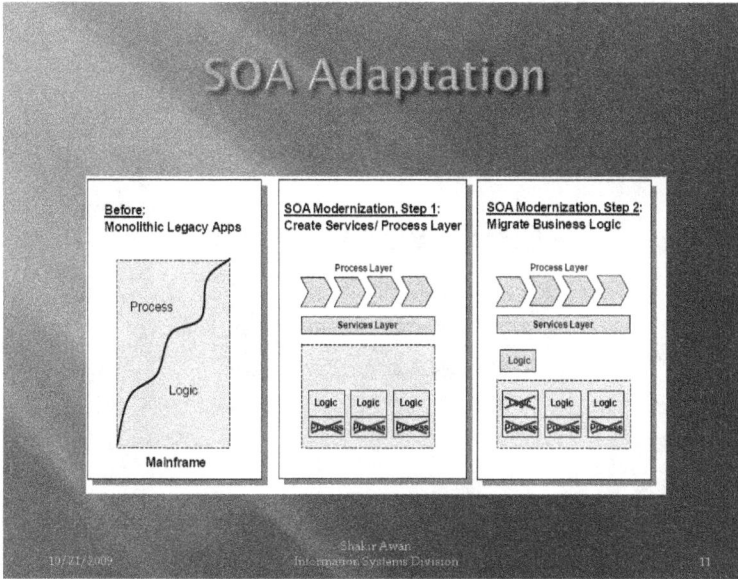

Figure 4.6: Evolution of IJIS Enterprise Architecture with SOA Modernization

As you can see in Figure 4.6 our use of SOA allows us to move from a high risk, tightly coupled legacy environment to Step 1 which abstracts our services and process layers. This then allows us the flexibility of then migrating our business logic out of the proprietary environments.

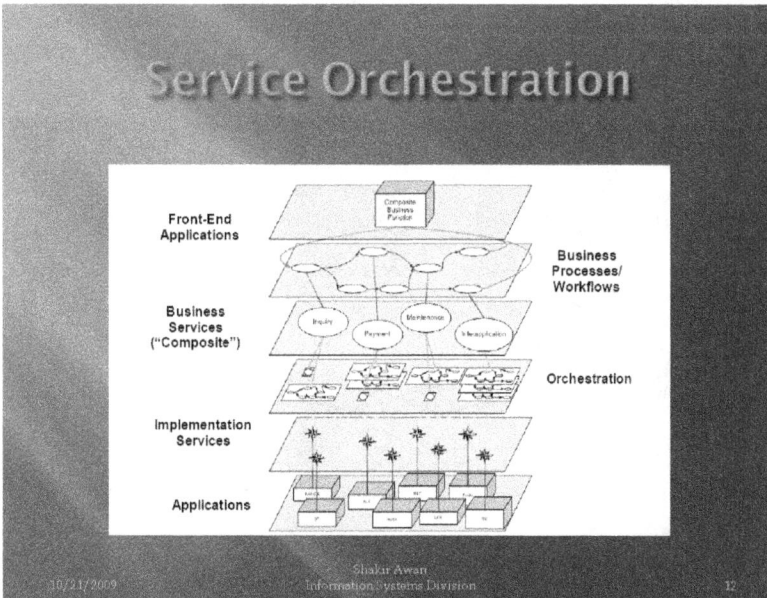

Figure 4.7: IJIS Using BPM and Workflows as key part of SOA Modernization

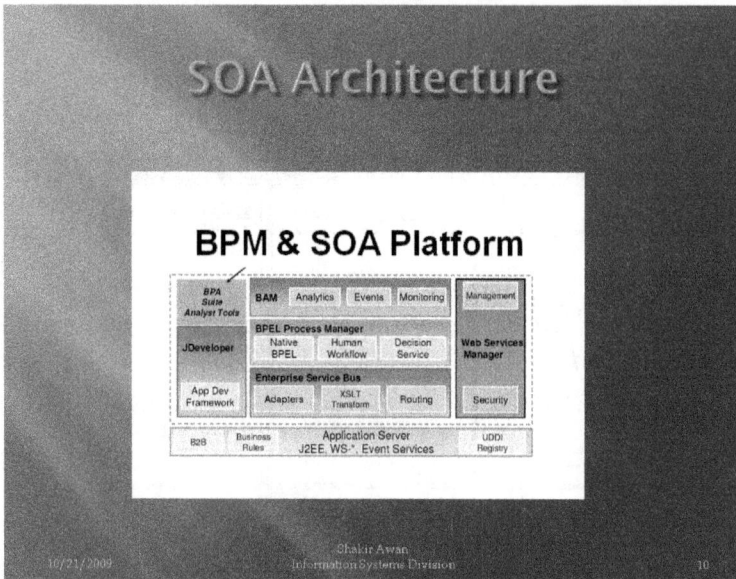

Figure 4.8: Specific BPM and SOA Components Used

Our end state objective is to abstract our EA capabilities into the appropriate layers to allow us more agility and flexibility to meet our future requirements.

Specific BPM and SOA components we took advantage of spanned the gambit. As you can see in Figure 4.8 we combine BPM, Service Bus, BAM, Application Development and scaled it with deployment onto Application Server and implemented Security and Governance SOA and Security Management technologies as well. We truly took a holistic approach to BPM and SOA and truly believe that the sum of the parts working together provides more value than just adding together each single component.

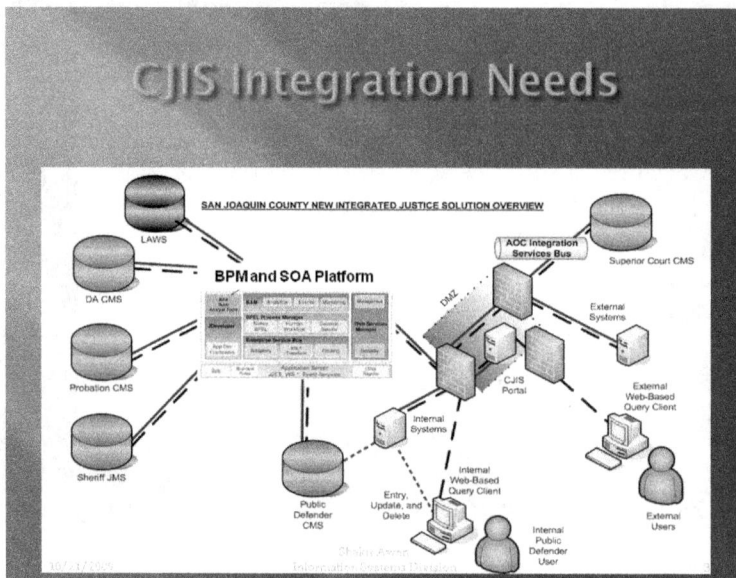

Figure 4.9: BPM and SOA as enabler of San Joaquin's new IJIS

This BPM and SOA Platform enabled us to modernize into a robust, scalable, secure, and agile Enterprise Architecture (see Figure 4.9 above).

4.4 Organization

A critical part our success has been the proper alignment of our Strategic Vision to the way our organization was enabled to plan and execute (and continues to execute) our modernization project.

We first established key project benchmarks to ensure our modernization effort met our key objectives:

* - Dedicate resources for SOA. (2006)
* - Enhance County SOA maturity. (2006-2007)
* - Development on DA-Courts-LAWS interfaces.(2007-2008)
* - Develop County SOA Hub (2008-2009)
* - Development for Probation-Courts-DA-LAWS interfaces (2008-2010)
* - Preparation and Development for AOC-County V4 Integration (2009-2011)

Communication of our Strategic Vision was critical in keeping our organization aligned and ensured we were executing to standard.

Our Best Practice Strategy:

San Joaquin County seeks to maximize the investment of each dollar spent on technology in order to improve overall business operation and service to the public. To accomplish this, the County will make appropriate investments in technology in order to:

* • Improve County Service Delivery
* • Expand County Services
* • Realize Efficiencies

To accomplish these goals the County will, with guidance from the County's Chief Information Officer (Director, Information Systems Division), focus on four strategies:

STRATEGY #1 The County will sponsor projects that provide secure public access to government services.

* • Wherever possible, the County will provide on-line public access to appropriate government information
* • The County will seek public input on what County services or information they would like available on-line
* • The County will promote electronic commerce as an alternative form of delivery of government services and transactions
* • The County will ensure security and confidentiality of information and electronic transactions, giving special attention to compliance with the Health Insurance Portability and Accountability Act.

STRATEGY #2 The County will provide standards, guidelines and training to facilitate innovation and a cohesive business operation.

The County will:

* • Develop and actively maintain a comprehensive IT Disaster Recovery Plan
* • Develop, maintain and actively enforce comprehensive Information Security policy and procedure
* • Establish a coordinated approach to automating shared business processes
* • Continue to support an Information Technology Management Committee responsible for the review of all major IT efforts in the County

- • Adopt and implement the Federal Enterprise Architecture (FEA) model for technology
- • Apply project management techniques to all IT projects
- • Establish, promote and enforce countywide IT standards
- • Establish tools, methods and policy that facilitate the concept of collecting information once and sharing the information with those individuals who have the right to use it

STRATEGY #3 The County will develop and implement a robust, interoperable information technology (IT) environment.

- The technologies and practices implemented by the County will:
- • Manage data to satisfy the needs of a diverse customer base
- • Support the collection, storage, and utilization of multi-media, including text, audio, images, maps, and video
- • Consolidate (where appropriate) like technologies to reduce costs, eliminate unnecessary redundancies and free up limited technology staff
- • Reduce the need to store paper documents
- • Provide flexibility and ease of access to County services and information
- • Foster greater collaboration and data sharing
- • Focus on selecting proven, "off-the-shelf" solutions wherever possible
- • Improve the reliability and responsiveness of the technology being used

STRATEGY #4 The County will utilize technology to control operational costs.

- The County's operational costs are likely to grow as the County strives to serve the needs of a rapidly growing population. The County will consider the following as a means of controlling costs:
- • The County will investigate software solutions as a means of reducing ongoing software maintenance costs
- • Where feasible and prudent, the County will seek to establish public / private partnerships for the implementation and support of technology
- • The County will review the replacement of computer hardware to determine if its useful life can be extended
- Adopted SOA as the integration standard
- Identified highly talented staff within our team
- Chose a product as integration software
- Selected a manageable project for proof of concept (Think Big, Start Small, Move Fast)

To make our organization aligned with our Vision and Strategy meant we had to invest in re-aligning and training our organization.

A core competency of Our Strategic Vision: Technology Skills and Training of Workforce

The County's reliance on technology increases each year. The County has made significant investments in enterprise wide systems that are now used daily for a variety of essential administrative and program functions. For the County to be effective and efficient, its workforce must be adequately trained in the use of technology. When we first started our Modernization Project in 2005, there was not a comprehensive technology training program in the County, and the technology skills of the County workforce varied greatly from department to department. One of the key benchmarks we set ourselves early on was to dedicate resources for SOA, which we met in 2006. We then established a structured project team directly supported and sponsored by the CIO. We also trained our team on SOA, BPM, Database, and JDeveloper technologies and maintained core staff on these technologies. Additionally, we used an Agile Development methodology which required a broader education process to ensure all stakeholders new what to expect as well rolled-out capabilities.

As we focused on our first effort, the modernization of Local Area Warrant System (LAWS), we stood up a Center of Excellence (CoE) sponsored by the CIO and led by a Project Manager and Systems Analyst V. The project team consisted of core IT staff and Subject Matter Experts (SMEs) matrixed into the project team throughout the project. This team expands and contracts based on the project development cycle. Key members of this team are also sit in the Governance Board that manages change management, project scoping, budgeting, and service level agreements from both a business and IT perspective. For our Change Management Process any change to the system or process is requested by the Business Users and Information Systems Change Management compiles a formal request to Change Management Board for approval.

For the technical change management IT uses Version Control for Change Management. This tool is being used by SOA and J2EE development team.

Overall, End Users, LAWS and SOA Technical and Functional teams, Managers and the Change Control Boards are part of our CoE.

All of these facets are essential teams within our CoE and ensure not only our continued success, but also our alignment with the Counties Strategic Vision.

5. HURDLES OVERCOME

There were a lot of cultural challenges that we faced, our End_users were not accustomed to Mouse and we had to provide both hot keys and mouse usage but slowly the Users found out the usefulness of mouse. Also the Users had to move to different screens on mainframe vs one page on LAWS showing all consolidated information including CLETS, CAD, NCIC and Local Warrants. This huge advantage was very quickly realized by the whole community. The development time for interfaces in SOA setup has a turn-around time of 4 weeks vs 24 weeks in the mainframe system. Another huge benefit of SOA is that the SOA development team is able to change the business logic very quickly due to Jdeveloper and development environment.

6. BENEFITS

After implementing the BPM & SOA Architecture, San Joaquin County realized the following benefits:

- Improved processing of Warrants by providing BAM dashboards to users
- Reduced interface development time from 6 months to 1 month
- Reduced implementation time for COTS applications
- Reduction in the number of system interfaces by adopting a publish/subscribe architecture
- Greatly reduced custom coding by adopting BPM/BPEL modeling tools
- Reduced maintenance needs for maintaining system interfaces
- Exposed CJIS information to be easily accessible by other applications
- Greatly improved manageability of Warrant processing
- Established standards-based security infrastructure
- Established a flexible core technology gateway that will allow for the future implementation and integration of new/COTS applications into a seamless workflow. (i.e. AOC CCMS)

The Enterprise Integration Gateway solution using BPM and SOA suites are a key component in San Joaquin County modernization initiative. By adopting the BPM & SOA technology the County was not only able to integrate internal and external systems but also use the newly developed frame work for future application development.

"With tools like Application Development Framework and SOA Suite, we have greatly reduced the complexities of our previous system, thus enabling development staff to focus on business logic and flow, and thereby saving time."– Jerry Becker, Chief Information Officer, County of San Joaquin Information Systems Division

One specific example of the benefits we derived was from the LAWS-SOA Application, which has been in production for over 18 months.

Description:

Local Area Warrant System (LAWS) is a web based Java J2EE Oracle ADF application integrated with Internet Directory and BPM and SOA suite. It is a mission critical application that serves from 5000 to 10000 transactions per hour.

The application uses cutting edge J2EE , Application Development Framework (ADF), Internet Directory, Real Application Clustering (RAC) and BPM & SOA suite to provide access to all Law Enforcement Users spread across 7 major cities and 18 separate agencies.

The application is unique in the state of California in that it provides web based CLETS access from LAWS application.

The application is the lifeline to the Law and Justice agencies including Sheriff, City Police Chiefs, District Attorney and Courts.

To date 16 million transactions have been done on the warrant system for 18 months of go-live system.

Usage:

18 San Joaquin Law Enforcement agencies with 1600 Users access this application each day.

The Police Car Units access this application from their mobile cars. For each inquiry submitted from the Police cars the response time is less than 3 seconds.

The City and County Police Agencies run searches on Local, State and Federal Warrants through this application. The response to the search comes from 400,000 local Warrants.

The LAWS application is customizable with each page section customized according to the role assigned to the User. The page authorization is easily customizable from the local admin console provided to each agency. All agencies administer security and authorization independently.

Features

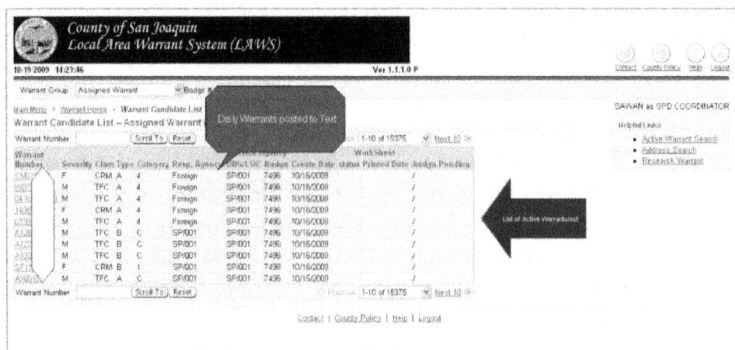

ActivX technology captures IP and MAC addresses

Single Page View to view 30 different warrant modules

Internet Directory provides authentication to LAWS Users.

LAWS application in integrated with CLETS and provides single point of contact for local, state and federal warrants.

LAWS application is integrated with CAD system in that all searches from Police Units are run in real time with less than 3 second response time.

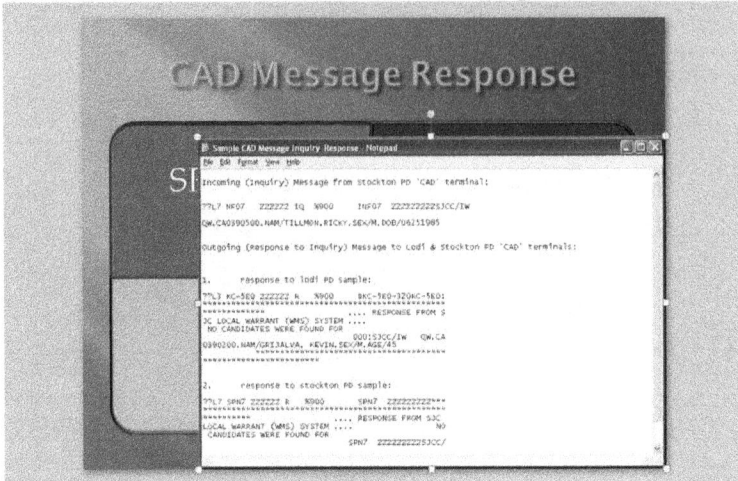

Admin Console for administration of User security and authorization provided to each Agency for Self Service.

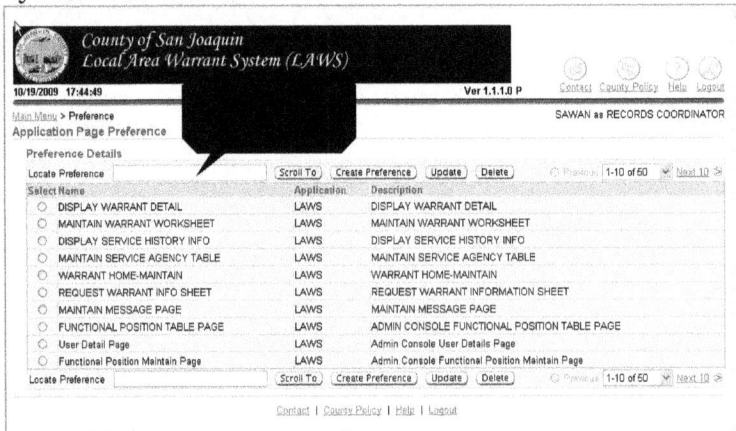

Help provided on each page for daily work routine.

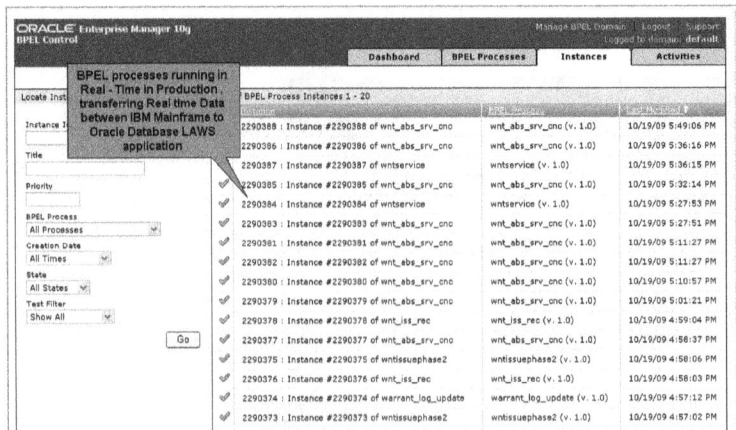

LAWS application is integrated with Courts Mainframe system using BPM and SOA suite.

The architecture of SOA integration is posted on California State Administrative

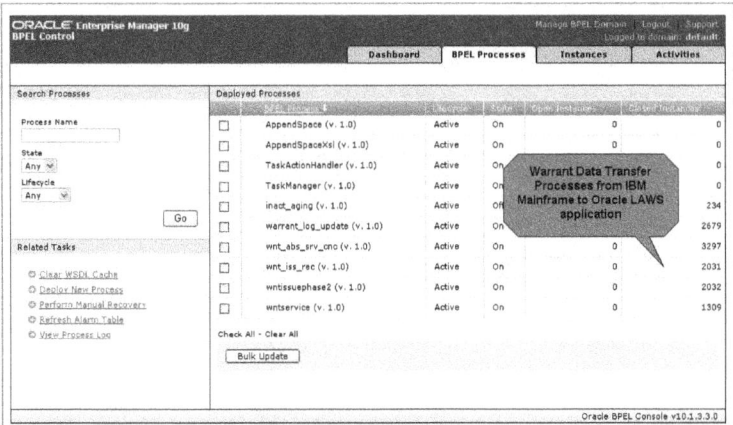

Office of Courts and is recommended by California State AOC to other counties. Integrated with California Telecommunication System (CLETS) and National

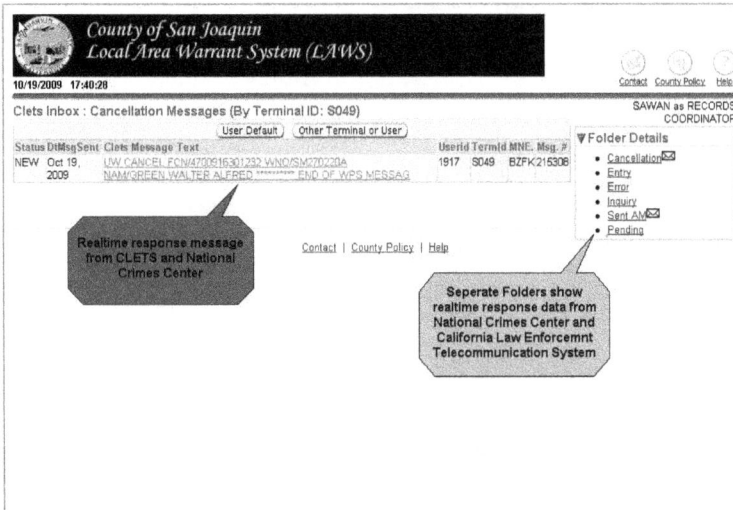

Crime Investigation Center

Single Entry Point for Local Area Warrants, California Law Enforcement

Single Entry Point for Local Area Warrants, National Crime Investigation Center

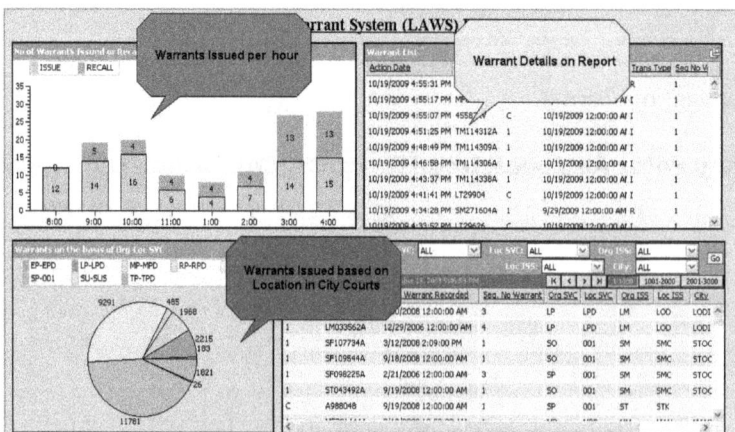

Real- Time Dashboards for Information Systems

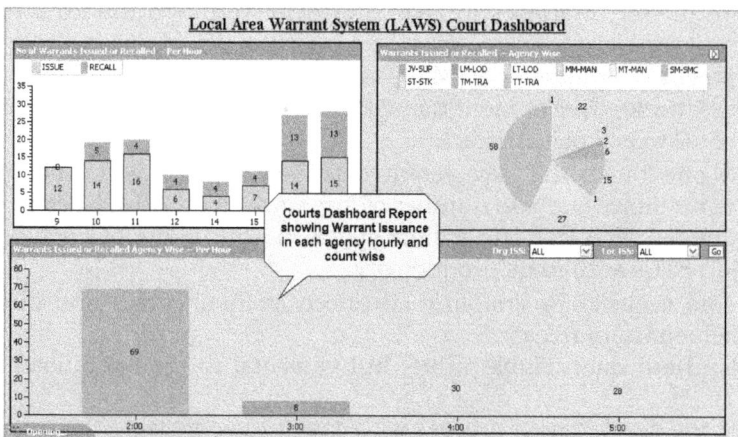

Real-Time Dashboards for Courts

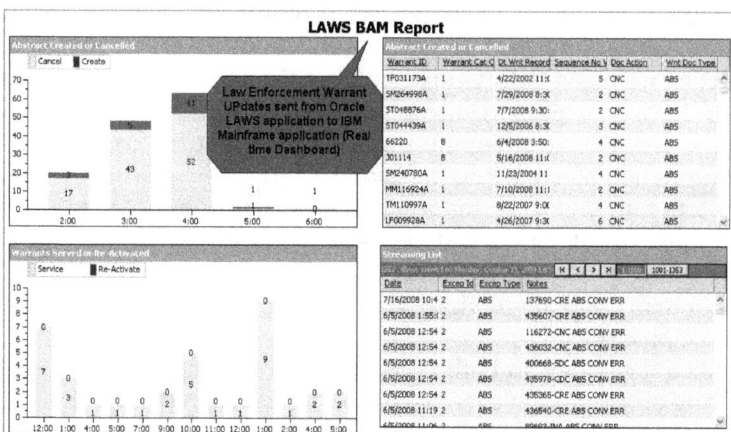

Real-time Transaction Reports between Mainframe and LAWS

Go-Green application

The application is web based and provided detail information on single based with customized links. This helps reduce the need to print data information and share with other Users.

The application uses CUPS for printer access and does not allow multiple copies of warrants thereby saving paper and preserve nature.

Since the application is accessible via web the Users don't need to take paper printouts to each other.

The 18 Agencies are spread across different geological locations. In case of support from Information Systems IT people would need to travel to different locations to fix problems, the web based application provides control from a single location thereby saving fuel and preserving nature.

The Warrant Reports are viewable in pdf format while previously these needed to be printed on line printers thus saving paper and time and preserving nature. With 1600 Users this saving is a lot.

6. (1 to 4) Cost Savings, Time Reductions, Increased Revenues, Productivity Improvements

We saved a significant amount of money with the Web-based system by eliminating the need to implement the application on individual desktops and by avoiding the need to hire 5 to 10 additional full time employees for support

Development of new Interfaces in BPM and SOA were 1/6 than the time on the Mainframe
- 24 weeks development on Mainframe
- Now 4 weeks development using BPM & SOA
- Save 20 weeks per Interface

Reduced by one-fourth the time required for law enforcement officers to create daily reports on topics such as number of arrests and status of warrants
- Estimated 25% less officer time spent on non-productive activities * 1600 = 400 FTEs additional productivity

Improved data security by enabling advanced authentication and authorization based on defined users roles
This is not a hard quantifiable value, but essential to the operations of a court system!
Streamlined the development process with easy-to-use tools
- Example 12 month reduced to 6 month implementation timeframe
- Example 9 Full Time Equivalents * 6 months = saving 4.5 FTEs per project
- Benefits of getting Solutions in half the time also

Implemented BPM and SOA Suite to integrate various heterogeneous systems across county agencies to integrate data with the court's mainframe—enabling improved information sharing and decision making
Example reports that had to be manually done are now out of the box
- Real-Time vs. Historical Data is much more accurate
- Time saved by Management and IT staff at an operational basis

Enabled dependent systems to share data to ensure accurate, timely handling of law and justice processes
- Significant savings on both infrastructure and maintenance
- Sharing of the data of over 16 million transaction during the 18 months in production

Going Green on-line processing and report viewing for 1600 users every day.
- Example estimate: 260 workdays * 1600 user * 50 pages = >3.3 million pages

Secure and Trustworthy Solution. Allowing Role and Policy based access control to underlying processes and content
- When it comes to Public Safety and Control of Sensitive Information this can prove to be "Priceless"
- The safety and/or life of our end stakeholders are can't be measured in pure monetary terms

Auditing and Reporting of processes
- Giving different levels of management real-time access to information means making the right decisions versus wrong decisions
- Value could be "priceless"

End to end access to field personnel (e.g. mobile access to officers) coupled with the efficiency gains from all end-users versus old mainframe access points
- Access times reduced to < 3 seconds
- On-site / Field Access were there was none before
- Single view of the operation versus Mainframe multi-application access
- All these provide not only efficiency and effectiveness gains
- Less busy work and more feet on the street
- Faster response times

Also, potential threats get the right response versus the wrong due to lack of information
- E.g. without real-time access to information on a suspect may result in additional risks to the public
- Allows field officers to cross check information to improve decision making

Improved inter-operability
- Easy and more reliable collaboration both internally and externally to other agencies
- Allows for future collaboration due to standards based end-points via secure web service layer

Reduce or Eliminate Risk of Wide Systematic Failure
- Modernized critical capabilities that were at the point of potential failure
- Avoiding potential wide spread system failures that could put the public (over 650,000 residence) at considerable risk
- Ability to continue to modernize legacy systems by priority without having to shut down and rebuild complex systems all at once
- Results in better EA planning and budgeting
- Reduces Maintenance Costs
- Better Disaster Recovery Planning and Support
- Reduces Technical Risk in upgrading systems
- Reduces project risks as modernization can be focused and prioritized
- Reduced potential down-times when upgrading to manageable levels

7. BEST PRACTICES, LEARNING POINTS AND PITFALLS

7.1 Best Practices and Learning Points

- ✓ *Think Big, Start Small, Move Fast*
- ✓ *Don't assume customer and/or partners will modernize at the same pace as you*
- ✓ *Develop and configure mainframe adapter in SOA environment. You need to look at what jdbc gateway solutions are available to connect to mainframe, then configure these libraries in SOA.*
- ✓ *Learn the mainframe transaction environment, is it data&time based transaction sequence or event based sequence of transactions, what it means is that if it is date&time no matter what order you send to mainframe these would be sorted correctly. In the other case if it is event based then make sure the SOA takes care of the sequence of transactions needed to be send to mainframe otherwise the system will not work properly.*
- ✓ *Maturity Level in SOA is extremely important. The local IT resources should be well versed with the technology. Choose a manageable project.*
- ✓ *Governance in SOA and transparency in transactions across systems is a must.*
- ✓ *Establish a clear Chain-of-Command, with appropriate sponsorship levels*
- ✓ *Establish a Center of Excellence (CoE) with a core team that includes SMEs from the customer(s) when possible*
- ✓ *Governance across the project and services is essential*
- ✓ *Processes (that matter) usually span and require interfaces with external partners or customers*
- ✓ *Include your external partners in project communication*
- ✓ *Know your "As is"*
- ✓ *Knowledge of legacy environment*
- ✓ *Skill sets, including SOA*
- ✓ *Get Buy-In (IT & Business & Leadership – Executive)*

✓ *Foster Business Desire for Change*
✓ *Push for the upfront investment – "not your father's system"*
✓ *Constant marketing*
✓ *Adhere to a Reference Architecture*
✓ *Take a phased approach to its implementation*
✓ *Phase I – Build Reference Architecture with initial business components*
✓ *Phase II – Technology pilot at select sites*
✓ *Phase III – Build out enterprise SOA services aligned with strategic plan and shareholder feedback and use metrics*
✓ *Maintain project management discipline*

7.2 Pitfalls

✗ *"Turning-off" legacy systems without understanding the business logic that connects it to other systems*
✗ *Scalability is not a given in mainframe, you have to send transactions in sequence. In other words you have to throttle the transactions send to mainframe.*
✗ *Re-publishing capability is a must*
✗ *Don't have a build and they will come philosophy*
✗ *Don't underestimate challenge of changing thoughts from IT infrastructure to providing Business Services*

8. COMPETITIVE ADVANTAGES

The Enterprise Integration Gateway solution using BPM and SOA suites are a key component in San Joaquin County modernization initiative. By adopting the BPM & SOA technology the County was not only able to integrate internal and external systems but also use the newly developed frame work for future application development. This also keeps us in alignment with the Counties Strategic Vision and Directives from the California AOC.

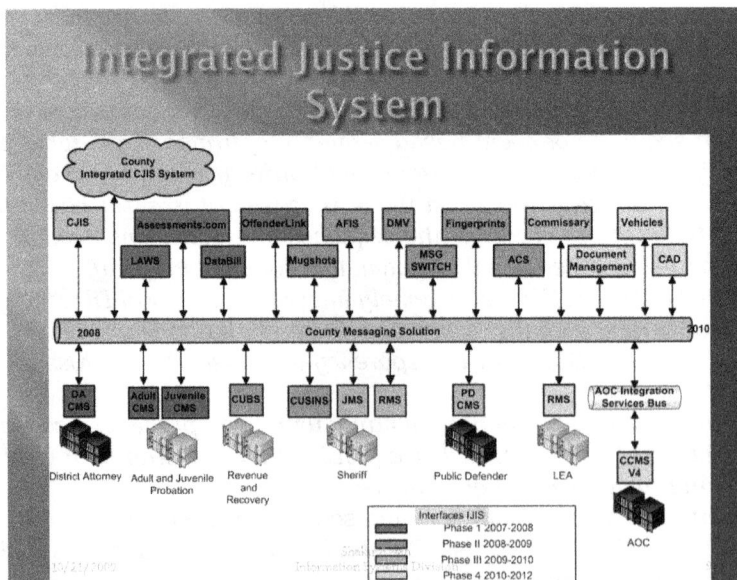

Figure 8.1: BPM and SOA Established a Successful Architecture for all our Future Modernization and Enables Agility

"With tools like Application Development Framework and BPM & SOA Suite, we have greatly reduced the complexities of our previous system, thus enabling development staff to focus on business logic and flow, and thereby saving time."–

Jerry Becker, Chief Information Officer, County of San Joaquin Information Systems Division

With the move to BPM and SOA we can now make interfaces in 4 weeks, when it took us 24 weeks on the mainframe. And these new interfaces are also much more productive for the end-users. After the LAWS went into production, we are continuing to build out capabilities with 4.5 FTEs augmented by SMEs when required. The San Joaquin County modernization initiative has been recognized by the California AOC as a Best Practice Implementation that not only provides continued value to San Joaquin County, but also a potential road-map for success State-wide.

9. TECHNOLOGY

Our modernization objective was to abstract our EA capabilities into the appropriate layers to allow us more agility and flexibility to meet our future requirements. And have this aligned with our Strategic Vision.

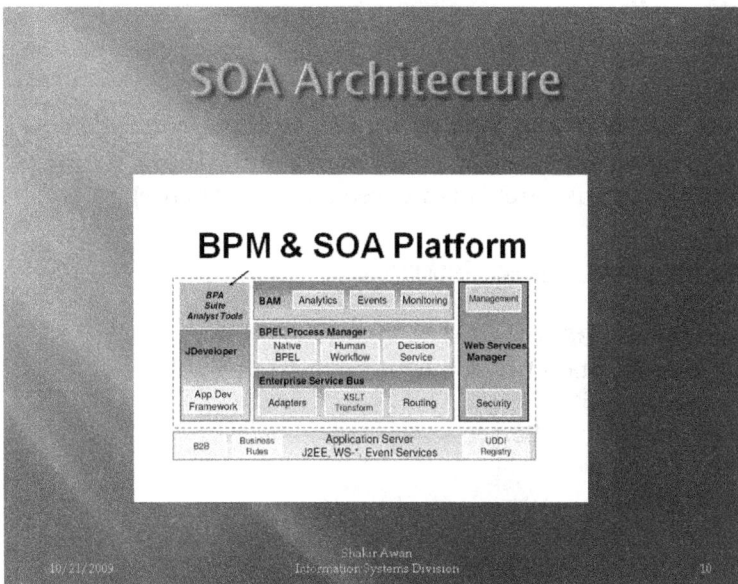

Figure 9.1: Specific BPM and SOA Components Used

Specific BPM and SOA components we took advantage of spanned the gambit. As you can see in Figure 9.1 we combine BPM, Service Bus, BAM, Application Development and scaled it with deployment onto Application Server and implemented Security and Governance SOA and Security Management technologies as well. We truly took a holistic approach to BPM and SOA and truly believe that the sum of the parts are worth more than any single component.

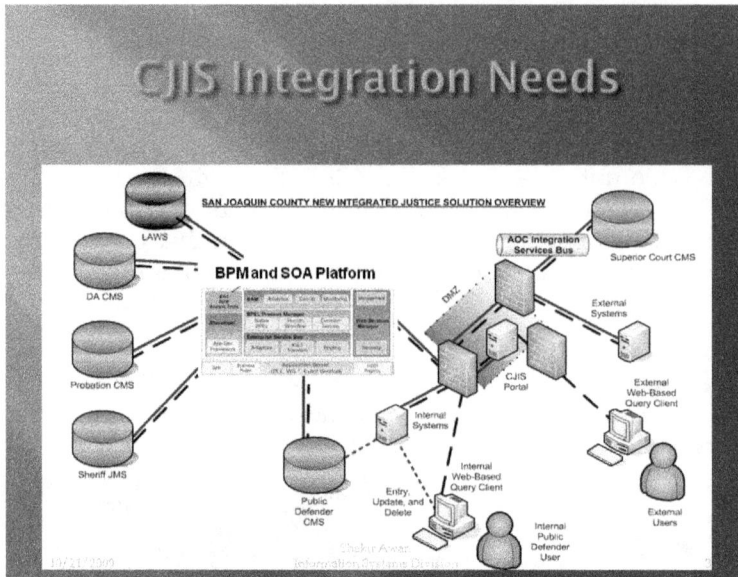

Figure 9.2: BPM and SOA as enabler of San Joaquin's new IJIS

This BPM and SOA Platform enabled us to modernize into a robust, scalable, secure, and agile Enterprise Architecture (see Figure 9.2 above).

10. THE TECHNOLOGY AND SERVICE PROVIDERS

Products Used:
- Oracle BPM / BPEL / BAM
- Oracle Application Development Framework
- Oracle SOA Suite
- Oracle Application Server
- Oracle Database
- Oracle RAC
- Oracle JDeveloper
- Oracle Internet Directory

Section 4

Pacific Rim

AEGON Religare Life Insurance Corporation, India

Finalist, Pacific Rim
Nominated by DST Global Solutions, USA

1 SUMMARY

AEGON Religare Life Insurance Company Ltd, is a joint venture between AEGON, one of the world's largest life insurance and pension companies, Religare, one of India's leading integrated financial services groups and Bennett and Coleman, India's largest media house.

The company was launched across pan-India with multi-channel operations in July 2008 with over 30 branches spread across India. The business philosophy for AEGON Religare is to help people plan their life better.

2 LIST OF ABBREVIATIONS USED

AHT   Average Handling Time

AWD   Automated Work Distributor

FOS   Feet on Street

RM   Relationship Manager

TPA   Third Party Administrator

3 OVERVIEW

In life insurance, the provider's relationship with the client is a long term one, from initial sourcing of the policy until settlement either at maturity or on a death claim.

Sourcing of the policy includes the following activities:

1. Receipt and verification of the proposal form
2. Receipt and verification of the agent's confidential report
3. Receipt and verification of the medical form
4. Receipting the initial payment
5. Receipting the financial statements (wherever required)
6. Receipt and verification of the various proofs (age proof, permanent tax number, address proof etc.)
7. Data entry of the input into the system[1] (refer to the Annexure for sample proposal form)
8. Classification into simple, medical and non-medical
9. Classification based age and sum at risk
10. Classification based on VIP and non-VIP
11. Identification of any additional requirements (can be medical or financial proof)

---

[1] The number of data entry fields will also differ based on the product type e.g. unit linked or term assurance.

12. Follow-up to closure of any additional requirements

13. Underwriting of proposal

14. Noting of underwriter's notes

15. Raising counter offer

16. Follow-up to closure of counter offer

17. Acceptance/declinature/postponement of proposal

18. Realization of the payment

19. Printing of policy schedule

20. Refund of initial payment for declined/postponed cases

21. Maintaining and uploading of policy schedule to image repository

22. Sending the all physical papers to storage[2]

Apart from the various steps/touch points involved in sourcing the business, there is need to manage a growing number of entities in a scalable manner. Some of these entities include:

1. Number of branches/collection centers across PAN India[3]

2. Number of distributors involved in sourcing the business[4]

3. Number of TPAs/doctors involved[5]

4. Number of products launched for new business[6]

5. Number of parties involved, i.e. outsourced entity, banks and internal new business and underwriting teams

Based on the above, a need was identified to implement a BPM solution.

4 BPM/Workflow Solution

To provide our clients and distribution partners with a better experience and to achieve a competitive edge in the life insurance industry. It was decided to implement AWD a BPM solution from DST Global solutions as it is an identified solution as part of AEGON's regional strategy.

Automated Work Distributor (AWD) from DST Global Solutions is one of the leading workflow and image processing products with a number of large multinational clients. DST Global Solutions' parent, DST Systems was established in 1969, listed in NYSE and has got more than 11,000 employees worldwide. Some of their clientele include Manulife, Standard Life, AXA, Lloyds and JP Morgan, apart from AEGON.

AEGON has used AWD for more than 10 years in a number of countries, including the USA, UK, and China. Apart from the benefits of control and im-

---

[2] Based on Indian Insurance Regulatory need all the proposals accepted need to be preserved for seven years from the end of the term or payment of claim

[3] 2008-09 – 48 Branches, 15 collection centers
2009-10 – 12 more branches to be added
2010-11 – 60 more branches to be added

[4] 2008-09 – 2500 Agents/FOS/RMs
2009-10- 12000 Agents/FOS/RMs
2010-11-25000 Agents/FOS/RMs

[5] 2008-09- 2 TPAs Managing thousands of doctors and clinical laboratories
2009-10- 5 More TPAs are to be added

[6] 2008-09 – 14 Products launched
2009-10 – 11 launched so far and 7 more to be launched
2010-11 – 10 products to be launched

proved efficiency realized by these countries, AEGON has benefitted from DST Global Solution's knowledge of BPM and implementation experience has also helped us, especially China, where it is also used in conjunction with FUTUREfirst/Asia, our core administration system.

Apart from the robust workflow technology, AWD has an internal image repository, which does not require any external image storage system. The application also has the capability of load balancing, guided data entry, strong BI analytics, and integration with fax, email, electronic documentation and phone call.

Having selected DST Global Solutions, the following are the additional benefits that AEGON Religare has accrued as a result of the AWD implementation:

1. Over 20 years of BPM experience plus knowledge on the insurance industry, resulting in less than 15 man months customization, which also indirectly means faster roll out to production
2. Increased user efficiency – customizable line of business values, user friendly GUI, etc
3. Consolidated image repository with workflow – no extra hardware and thus a differential savings in hardware of around USD 150K
4. Minimal numbers of support incidents with around 5 support calls raised per month.
5. Ability to accept images from different sources, thus enabling real time association with medical test centre, external printing vendor, etc.

5 IMPLEMENTATION METHODOLOGY

The implementation of BPM was spread across three phases to leverage the learning and focus on the business plan.

Phase 1 – Implementation of new business and underwriting workflows with integration to core system and reporting systems – 4 major workflows comprising of new business, underwriting, cancellation and refund

This phase was implemented from Go-live of the Company and has been in use for 15 months at the time of this writing.

Phase 2 – Additional enhancements for integrating with TPA and automatic classification of underwriting limits

This phase was implemented four months after Go-live of the Company and has been in use for 11 months at the time of this writing.

Phase 3 – To implement workflow for policy servicing and agent recruitment and licensing

This phase is yet to kick-off, as most of the policy servicing aspects are required only after 2 years of operations.

6 BENEFITS REALIZED FROM THE IMPLEMENTATION:

6.1 FOR OUR CUSTOMERS:

- Fast turnaround time or reduced average handling time (reduced by 60% when compared to manual operations)
- Reduced errors
- Consistent service standards – giving one view of the policy at its various stages of completion in real time.

- Easy access of insurance documents on demand - policy document, premium receipts, etc available on customer portal for ready reference

6.2 FOR TRADING PARTNERS (AGENTS/FOS/RMS)

- Input at the right time (e.g. outstanding requirements informed through portal)
- Reduced touch points (customers only log-in in through the portal, which is integrated with our BPM solution)
- Tracking of customer and trading history

6.3 FOR OUTSOURCED PARTNER

- Quality output
- Effective utilization of resources
- Highly motivated employees
- Better managed processes
- Ability to measure the productivity of its employee on run time basis
- Win-win situation on commercials

6.4 OTHERS (TPA)

- Integration with their current systems – direct upload of medical reports and doctors statements into workflow
- Better management of appointments

6.5 FOR ORGANIZATION:

- Faster and accurate data entry in the system
- Better case tracking
- Increased productivity
- Reduced staff strength (even in an outsourced model, this gave us increased flexibility to choose between various commercial models)
- Well integrated with other back-end systems
- Process consistency
- Location Independent
- Reduced manual touch points
- Automated work prioritization
- Better operations risk management
- Better reporting
- All documents (images) at one place for better retrieval
- Increased/higher decision making capabilities at each processing level

7 COST BENEFITS AS A RESULT OF IMPLEMENTING A BPM SOLUTION

This section gives a summary of the costs and benefits accrued (in US dollars) as a result of the BPM implementation

Description	Value	Remarks
Number of Contracts Processed in the past 15 months	36000	
Without BPM		
A1. Number of hours that are required to process the above contracts	60,600	AHT per contract is 101minutes.
A2. Number of resources that are required to process the above contracts	20	
A3. No. of resources required to manage the overall coordination and towards MIS Support towards Issuance in absence of AWD	2	AHT per contract is 11 minutes.
With BPM		
B1. Number of hours that are required to process the above contracts	36,000	AHT per contract is 60 minutes.
B2. Number of resources that are required to process the above contracts	12	No. of resources currently employed
Benefits		
Savings in no. of resources	8	Calculated as (A2-B2)
Average cost of savings on resources - includes savings arrived from reduced no. of resources	$80,000	1.The annual average salary per agent is taken as 8,000 USD 2.Recurring expense
Average cost of savings on resources due to reduced effort on Overall Coordination & MIS Support with AWD	$30,000	1. The annual average salary per employee is taken as 12,000 USD 2. Recurring expense
Savings on image server	$150,000	Capital-one time, savings under due to differential cost from in house AWD image repository when compared to an external content management solution plus workflow
AMC on image server	$27,000	Recurring every year @ 18% on the differential cost
Total Savings so far	**$287,000**	
Total Savings so far	**INR 24,700,000**	**1 USD = INR 50**

Docu-ment	Description
Issuance life cycle solution architec-ture	This diagram explains on the process flow at the major touch points –
	Branch – How does a branch accept a proposal form, logging a cheque in FFA, banking of cheques, etc
	Head Office customer service – scrutiny of the images in AWD, data entry, policy set up in FFA, etc.
	Head Office underwriting – checking of the scanned images in AWD, creating underwriting worksheet in AWD, seeking clari-fications (internal /external), underwriting decision
	Printing interface, agency commission, actuarial extract, etc.

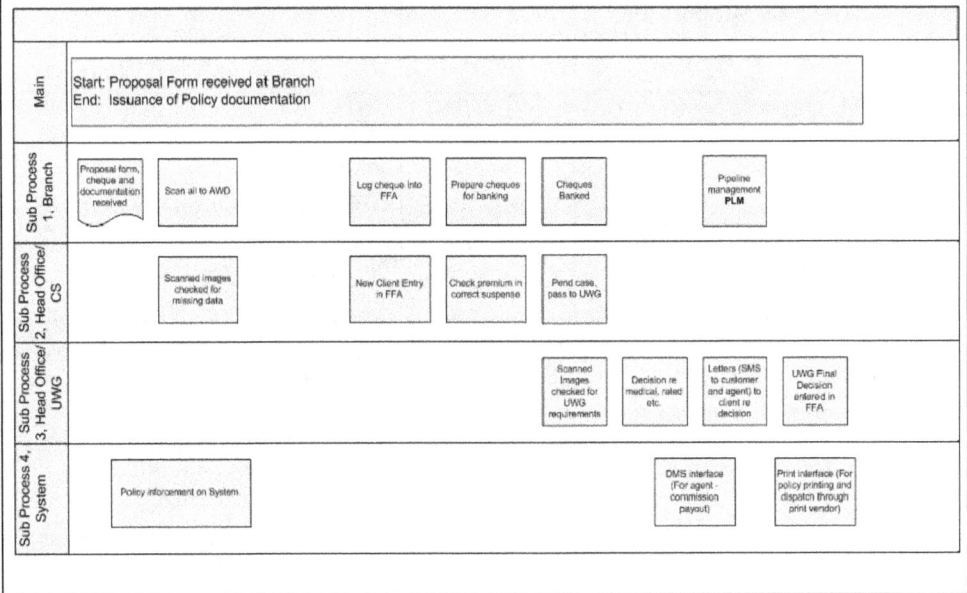

9 CONTACT INFORMATION

AEGON Religare Life Insurance Company LTD
Website: www.aegonreligare.com
DST Global Solutions
Website: www.dstglobalsolutions.com

Reliance Life Insurance, India

Silver Award, Pacific Rim
Nominated by Progress Software Corp., USA

1. EXECUTIVE SUMMARY / ABSTRACT

Life insurance is a hugely competitive industry in India. It is also seasonal with the bulk of policies purchased during the end of the year. Reliance Life Insurance (RLIC) is an associate of Reliance Capital Ltd. which ranks among the top 3 financial services firms in India. In just two years of operation, Reliance Life Insurance has exceeded 2 million policies and is among the country's fastest growing life insurance firms in new business premiums with a year-over-year growth rate of 195 percent.

However, its technology infrastructure systems were not keeping pace with its rapid rate of development, limiting its growth, proving to be a bottleneck and preventing the company from scaling fast enough. A number of processes were manual and resulted in lack of visibility into operations. The absence of automation was impacting productivity and the ability to book revenue in a timely manner. RLIC needed to find a solution that could improve process control, enhance visibility, reduce policy turn around time, as well as accelerate time to market and agility to react to changing market conditions. They discovered the solution in BPM.

2. OVERVIEW

The underwriting process required insurance policy underwriters and application process agents to manually assemble all the information they needed from large paper files, analyze the data, and determine what premium rates should be, or whether the customer should be offered coverage at all. Because of the lack of visibility of the end-to-end process, underwriting often took two weeks to complete and was prone to errors. The problem was getting worse over time due to the rapid growth of the company.

The absence of automation was impacting productivity and the ability to book revenue in a timely manner. RLIC needed to find a solution that could improve process control reducing average underwriting turn around time (TAT) from weeks to hours. The solution also needed to provide scalability to meet future needs, flexibility and agility to react to changing market conditions, and support for new products and markets.

Implementation of BPM has resolved some of the gravest underwriting issues confronting Reliance Life. They have actually reduced the TAT from two weeks to a single day now! This reduction has ensured the lag period to shrink and hence tasks are not dropped or affected adversely. Instead of disconnected silos, there is now one single integrated platform. Automated processes have also eliminated the inaccuracies that emerged earlier. This improvement not only boosts productivity but also enhances customer service significantly. Progress Savvion also answered the need for scalability - the solution easily supports 900 concurrent users and volumes of up to 10,000 new policies per day during the peak season of January through March. In case of expansion of offerings, the Progress Savvion solution can accommodate new types of policies within two to three weeks.

3. BUSINESS CONTEXT

Reliance Life Insurance (RLIC) had an IT infrastructure in place that included four standalone systems: LifeAsia running on an AS/400 was their core business engine. In addition they also used a document management solution and a policy tracking system. However, the company lacked a formal system for managing the steps involved in underwriting: receiving submissions, analyzing data, and providing approvals.

The customized BPM solution helped RLIC to not only leverage all these systems and deliver a superior technical solution but also promptly achieve the business objectives of faster policy processing and lower operational costs. As a part of their business operations, RLIC has a decentralized workflow model in place, with a number of external stakeholders to the processes. The BPM solution has allowed them to serve all these stakeholders in an unprecedented manner and expand their network of external business partners. Earlier there was only one BPO vendor but now there are 12 processing hubs who handle the localized content and data entry thereby improving the productivity and service delivery.

BPM implementation has resolved RLIC's biggest underwriting issues. With the automated processes in place, BPM helped RLIC reduce turn around time (TAT) from almost two weeks to a day, reducing lag time and ensuring that tasks don't fall through the cracks. In addition, transaction costs for auto underwriting have been significantly reduced. What were once siloed systems now work together. Progress Savvion seamlessly integrates all the systems, giving RLIC end-to-end visibility and control of the complete policy underwriting life cycle in real time. This visibility and control also reduces errors, increasing the quality of the process that in turn increases customer satisfaction.

The implementation team was a good mix from business and IT side, where the business team had good knowledge of the processes that were to be automated, the IT team had know how of BPM technology. The processes too were a combination of human intensive and system centric, straight through processes. BPM provided the backbone and orchestrated with multiple systems like Documentum content management system, LifeAsia which was on AS/400, Policy Tracking system and InsureConnect. This integration was delivered through SOA based webservices integration and asynchronous communication with some of the systems using messaging.

RLIC has seen a significant return on their investment in the BPM solution. With the business growth, head count has increased only by 30 percent since BPM was deployed. Without BPM technology, however, the increase would have been 100 percent. RLIC estimates the solution paid for itself within the first three months after deployment.

4. THE KEY INNOVATIONS

4.2 Business

With BPM methodology and technology, Reliance Life was able to reduce turn-around time for processing new policies from two weeks to four hours. Transaction costs for auto underwriting were significantly reduced and the quality of process was enhanced by reducing errors. Customer satisfaction was assured by meeting SLAs and enabling services via multiple channels.

4.3 Process

RLIC had a requirement of the system managing 1000 concurrent users and around 30000 policies during the peak time. This process is a critical business process and had to be very scalable and highly available as any kind of downtime would mean tremendous loss of revenue. With the BPM implementation, RLIC was able to ensure that there is no downtime in operations - especially during the peak season when most of the business is done.

The branch CE, New Business and the Underwriting teams consume the processes and use the system. The workflow ensures that no cases/proposals remain unaccounted for. The TATs will improve and will be monitored while MIS is expected to be simpler. Change management will be handled jointly by the IT and Business teams.

The critical process is designed for high policy volumes and scalability, currently supporting 400 end users on considerably large process of 100+ activities. The team can now process more than 30,000 policies per day during the peak activity season. The project involved multiple teams/departments across geographies from Branch operations, outsourced BPO for client contract data entry, rural BPO, New business, Underwriting, Issuance, and finance. These teams are also the end users of this solution.

4.4 Organization

The process being highly distributed, multiple departments were involved. Branch operations, outsourced BPO for client contract data entry, New Business unit, Underwriting, Issuance, finance were some of the key participants and the users of the implemented process.

RLIC initiated a BPM governance council under the leadership of CTO and concerned HODs to review and suggest changes in the BPM projects. Their brief is to monitor the results and suggest new areas wherein BPM can add value to the organization. The project managers implementing the projects give their updates to the CTO who is leading the BPM governance at Rlife. Decisions on issues of executive sponsorship are taken by the CTO in consultation with the CEO.

5. HURDLES OVERCOME

RLIC faced initial skepticism as stakeholders were privy to and wary of automation replacing the manual mode. But soon they realized that it would create and add value for themselves and the back-office team. After buy-in from the senior management, they were geared for and embraced the change. RLIC has a full-fledged team of trainers who assist staff who need help or hand-holding. They also have a production support team in place and a 16-hour helpline. Training is provided in classrooms and on the job.

6. BENEFITS

6.1 Cost Savings

After the BPM implementation the transaction costs of underwriting significantly reduced due to the automation achieved. This also led to process much more policies with the same level of resources.

6.2 Time Reductions

Turn-around time for processing new policies slashed from two weeks to four hours. The substantial time reduction provided a definite competitive edge in the industry.

6.3 Increased Revenues

As Reliance is now able to process many more policies especially in the seasonal environment, the BPM implementation has had a high impact on the growth revenues.

6.4 Productivity Improvements

Turn-around time for processing new policies slashed from two weeks to four hours and also impacted the customer satisfaction assured by meeting SLAs and enabling services via multiple channels. The system also ensured the real-time visibility and control over status of every policy in the process and last but not least the quality of processing the policies was enhanced by reducing the errors.

This allowed Reliance to easily scale to support anticipated exponential growth via seamless, end-to-end processing achieved through integration with multiple external systems.

7. BEST PRACTICES, LEARNING POINTS AND PITFALLS

7.1 Best Practices and Learning Points

✓ *Webservices enabled*

✓ *Lean customized login screen enabling faster access and less consumption of bandwidth*

✓ *Business has adapted well to using a completed automated workflow solution*

✓ *Workflow solution tweaked to include case allocation to rural BPO during downturn for resulting in enormous savings for the company*

✓ *Solution integrated with WS process server, auto underwriting engine , MQ for access to other systems and DCTM content management system*

7.2 Pitfalls

✗ *Biz event table truncation required every month-end*

✗ *Business completely dependent on solution hence uptime requirement is 100 %*

8. COMPETITIVE ADVANTAGES

As mentioned earlier, life insurance is a hugely completive industry in India. It is also seasonal with the bulk of policies purchased during the end of the year due to the tax advantages offered by the government. What this peculiar situation means is that the organizations need to be very efficient and process as many policies as possible to take advantage of this short period when most of the people will buy policies. Due to this constraint of deadline to complete the processing of policies, the automation and process efficiency gives a competitive edge to Reliance in order to process more policies and at higher efficiencies.

9. TECHNOLOGY

Progress Savvion BPM was integrated with Documentum (EMC). Since MQSeries was already part of the system it was also integrated to use the messaging feature. RLIC had WebSphere process server, hence SOA based services were used to integrate with it.

10. THE TECHNOLOGY AND SERVICE PROVIDERS

RLIC selected Progress Savvion Business Process Management System for its BPM needs. More than 300 of the world's top-performing companies, including 24 of the Fortune 100, choose Progress Savvion to operate more productively and profitably. As the business process management trailblazer, Progress Software moves enterprises beyond ordinary

BPM with groundbreaking business-critical software solutions and services that make them more competitive and cost-efficient, including a return on investment as high as 300%. Progress Software has a proven track record for turning process improvement ideas into real world solutions within 30 days, providing the highest ROI for the lowest total cost of ownership. Headquartered in Bedford, Massachusetts, Progress Software Corporation can be reached at www.progress.com

About Progress Software Corporation

Progress Software Corporation (NASDAQ: PRGS) is an independent enterprise software company that enables businesses to be operationally responsive to changing conditions and customer interactions as they occur – to capitalize on new opportunities, drive greater efficiencies and reduce risk. The company offers a comprehensive portfolio of best-in-class enterprise software spanning event-driven visibility and real-time response, open integration, data access and integration, and application development and deployment – all supporting on-premises and SaaS/Cloud deployments. Progress maximizes the benefits of operational responsiveness while minimizing IT complexity and total cost of ownership. Progress can be reached at www.progress.com

South Australia Department of the Premier and Cabinet, Australia

Gold Award, Pacific Rim
Nominated by HandySoft, USA

1. EXECUTIVE SUMMARY

The Department of the Premier and Cabinet (DPC) is the principal government agency in the state of South Australia responsible for strategic planning and policy development. Under the leadership of the Premier and Executive Council, these matters of state business require collaboration and negotiation across more than 20 directorates and agencies with more than 40,000 potential participants. The workload, as a result, became highly dynamic, heavily paper-based, and prone to security breaches.

Rolled out in 2009, the Electronic Cabinet Online (ECO) system is DPC's answer to streamlining business processes, improving the quality of work and ensuring information security. The fundamental purpose of ECO is to create a paperless government.

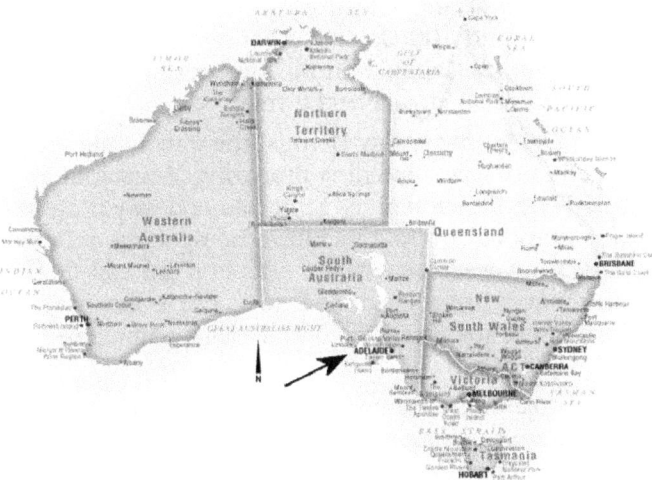

2. OVERVIEW

Based in Adelaide, the Department of the Premier and Cabinet (DPC) is the principal government agency in South Australia, a state with about 1.5 million people.

Cabinet Office is a division of DPC that provides support for the deliberations and decision-making of the Executive Council, Cabinet and Cabinet Committees. It drives implementation of South Australia's Strategic Plan, coordinates and advises on policy development, and has overarching responsibility for federal-state relations.

Midway through 2007, the Cabinet Office underwent a major overhaul. On the recommendations of the Government Reform Commission, headed by former Queensland Premier Wayne Goss, the Government agreed to expand the office and equip it with the right mix of skills to take a more assertive role in public policy development and coordination in South Australia. The former Office of the Executive Committee of Cabinet was merged with Cabinet Office, and staffing expanded through second ments from each of the other government agencies.

Adelaide, South Australia

The Cabinet Office contains the following directorates:

- Cabinet Secretariat and Implementation
- Office of Intergovernmental Relations
- Office of the Executive Committee of Cabinet
- Policy Co-ordination: Innovation and Opportunity
- Policy Coordination: Prosperity and Sustainability
- Policy Coordination: Wellbeing and Communities

The Cabinet Secretariat and Implementation directorate services the meetings of Cabinet (Premier and Ministers) and Executive Council (Premier, Ministers and the Governor). There are around 100 Cabinet meetings a year, with about 10 of these conducted as Community Cabinets in different regions of the State. There are approximately 50 Executive Councils held a year.

With a small staff headed by Manager Ray Dennis, the directorate also performs a constitutional and governance role, including preparing Ministerial appointments and delegations, advising on Parliamentary protocols and swearing in new State Governors. Its Parliamentary liaison role includes the opening of Parliament and managing the machinery of government when elections are called. Recently, the directorate's functions have been expanded to include an implementation-monitoring role to ensure that the decisions of Cabinet are implemented effectively.

The directorate's central role as a secretariat for Cabinet and Executive Council meetings traditionally required a tremendous amount of paper.

3.   BUSINESS CONTEXT

As the central decision making body of the executive government in South Australia, Cabinet deliberates on matters brought to it by Ministers in the form of Cabinet Submissions or Cabinet Notes.

Cabinet Submissions are required to gain approval for:

- Significant or sensitive strategic Government policy changes
- Creation or amendment of legislation
- Projects requiring significant expenditure
- Inter-governmental matters
- Appointment of senior Public Servants and other senior Government appointments

Cabinet Notes are more informal requests for discussion and guidance in Ministers' own decision-making within their portfolios. Meetings happen weekly. The submissions process timeline is fixed.

Some Cabinet decisions result in the initiation and subsequent enactment of legislation; other decisions become legally binding through ratification by Executive Council or through powers vested in individual Ministers.

In preparing Cabinet Submissions and Notes for Cabinet and the associated policy briefings for the Premier and Ministers, Cabinet Office handled a massive amount of paper. For example, thirty (30) copies of a normal Cabinet Submission were required, together with the original, in a Cabinet Submission file cover. Twenty-three (23) copies in the case of a Cabinet Note. These paper copies were then circulated to other Ministers and agencies for comment on proposed decisions, providing a rounded view of possible policy implications.

Files, folders and correspondence passed among the many departments briefing Ministers and were collated in a mass of documents circulated to Ministers in advance of every meeting in what were called the "Cabinet Bags". Not only did this create operational costs, but also put extremely sensitive documents in potentially unsecure spaces. Cabinet Office has a responsibility to eliminate the possibility of lost documents or policy leaks.

Furthermore, all the Departments and agencies involved in preparing or commenting on Cabinet documents have different systems for processing and tracking correspondence. Trying to create a platform for all to use with associated plug-in or integration points presents a high hurdle.

DPC conducted research on ways to reduce paper and tighten security. It found excellent examples at the Irish Government and the Federal Government in Australia.

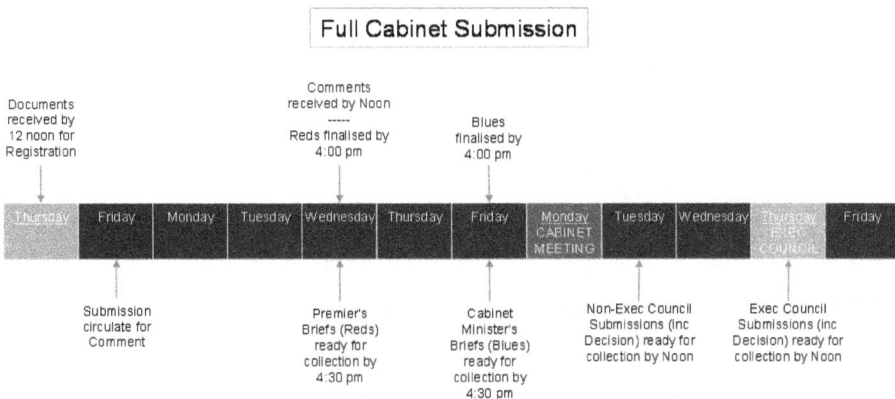

Full Cabinet Submission

By 2007, DPC obtained approval to issue a tender – "Project Name: BPM Implementation Partner for the Electronic Cabinet Online (ECO) Project" – to develop a system creating a paperless environment for Cabinet proceedings. As other agencies in the South Australia Government were using workflow solutions created with business process management (BPM) software, Cabinet Office believed that the right BPM platform could support the ECO project. The ECO solution would need to integrate with the existing Cabinet Secretariat Support System, itself made up of the Cabinet Submission Information System, the Boards and Committees Information System, and the Candidate Register Information System.

ECO Project sponsorship came from the Deputy Chief Executive, Cabinet Office and the Minister Assisting the Premier in Cabinet Business and Public Sector Management

Key objectives included:

- Improving the efficiency of processing of Cabinet business by the Cabinet Office;
- Streamlining the process for agencies submitting documents to Cabinet;
- Improving tracking of the implementation of Cabinet decisions;
- Improving the quality and consistency of Cabinet documents; and
- Ensuring that the security of Cabinet business is not compromised.

4. 4. KEY INNOVATIONS

4.1 Business

Whether real estate projects, health care programs, or environment protection laws, DPC tackles all sorts of issues.

For example, the Minister of Industrial Relations wants to sponsor a new development near the beach. Any new construction project will affect transportation, infrastructure and the environment. The project will also affect local communities and families as new people move in who require services such as housing, education and law enforcement. Before any construction commences Parliament may have to examine the project and Cabinet authorize public expenditures.

The way DPC managed this process in the past was to produce mountains of paper for review. Things would get lost, forgotten or in the worst case stolen. Status was difficult to know. Control was limited.

Today, the business has one location in ECO to initiate, track and archive projects. They have control on distribution. They produce and pass no paper. They have visibility into who is doing what at any given time. And they can fully account for all personnel actions related to any one work item.

4.2 Process

There are seven stages in the Cabinet submission lifecycle:

Cabinet Submission Life Cycle

1 - Drafting	Performed by the Submitter – ends when a Submission is Registered with the Cabinet Office.
2 - Registration	Performed by the Cabinet Office – records the formal lodgement of a Submission for consideration by Cabinet.
3 - Commenting	Managed by the Cabinet Office – requires distribution to, and responses from a Submission-specific community of Reviewers.
4 - Briefing	Managed by the Cabinet Office – involves time-critical delivery of Briefs to the Premier and Cabinet Ministers.
5 - Decision	Managed by the Cabinet Office – records the Cabinet Decision.
6 - Notification	Performed by the Cabinet Office – involves prompt communication of a Decision to the Submitter.

7 - Implementation	Performed by the Submitter and monitored by the Cabinet Office – taking action to implement Cabinet Decisions.

During these Stages, as many as 40,000 people can take part. Roles include:

- Administrators
    - Creates meeting
    - Creates agenda
    - Creates folder
    - Registers documents
    - Circulates documents
    - Collates comments
    - Mediates/coordinates comments
- Cabinet Participants (e.g., Ministers, Members)
    - Downloads documents
    - Reviews electronically
    - Adds comments and recommendations

Every Monday, the Cabinet meets to review new submissions, such as the proposed development. Administrators have the responsibility to establish meeting dates, start meetings, receive and validate submissions, and coordinate the review and approval process. ECO streamlines this entire process. It gives everyone in affected agencies an opportunity to contribute their expert input.

Submission Process – Registration

Users based in Cabinet Ministers' Offices can register Cabinet Submissions through ECO to initiate review. Depending on the type of Submission, Users will fill in one or many forms (note grey tabs depict extra sub-forms). Behind each option in the forms are sophisticated rules governing policies and routing procedures.

Policy changes often involve legislative amendments, for example new crime control initiatives. In this example the Attorney General (via his office) creates a new submission that is registered with the Cabinet Secretariat and then circulated by us for commentary and review. Cabinet Office receives comments from officials overseeing policy in areas such as family and community, courts and police. Another example is an appointment to a major board. In this case the Office for Women may comment on gender balance. In a major project DPC get comments from up to 20 agencies.

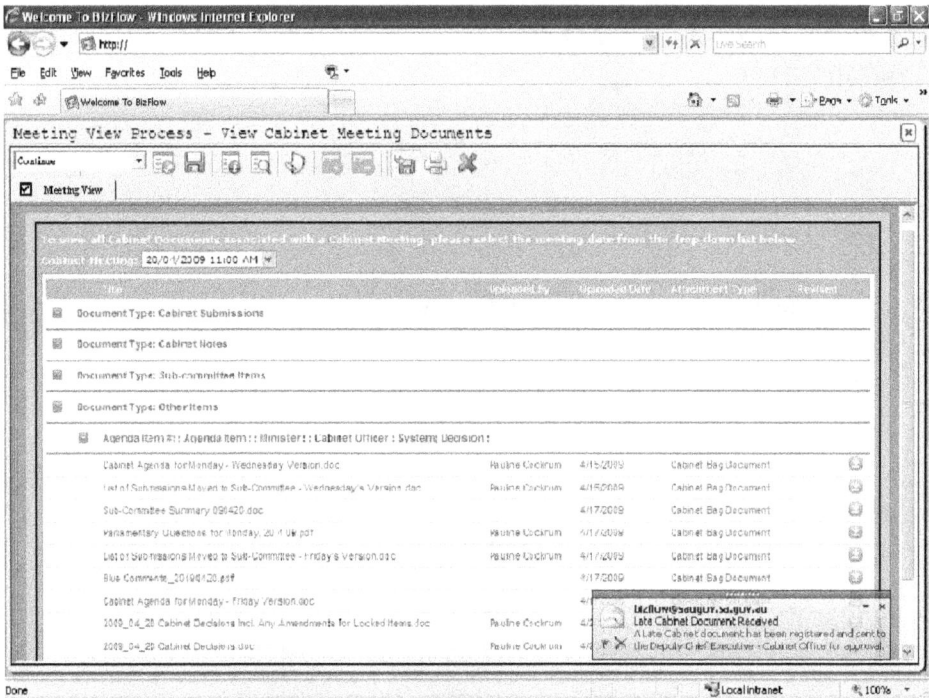

Submission Process – Briefing

Most high-level users will access this form during the Submissions process. They are notified of new tasks via email and BizFlow pop-ups. All details, and their corresponding documents, are available to Users by clicking on the appropriate orange icon. Ministers' Offices normally access all of the items under the expanded tab on Friday afternoons for review. At this time they can review online, offline, or in print when required in order to prepare for Monday meetings. ECO's "e-bag" replaces the voluminous paper previously collated by Cabinet Office, stuffed into large locked Cabinet bags and carried by couriers from Cabinet Office to Ministers' offices scattered throughout the square mile of the Adelaide CBD.

In each of the seven stages in the Cabinet submission lifecycle, there are structured and potentially unstructured processes and sub-processes. Furthermore, a submission may cycle back through previous stages up to the point that a decision is made. Task routing can change based on topic, role and responsibility.

The beginning of the process is largely structured. Rules are incorporated into the ECO processes that govern roles, policies, procedures, routing, etc.

As DPC learned during process analysis there are many areas within case management and correspondence and action tracking operations where unstructured workflows exist. Participating in these dynamically changing interactions are mainly Knowledge Workers that work deep inside DPC to gather, analyze and review issues, incidents and policies.

ECO enables both structured and unstructured process execution and monitoring. For example, the Administrator kicks-off a workflow regarding a proposal to build a park. The proposal is routed to the appropriate personnel for review. At this point, people within each department decide whether others should review and opine. Because knowing who is best fit, qualified or available to comment up front is near impossible, DPC added flexibility in ECO allowing department personnel to dynamically include others in the action review and approval processes.

The department official reviews the action to decide whether to include others. If there is a need to task others, the official creates subordinate tasks, selects key categories, sub-categories, and deadlines, adds users (aka Knowledge Workers), attaches pertinent documentation, and submits for execution. All users then receive actions via ECO. They individually review and complete work. They can also choose to sub-task others. DPC often has actions that move from Office to Division to Branch to Team to Individual levels. Each level knows who is involved, what have been assigned, and corresponding materials, comments and deadlines.

Agility is key to the overall effectiveness of the case management and action tracking processes. While the first and last steps to any action are formalized, the real work gets done through dynamic collaboration. Those tasked can task others (aka Knowledge Workers) who have access to or knowledge of the requested information, thus actions can take innumerable routes to find the "right" people to get the work done efficiently and completely. Meanwhile, those involved do not lose visibility into action status. Furthermore, DPC learns over time that certain actions always take the same course and certain people seem to be key team assets. This form of on-the-fly process discovery can lead to more formalized (or structured) workflows. It can also pinpoint people for promotion, people who require training, and people who should be reassigned or let go.

ECO pushes the very limits of BPM. When DPC started the project the team felt that is could model and design workflows with formal or rigid business rules. They quickly discovered, however, that program success boiled down to giving Knowledge Workers the flexibility to assign actions based on their own experience and networks. DPC worked with its business partners to expand the limits of BPM to executive unstructured or dynamic workflow applications. By working together with its partners DPC has created a BPM-enabled application unique to the world, which can now be easily replicated by other organizations wanting to automate dynamic business processes.

Structured Process
(Definitive Rules & Roles)

Unstructured Process
(Flexible Rules & Roles)

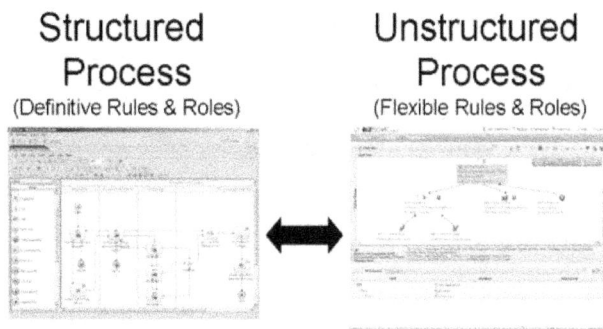

Process Use Cases

5. HURDLES OVERCOME

The most significant hurdle during the initial stages of the project predominantly came from the mapping of existing paper based processes into an electronic form. Although the process was defined by policy and procedure, on investigation for mapping purposes it was discovered that a large amount of the procedure actually resided within the knowledge base of an individual and differed slightly from the documented process.

This knowledge-worker know-how necessitated considerable effort to align the documented process with actual day-to-day operations within each department participating in policy matters.

5.1 Management

The existing paper-based process was extremely well structured but required a considerable amount of time to manage due to lack of visibility. Daily workflow management was predominantly undertaken though continual follow-up by individuals to ensure work was completed within the defined '10-day' rules.

The implementation of the new ECO systems has given management a level of confidence, through controlled and regulated processes, alerts and process transparency that tasks are followed correctly and in a timely manner.

Now management has more time to perform strategic tasks as opposed to resource-draining, low-level administrative duties.

5.2 Business

With ECO, DPC has not only created a paperless environment, the organization has significantly improved security. Process participants need a piece of hardware in addition to User ID and password to initially access ECO. All documents sourced from our secure system are watermarked as "Cabinet-in Confidence" when they are downloaded and are also marked with the name of the person who downloaded them and the date and time they were accessed. A complete audit trail of users is automatically created in the background as the system is used every day.

5.3 Organizational Adoption

The vision is to go completely paperless by 2010. Ministers have already embraced the concept by taking their laptops to Cabinet meetings loaded with the submissions and briefings to be considered at the meetings, rather than bringing masses of paper.

As people become familiar with the new system and the inevitable bugs attending a complex, State-wide, IT project are ironed out, DCP expects to realize savings in time and money. Courier costs are already down and the time taken to process documents is being dramatically reduced. Expert comments on submissions and briefings by Ministerial advisers will be delivered in a much more timely fashion, leading to improved decision-making and a better outcome for the whole community".

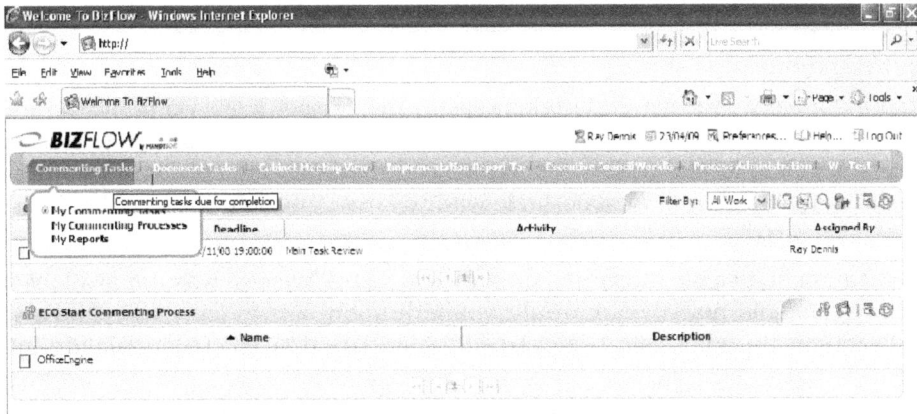

User Screen – Commenting Tasks Work List

After logging in to ECO, Users will immediately view their work list. Clicking on a task will open the form (aka business process application) that captures user commentary. Power Users such as the Manager of the Cabinet Secretariat and Implementation Unit have a wider range of views (the orange tabs).

6. BENEFITS

6.1 Cost Savings

Although the ECO project was not undertaken with cost savings as a target, it has resulted in significant savings through paper reduction, courier costs and smarter resource utilization. For example, each fortnight reams of paper were printed to support the Cabinet Submission process both within the Cabinet Office and also each individual department. The paper was couriered from one to many locations and back. And in the case of lost or missing files, new printed materials had to be made and shipped as well as analyses done to investigate security breaches. ECO has results in hundreds of thousands of dollars saved or applied to other noteworthy programs.

Furthermore, ECO supports the targets set by the South Australia Government for not only efficiencies but also the impact Government has on the environment.

6.2 Time Reductions

An evaluation of 'return on investment' is planned for the near future, but anecdotally this initiative has not only generated great efficiencies but also reduced the time commitment of all staff involved throughout Government.

The mere fact that these documents are now available online has changed the manual handling, printing and distribution processes from days to hours.

6.3 Productivity Improvements

DPC has realized "time reductions" as well as "productivity improvements." DPC plans a full ROI analysis in 2010.

7. BEST PRACTICES, LEARNING POINTS AND PITFALLS

7.1 Best Practices and Learning Points

The ECO project was significant and complex. The processes as mapped required greater flexibility than realized as the project rolled out to more and more knowledge workers. Minor variances created short delays to understand user roles and redefine process interactions. This is where the functionality in the product selected played a key role in delivering the dynamic and unstructured process execution required by knowledge workers.

The DPC project team and the consulting team also put in risk mitigation strategies up front to help quickly resolve issues in the misalignment between IT architecture and business strategy

If the initiative was to be undertaken again, the project team would spend more time analyzing up-front the subtle and dynamic ways people interact. Workflow models detailing formal rules need to also capture informal, collaborative interactions to make users really comfortable with the resulting solutions.

7.2 Pitfalls

The creation of a single integrated or standard 'LDAP' system was not available for this project. This now means until standardization occurs (currently underway) ECO requires an administrative overhead to ensure that all credentials are up to date.

Another pitfall uncovered was the different information handling processes between Government agencies. For the ECO project it was important to define a standard for inter-agency user communication. This was true for both structured and dynamic interactions. For example, ECO has many formal steps on how people pass and review information. But there is a point in the process where users may break out of the formal process pattern to initiate and assign dynamically tasks to one or many individuals. Tasking – assigning, sub-tasking and completing dynamic tasks – is done in the solution itself. It also enables users to upload and download documents without using email, which is to say keep all the dynamic collaboration and comments remain within the solution itself. But the implementation team found that some agencies would 'download' documentation from ECO to transmit via email. One primary reason for ECO is to track the status user interactions. Moving from ECO into email can undermine the integrity of the entire process. By both educating users on how to use the solution and the importance of the entire process and not just their task, DPC has effectively overcome this issue.

8. COMPETITIVE ADVANTAGES

Considering that DPC is a government organization, there are no real competitive advantages. However, ECO enables DPC will provide more efficient policy development, and thus improved citizen-centric services.

9. TECHNOLOGY

Technical requirements included:

- Architecture
    - Integrated, single-vendor environment for modeling, workflow execution, system integration, business rules and process monitoring,
    - Central repository for storage and synchronization of model and executable elements – round-trip integration,
    - Conversion of model to executable with minimal need for programming, standard connectors for Microsoft SQL Server database – 2000, 2005, scalable
    - J2EE or equivalent software platform services
- Modeling
    - Existing or planned support for standards
        1. BPMN 1.1 (mandatory)
        2. XPDL 2.0

- Ability to create multi-layered, integrated models that meet the needs of business users (conceptual), process analysts (simulation) and system implementers (deployment)
- Support for collaborative development – modeling versioning,
- Versioning to support RAD/iterative development,
- Components discovery and re-use
- Business Rules
  - Discrete, built-for-purpose business rules management functionality,
  - Full integration of business rules functionality with process modeling and process execution.
- Process Simulation
  - Create and store simulation scenarios
  - Retrieve and manipulate stored process statistics as process simulation scenarios
- Human Task (Workflow) Support
  - Production workflow support
  - Integration with Windows Desktop – in particular, task lists in Microsoft Outlook
  - Email notifications and alerts
  - Flexible routing
  - Dynamic task assignment – reassign or delegate task
  - 'Team Room' features for collaboration
- User Interface
  - Ajax web forms or equivalent with full-featured form designer
  - Guided task performance
  - User sort/filter/query work list
  - 'Live' instance status information
- System Integration
  - SOA standards support
  - Pre-developed adapters for Microsoft SQL Server; introspection capability
  - Data transformation and mapping
  - Integrated registry/repository
- Document Management
  - Discrete, built-for-purpose, secure document management functionality
  - Folder/container document repositories
  - Document upload
  - Document versioning
  - Document viewing
  - Document printing, with print auditing and dynamic page watermark/header creation at print time
  - Document archiving
  - Document meta-data and optional content indexing
  - Document search
  - Full integration of document management functionality with process modeling and process execution
- Process Execution

- Existing or planned support for standards
- WS-BPEL 2.0
- BPEL4People 1.0
- WS-Human Task 1.0
- Dynamic process change propagation management
  1. Ability to choose whether or not process changes are applied to existing process instances
  2. Ability to flexibly select which existing process instances process changes are applied to based on process instance data attributes
  3. Ability to flexibly select which existing process instances process changes are applied to based on process instance stage in the process.
- Business Activity Monitoring
  - Create and change process metrics and KPIs
  - Customizable monitoring dashboard – charts, reports, alerts and notifications
  - KPI triggered rules and actions
  - Instance monitoring

10. THE TECHNOLOGY AND SERVICE PROVIDERS

ECO incorporates BizFlow® BPM from Handysoft as its foundation for process design, execution and optimization. BizFlow BPM also includes BizFlow® OfficeEngine™ to enable dynamic action assignments.

Websites:

Department of the Premier and Cabinet	www.premcab.sa.gov.au

For the ECO project, DPC used the following business partners:

Service Provider	Product / Service Offering	Website
HandySoft	BizFlow® BPM BizFlow® OfficeEngine™ Customer Support	www.handysoft.com
Brabham Consulting	Business Analysis and Specification Development System Design and Configuration Application Development Application Support Project Management	www.brabhamconsulting.com

Section 5

South and Central America

Quala SA, Colombia

Gold Award, South & Central America
Nominated by PECTRA Technology, USA

1. EXECUTIVE SUMMARY / ABSTRACT

Quala, a multinational mass-consumption corporation dedicated to the production and commercial distribution of food, implemented a technology plan which included the adoption of a process management philosophy and the incorporation of a BPMs tool to gain agility in front of market changes and greater scalability in the operations of: Logistics, human resources, promotions/prices, with the same organizational structure.

The BPMs project allowed for integration of all the members of the value chain associating tasks from over 500 users in 6 Core processes. Time reduction (-250%) and a productivity increase (145%) stand out among the main benefits in human resources processes and expense reduction in the purchase of materials (USD 55,000 monthly).

2. OVERVIEW

The adoption of a work philosophy that enables for the management of the organization through processes and the incorporation of a BPMs tool rises as a need to give an agile and effective answer to the pillars on which Quala designed the strategic growth in the region.

With the objective of supporting the strategic vision of the company, an opportunity in process automation was identified. These processes were documented but due to the dynamics of the business they would quickly grow outdated and go unfulfilled, causing operating cost increases, loss of market opportunities and lack of focus in the business.

"The project represented a considerable challenge for the entire organization. We identified three key stages, which allowed us to carry out the transformation of the company. The first stage was to identify the objective the newly incorporated technology should achieve. This objective should be aligned with the strategy of the business, count on the support of interested stakeholders, and relate directly to cost reduction, customer and supplier service improvement, and the ability to respond to changes in the rules of business. Our IT department had to integrate to the business, and the way to achieve that was through process automation.

The second stage was to define the most important process of the organization, which might give us a competitive edge to face the market and integrate all the participants of the value chain.

As the third stage we visualized the need to organize a report structure that enabled us to conduct tasks in a more planned manner, including IT and business profiles", explains David Enrique Moreno (CTO Chief Technology Officer).

The project included the survey, mapping, automation and integration with other systems of the company of 6 core processes; supply and logistics, investment project evaluation, prices and promotions, traceability of products and temporary staff management.

The dimension of the project involves over 300 internal users at 6 different locations, and over 200 external users that make up the value chain and conduct over 5,600 transactions per day. This enables us to identify bottlenecks in the processes, apply improvements where needed and keep all areas of the company involved in the fulfillment of processes.

The benefits evidenced after implementation are:

- Assurance of application of the required authorization levels in internal supply processes, human resources, sales, marketing and finance.
- Decrease in expenses and money reclassifications for the inappropriate execution of processes. Over USD 55,000 in monthly savings. This translates into:
    - Reengineering staff, reducing labor costs.
    - Elimination of expenses generated by the delivery and printing of 700 purchase orders to the suppliers.
    - Reduction in maintenance costs of printing equipment.
    - Reduction in phone expenses per confirmation calls of purchase orders delivery from providers by fax.
- Generation, approval and automatic shipment of 800 to 1000 monthly purchase orders (OCs) to the supplier with an average of 3,500 national products.
- Product availability to support growth in sales leading up to the year 2011, which equals 70% more sales than in 2006.
- Control of the use of resources invested as process raw materials.
- Integration with 800 suppliers.
- Standardization of process execution. All should execute identically in order to guarantee an efficient result aligned with company policy.
- 250% reduction in the time invested in the process of requisition requests for temporary staff: (before: 5 days - now: 2 days).
- Increase in the productivity of the capture process and payroll update registration in 145% (before: 45 monthly updates, now: 173 monthly updates).
- Timely and sufficient historical information for the different implemented processes which enables appropriate management and decision-making.

"The main economic advantage brought forth by the implementation of BPMs translates specifically in the ability of assisting the growth of the business from the IT department. Quala has been able to identify the drivers of the business in the sector and based on that delineate a growth horizon supported in processes, product development and flexibility and agility to adapt to market changes. The automation of core processes enabled us to leverage the growth and give a solid and effective response to three requirements weighing over the IT departments; alignment (lining up the entire corporation behind the fixed business objectives), compliance (the development of activities in accordance to current regulations) and governance (manageability of the company understood as the ease with which rapid changes can be introduced in the operational foundations)", explains David Enrique Moreno (CTO Chief Technology Officer).

3. BUSINESS CONTEXT

Quala has been present in the regional market (Colombia, Venezuela, Ecuador, Dominican Republic, Mexico and Brazil) for over 30 years, has 2,500 employees, 1,200 subcontractors, and thirty-nine own leading brands in the main market segments. Production and distribution of its products reach over 140,000 direct customers in over 600 municipalities and manages over 800 consumer goods suppliers. Such numbers place Quala among the top five mass-consumption food production and distribution centers.

The keys to success in the mass consumption sector answer to three processes which, by leaning on strategic and tactical marketing translate into market differentials; these are: Evaluation of projects investment, logistics, supply, prices and promotions. In each of these processes, Quala should, by aligning the IT area to the business, achieve its main competitive advantages and leverage its growth.

Initially, Quala operated a system whose functionalities did not satisfy the needs of the company nor the sector.

This system administered the requirements for the production area and generated over 2,000 purchase documents automatically. Said documentation had to be analyzed and processed by an employee in the supply area. In turn, this employee had to sort the paperwork by type of supplier, and manually enter over 800 purchase orders.

After the aforementioned task was completed, the purchasing employee had to conduct manual tasks which involved the issuance of reports for data verification, high management costs, and margins of error with high impact in productivity and reprocesses which had to be handled by a large support structure.

Among such manual tasks we can highlight:

1. Printing and having the purchase orders signed.
2. Scanning or photocopying the purchase orders.
3. Sending the purchase orders by courier.
4. Confirming by telephone the reception of the purchase orders.

Once point 4 was completed, the supplier had to contact the Supply area, identify the purchaser and initiate a negotiation, which, once finished, was confirmed by email.

Once the product delivery time had expired, the receiving employee carried out the entry of the raw material, with prior validation, support and security, while the depot employee received the raw material and entered it into the system at the end of the day. This generated a difference between the actual inventory and the theoretical inventory thus affecting the production process, and in turn, the possibility of having a real inventory available to forward to the points of sale.

The survey of this process resulted in finding the need to adopt a technology that enabled the integration of all the members of the value chain whether internal or external, since the structure grew in terms of management and support to cover the needs of the market dynamics and not in the strategic management which the company required.

The decision of the Systems area within Quala was the adoption of process Management as a work methodology and the incorporation of a BPM tool as solution to the problem of achieving efficiency and agility in its processes.

4. THE KEY INNOVATIONS

The development of the project has a deep impact in the main members of the value chain, linking internal and external participants of the organization distributed in the main regions of Colombia.

The core process of supply and logistics was mounted on a BPM tool through the survey, mapping, automation and integration with internal and external systems.

Currently, the purchase requisitions are automatically generated and transmitted via web service to BPMs so that the purchasing employee can automatically sort them by supplier. Once the purchase order is created, it goes through the different required levels of authorization, and once the respective approval is granted, two events occur:

- They are automatically generated in a proprietary system
- They are sent by certified mail to the supplier.

The following screen captures of the tool are shown here for illustration purposes.

Validez desconocida
Digitally signed by QUALA S.A.
Date: 2009.09.28 14:56:15 -05:00
Reason: Aprobación Orden de Compra
Location: Bogotá D.C , Colombia

ORDEN DE COMPRA

Fecha	28/09/2009 14:07:05	No OC	OM002508
Proveedor	60003956 - LITO-PRINT LTDA	Nit	860003956
Dirección	CLL 12 # 42 B 05	Teléfono	091 335 01 11
Atención	JORGE GAITAN	Fax	091 268 51 35
Ciudad	BOGOTA		

Ítem	Código	Descripción	Cantidad UM	Entrega	Precio	Costo Total	Almacén
1	13220791	PLEG JUNIOR 16X10 VEN	20.000,00 UN	06/11/2009	174,08	3.481.600,00	QUALA5
2	31200108	PLEG BI 16X10 R04	20.000,00 UN	17/11/2009	187,34	3.746.800,00	QUALA5
					Total Orden	7.228.400,00	

Valor en Letras	SIETE MILLONES DOSCIENTOS VEINTIOCHO MIL CUATROCIENTOS PESOS Y CERO CENTS
Moneda	PES
Término Crédito	45

Compras de materiales

Bienvenido

Gestión y seguimiento de órdenes de compra

Idioma:

Empresa:

Nit:

Usuario:

Contraseña:

Ingresar

Olvidó su clave

| Orden de Compra | Modificadas | Aceptadas | Venadas | Idioma: Español | | | Salir |

.:: pperez - Pedro Perez - 860070605 ::.

| Exportar XLS | | | | | | | | | | | Aceptar Órdenes de Compra |

Aprobar	Modificar	Dividr	Código	Ítem	Artículo	Descripción	Cantidad	UM	Despacho	Llegaca Quala
☐	Modificar	Dividr	OM000891	1	78100294	FRASCO F SH X350 LYF-DCR	5010	UN		01/05/2009
☐	Modificar	Dividr	OM000892	1	78100439	FCO SAV AC SAB350 R02VE	1000	UN		26/01/2009
☐	Modificar	Dividr	OM000892	2	78100439	FCO SAV AC SAB350 R02VE	1000	UN		26/01/2009
☐	Modificar	Dividr	OM000890	1	78100294	FRASCO F SH X350 LYF-DCR	5000	UN		01/05/2009

"We have involved over 200 main suppliers of raw materials that may check their information on the website. The automation of this process enables us as a company to be very timely in purchasing and thus maintaining effective communication with the supplier," explains David Enrique Moreno (CTO Chief Technology Officer).

Processes:

COMS-Compras Suministros

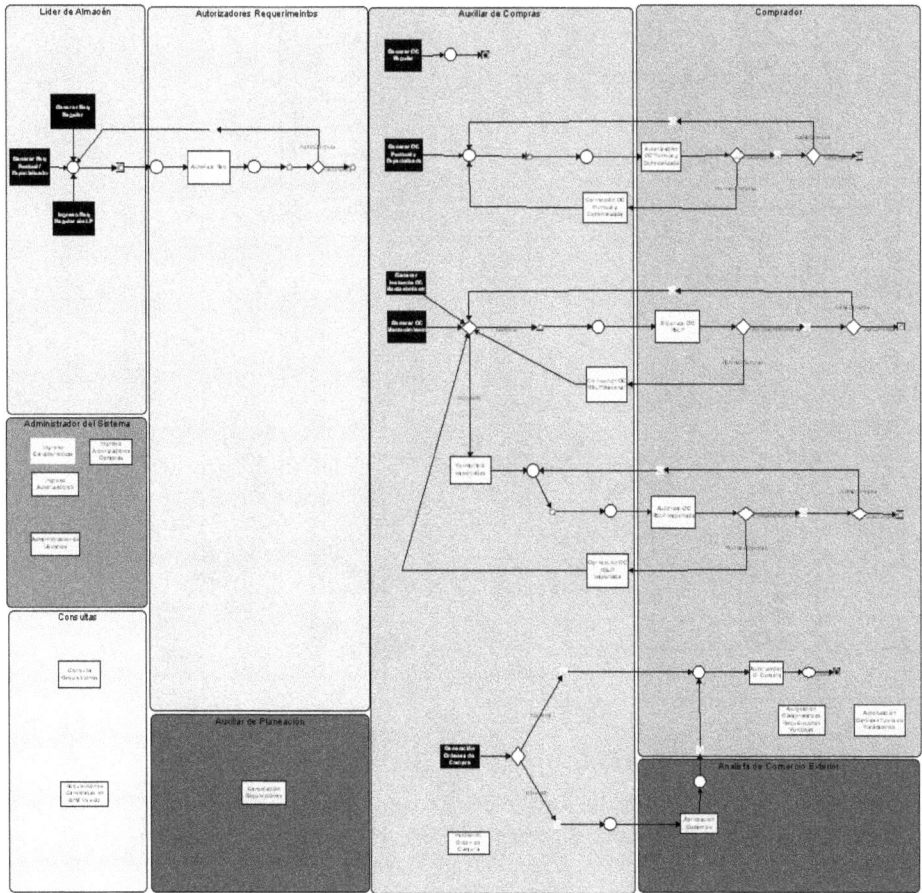

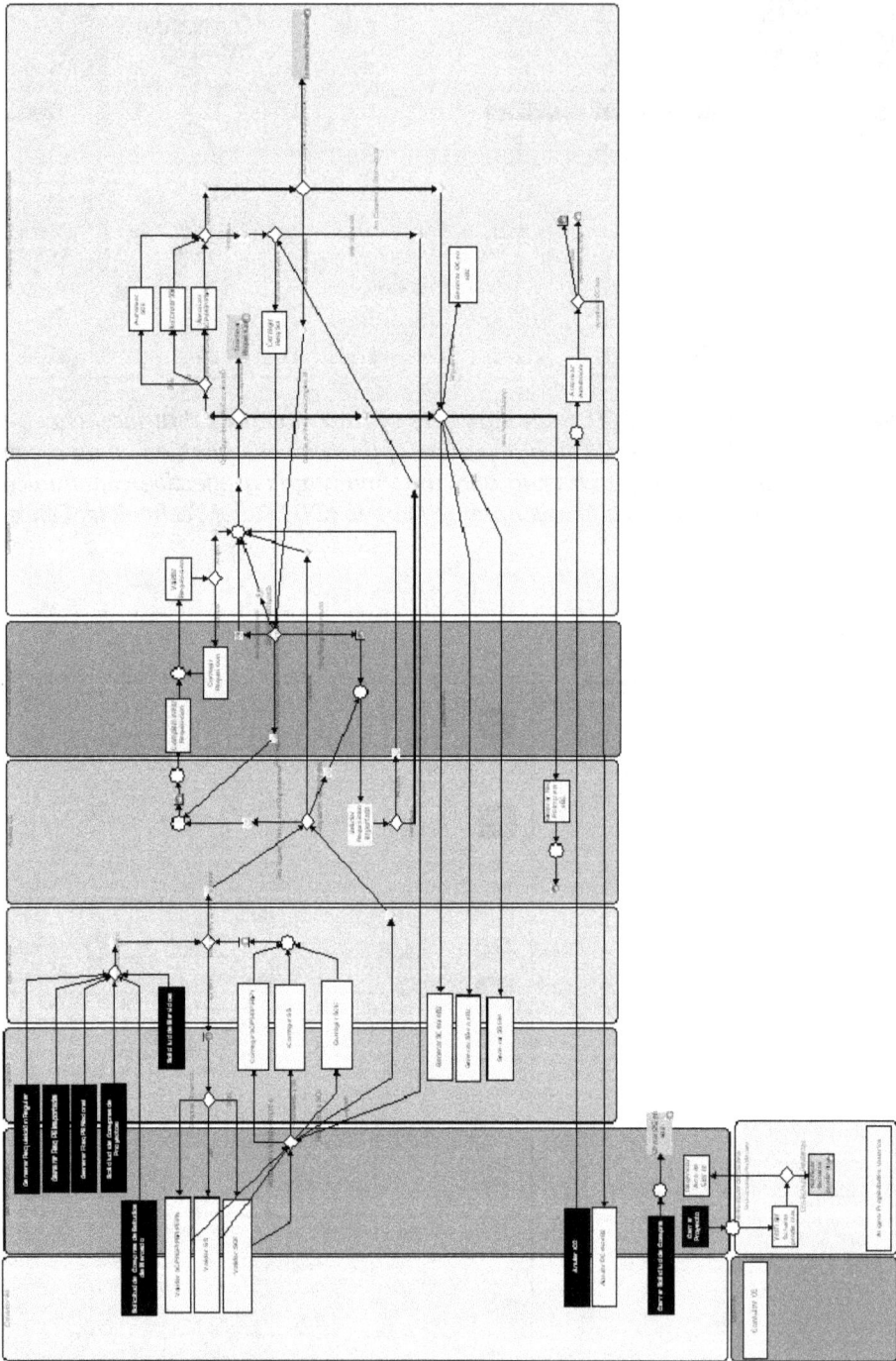

Structure of the solution:

Applications with components that support the development of process flows implemented on BPM have been created. These components carry out the integration with ERP, payroll systems, Mail, among others, achieving the standardization of development and implementation of new processes, the scalability and agility in the timeframes of process initiation.

Diagrama de componentes
PECTRA

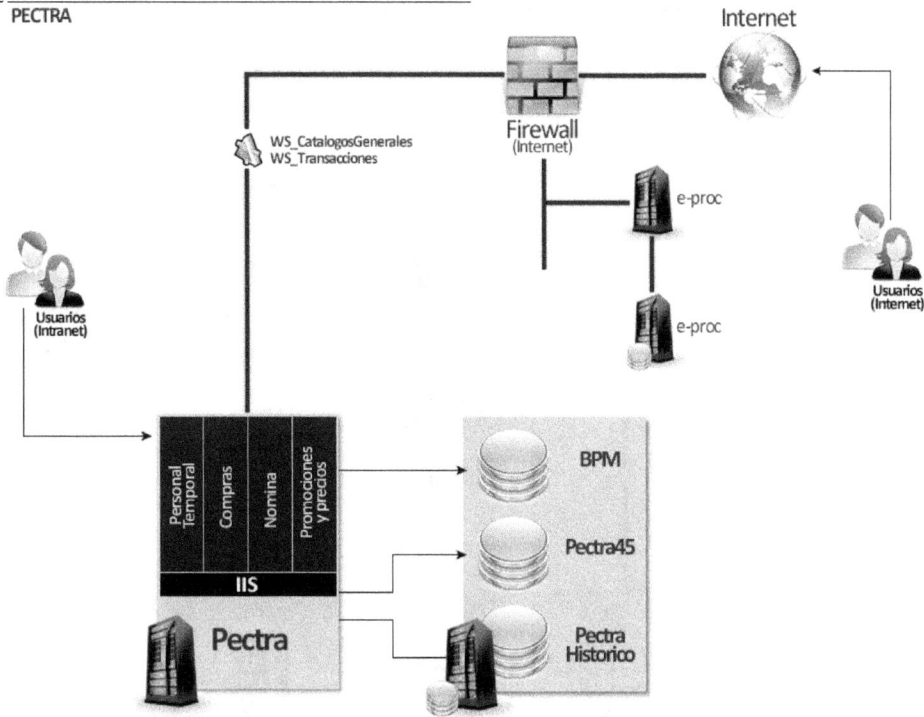

Components Diagram

Infrastructure:

Quala is a multinational enterprise with standardized processes, among them is the development of corporate applications. The implementation of all the projects has as its base the structure diagrams defined in the Technology area. They divide the web application services in two layers: a server for web-intranet applications and a server for OLTP databases. The BPM tool components are distributed in these two servers, thus ensuring availability, response time and application continuity. With the good results obtained through this scheme, the technology area is able to ensure the support required by the corporation for its growth.

For the services exposed to the Internet, the structured used is three-layered; a safe zone where we deploy all our applications with the security guidelines that have been established as better practices (SSL, Digital Certificates, etc).

Diagrama de infraestructura

PECTRA

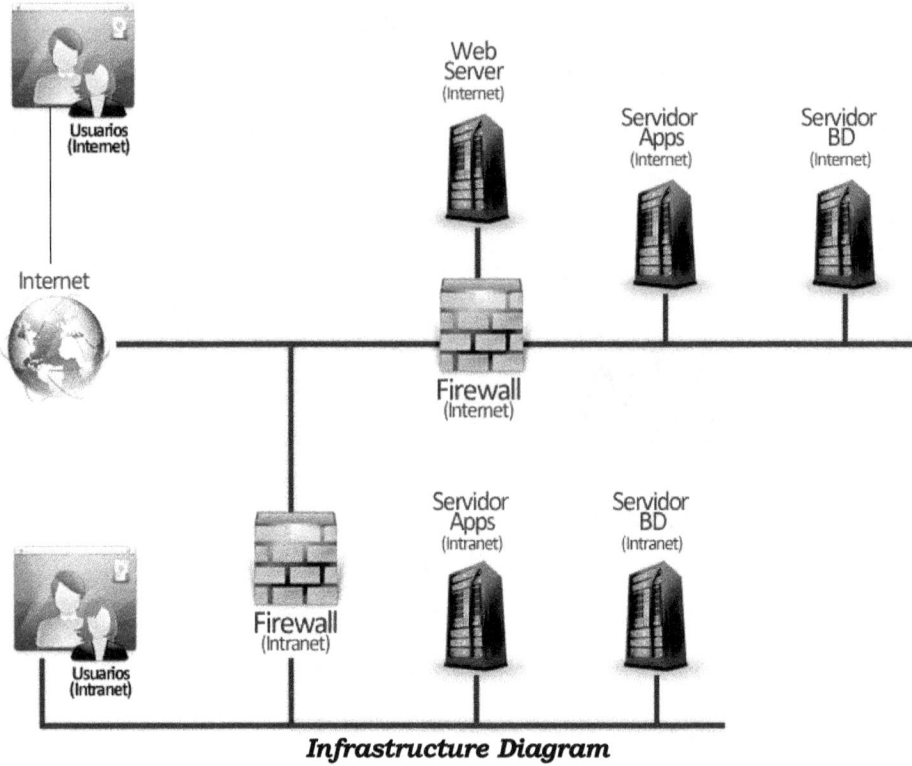

Infrastructure Diagram

Examples of some BPM processes:

1. **Temporary staff hiring:** Enables us to conduct temporary staff management (hiring, follow-up, assignment, budgeting) for marketing activities and sales in sales support, controlling authorization schemes and assigned budgets.

CONTRATACION DE PERSONAL TEMPORAL

2. **BPM Payroll Updates**: Online updates of the changes in positions and salaries of the company employees, insuring compliance with authorization levels. Manually, up to 75 updates were registered, and today, due to automation we are able to register approximately 350 updates per month.

Proceso Novedades de Nomina

3. **Promotions and pricing:** Enables controlling the definition and modification of promotions minimizing the risk for error in the inadequate parameterization of products.

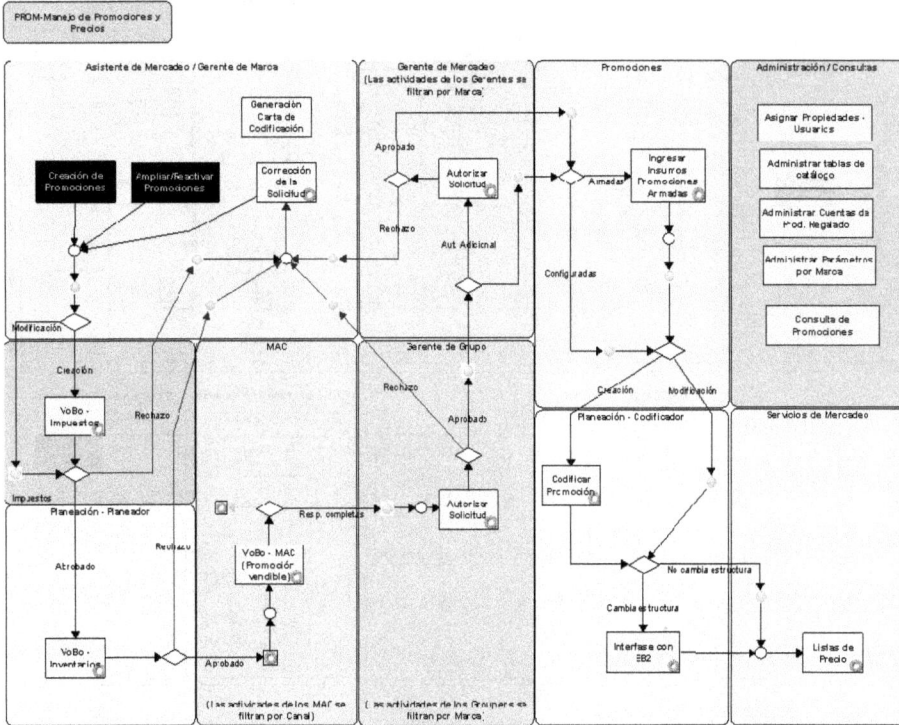

4. **BPM Product encoding:** Ensures the proper creation of a new product and the planning, purchasing and marketing parameters necessary for a product code, materials or shipping materials.

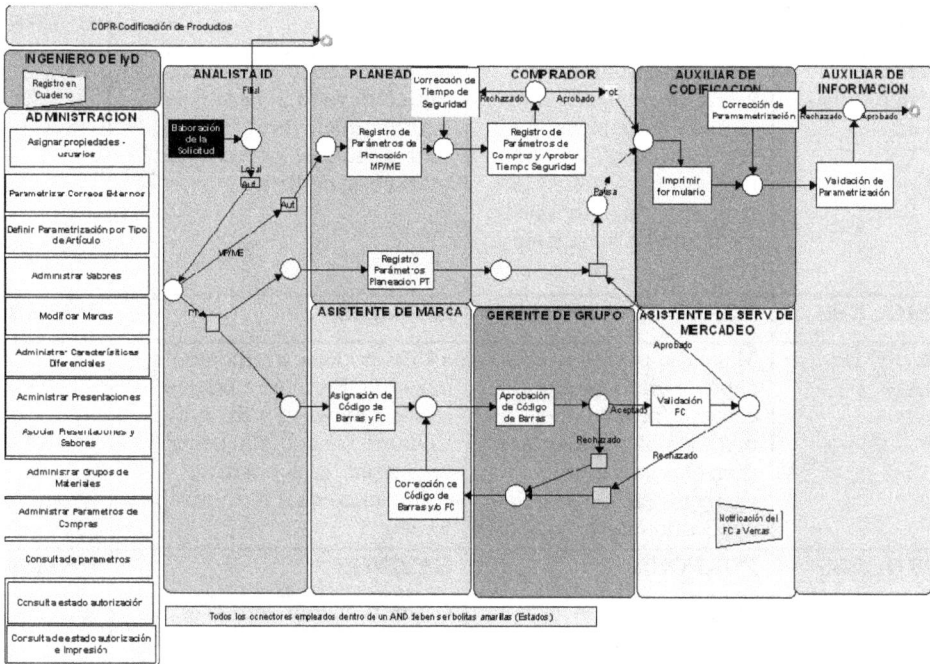

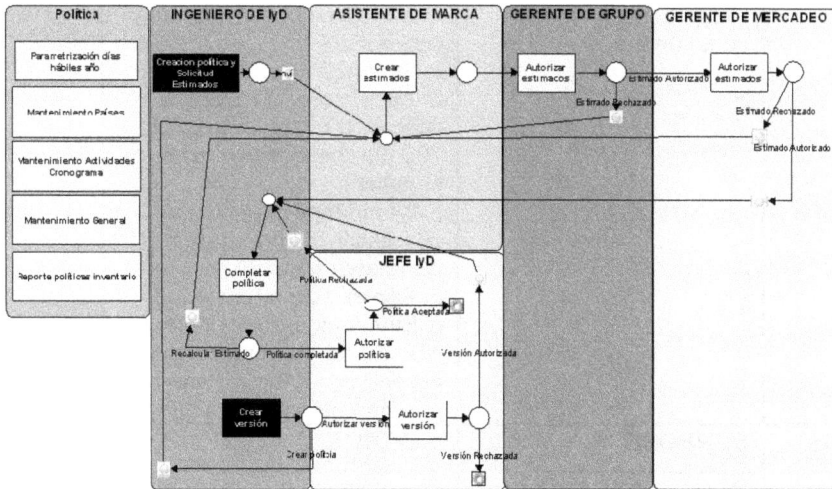

5. BENEFITS

As an introduction, we present the metrics of the Quala activities and the main processes implemented, detailing the benefits in accordance with the 4 axes requested: cost reduction, time reduction, profit increase, productivity increase.

PROCESS	PURPOSE	SAVINGS	USERS
Temporary staff requisition:	Reduction in time invested in the process of requisition requests for temporary staff from the moment it is created to the time it is authorized by all the persons necessary.	Reduction in process time from 5 days to 2 days. Ensuring the timely hiring of support personnel for sales and marketing activities.	52
PROCESS	**PURPOSE**	**SAVINGS**	**USERS**
Payroll Updates	Make the payroll update capture and registration efficient (promotions, methods of transportation, changes in management, etc.), immediate application in the payroll.	145% increase in update registration. From 45 updates registered per month, 173 updates are actually being registered, thus ensuring compliance with authorization levels.	48
PROCESS	**PURPOSE**	**SAVINGS**	**USERS**
Material purchasing	Insure the supply of a product according to the monthly estimates through the timeliness in the generation of purchase orders.	Communication and effective collaboration with the supplier. Savings of USD 55,000 per month given by the following concepts: a. Staff decrease. b. Elimination of expenses generated by the delivery of 700 purchase orders to the suppliers. c. Elimination of paper expenses for the printing of purchase orders. d. Printer maintenance. e. Elimination of telephony charges for the confirmation of fax delivery of the supplier's purchase order.	30
PROCESS	**PURPOSE**	**SAVINGS**	**USERS**
Promotions and pricing:	Process for the definition of promotional items, authorization of said definitions and registration of promotions and pricing in eB2	The promotions in the company are critical since they account for 20% of the monthly sales revenue of the company. It is for this reason that it is critical to insure that the definition of a promotion has passed through all the steps required by its definition and authorization.	60

6. BEST PRACTICES

The development and implementation of the project was based on Pectra Technology's methodology, with 10 years of ISO 9000:2000 certified quality. From this successful implementation we are able to highlight as Best Practices & Learning points the following items:

✓ *1) Follow-up of technology with implementation certified by global standards.*

✓ *2) Exhaustive evaluation of the business context and customer needs, both present and future.*

✓ *3) Exhaustive documentation of processes and surveys.*

✓ *4) Joint execution and monitoring of the project with the customer, with deliverable milestones defined at the beginning of the implementation.*

✓ *5) Application of risk and deviation management methodology.*

✓ *6) Satisfaction of the needs of all the participants involved in the market value chain at which the solution aims.*

Methodological framework:

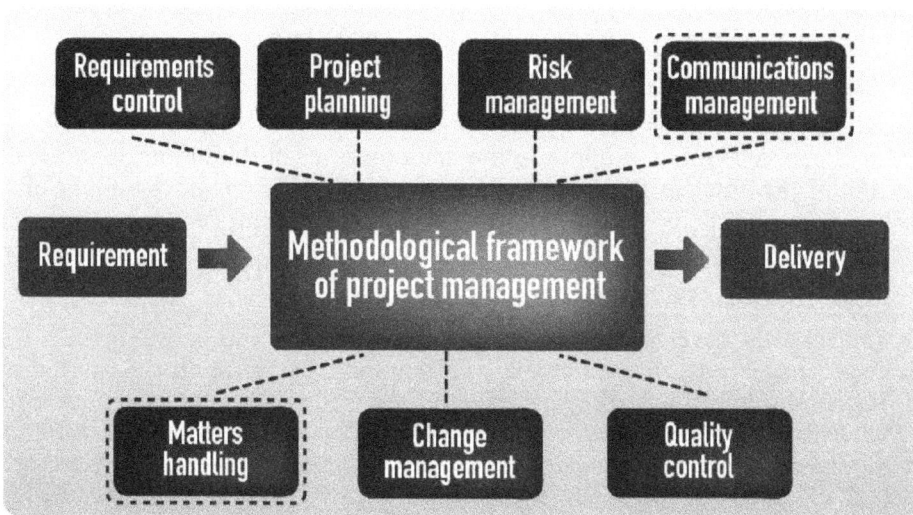

Implementation:

One of the most important points taken into account for the adoption of process management methodology and for the incorporation of a BPM tool was to gain the awareness that this was clearly an interdisciplinary project since it demanded knowledge in business development, key process identification to obtain competitive advantages, and technological applications that supported its execution.

These key issues provided a methodological framework for the definition of the optimal architecture of the integration process, thus enabling the juncture of defined business processes with the integration of existing applications.

In the project's beginning, it was necessary to know the current state of affairs for the organization, i.e., specific needs, short-, mid- and long-term objectives, real possibilities, expected positioning, and the focus and general vision of its directors in order to arrive at the ideal solution.

The project started with an analysis of defined Process Maps, over which work was started, and design, execution and control of the activities of the project was carried out to achieve the implementation of the Process Management tool. This first stage was the most critical due to the innovation and impact it caused throughout the organization: it lasted two months, and was managed under PMI methodologies.

In the next stage, process modeling began taking place. Different existing alternatives were analyzed, and BPMn was chosen to achieve the greatest scalability in the business structure (regional growth). The modeling allowed for the identification of bottleneck and activities that did not add value, which in turn helped redesign the processes and give birth to a stage of revision of responsibility levels and key tasks for the optimization of work.

The third and last stages were developed through a period of 7 months, which is when the project (automation and integration) was implemented, allowed for the integration of all the members of a value chain where over 500 users (both internal and external) in 6 key processes began using the BPM tool and visualizing the metrics of management in real time to the indicators of critical performance of the company.

The solution helped those responsible for the different management areas to have information available to take better decisions and be automatically alerted in case any problem should arise which could jeopardize the business.

7. COMPETITIVE ADVANTAGES

The adoption of process management methodology and the incorporation of a BPM tool enabled Quala to optimize the key processes of the industry and obtain competitive advantages from then which support the strategic planning of the company. Among them, we have the "Go To Market", "Time To Market" and pricing policies activities.

8. TECHNOLOGY AND SERVICE PROVIDERS

The project was developed by PECTRA Technology: a company specialized in Process Management, with more than 12 years of experience on the market and 200 successful implementations in the USA, Argentina, Mexico, Colombia, Spain and Chile. We have an extensive network of partners in the entire Latin American region and we offer services to more than 50,000 end users who, in turn, serve more than 6,000,000 users/customers. For more information, please visit: www.pectra.com .

Section 6

Appendix

APPENDIX

GUEST CHAPTERS

Linus Chow
Principal Consultant
Oracle, USA
linus.chow@oracle.com, 703 203 2178

Clay Richardson
Senior Analyst
Forrester Research, Inc., USA
crichardson@forrester.com, 703 584 2630

Christine Robinson
President
Christine Robinson & Associates LLC, USA
Christine@RobinsonChristine.com, 202 316 1068

Dennis Wisnosky
Business Mission Area Chief Architect & CTO
ODCMO, US DoD, USA
Dennis.Wisnosky@osd.mil

Award Winners and Nominators

EUROPE

Finalist Award
Faculty of Manufacturing Technologies, TUKE
Presov, Slovakia
Vladimír Modrák, Professor, Head of Manufacturing Management
Department
vladimir.modrak@tuke.sk, 421 7722828

Nominator:
Czestochowa University of Technology
Czestochowa, Poland
Sebastian Kot, Assoc Prof. Dr./Lecturer
sebacat@zim.pcz.czest.pl, 48 343250330

EUROPE

Silver Award
Homeloan Management Limited (HML)
North Yorkshire, UK
Paul Swinson, CREWS Programme Manager
Paul.Swinson@hml.co.uk, +44 (0) 1756 709959 Ext 2295

Nominator:
Lombardi, an IBM Company
Austin, TX, USA

Wayne Snell, Senior Director of Marketing
wsnell@us.ibm.com, 1 512 382 8200

EUROPE

Silver Award
SNS Bank IT
Hertogenbosch, Netherlands
Ronald van Tienen, Project Manager IT (Java Department)
Ronald.vanTienen@sns.nl, +31 622556139

Nominator:
Red Hat
Amersfoort, Netherlands
Danna Drion, Sr Marketing Manager Benelux
ddrion@redhat.com, +31 611561406

EUROPE

Gold Award
Swisscard AECS AG
Horgen, Zurich, Switzerland
Oezlem Civelek, Application Owner / Project Leader AP Processing
oezlem.c.civelek@swisscard.ch, +41 44 659 64 42

Nominator:
Action Technologies Inc.
San Leandro, CA, US
Bill Welty, CEO
bill.welty@actiontech.com, 1 510 903 1739

MEA

Finalist Award
Abu Dhabi Commercial Bank
Abu Dhabi, United Arab Emirates
Mr. Mansoor Ali, Sr. Project Manager
mansoorali@adcb.com, +971 2 6962222

Nominator:
Newgen Software Technologies Ltd
New Delhi, Delhi, India
Mr. Rohit Thakur, Manager Products & Solutions
rohit.thakur@newgen.co.in, +971 2 40773620

MIDDLE EAST - AFRICA

Silver Award
NAFITH Logistics PSC
Amman, Jordan
Nourah Mehyar, CEO
nmehyar@nafith.com, 962 6 5563629

Nominator:
TraxAware Software LLC
Amman, Jordan
Sameer Mubarak, CEO
smubarak@traxaware.com, 962 6 4618081

MIDDLE EAST - AFRICA
Gold Award
Nokia Siemens Networks
Dubai Media City, Dubai, U.A.E
Nick Deacon, CSI Head of Global BPM
nick.deacon@nsn.com

Nominator:
Appian
Reston, VA, USA
Ben Farrell, Director, Corporate Communications
ben.farrell@appian.com, 703 442 1067

MIDDLE EAST - AFRICA
Silver Award
South African Post Office
Pretoria, Gauteng, South Africa
Marietjie Lancaster, Group Executive Strategy
Marietjie.Lancaster@postoffice.co.za +27 8282 89977

Nominator:
Petanque Consultancy
Cape Town, WC, South Africa
Michélle Booysen, Managaing Director
drmich@petanque-c.com, +27 82 4452192

NORTH AMERICA
Silver Award
AmerisourceBergen Corporation
Chesterbrook, PA, USA
Manoj Kumar, Manager, Business Process Automation
mkumar@amerisourcebergen.com, 610 727 7054

Nominator:
Metastorm
Baltimore, MD, USA
Laura Mooney, Vice President, Corporate Communications
Laura.Mooney@Metastorm.com, 443 874 1300

NORTH AMERICA
Gold Award
Lincoln Trust Company
Denver, Colorado, USA
Joan Manning, EVP Operations
joan.manning@lincolntrustco.com, 303 658 3636

Nominator:
Lincoln Trust Company
Denver, Colorado, USA
Bob Beriault, CEO
Bob.Beriault@lincolntrustco.com, 303 658 3777

NORTH AMERICA

Finalist Award
Pinellas County, Florida
Clearwater, Florida, USA
Ken Burke, Clerk of the Circuit Court, Pinellas County
kburke@co.pinellas.fl.us, 727 464 4825

Nominator:
Global 360, Inc.
Dallas, Texas, USa
Jennifer Troxell, VP Product & Corporate Marketing
jennifer.troxell@global360.com, 214 520 1660

NORTH AMERICA

Finalist Award
San Francisco Public Utilities Commission
San Francisco, California, USA
Andrea Pierce, ITS - Business Applications and Development
APierce@sfwater.org, 415 551 4326

Nominator:
Interfacing Technologies Corporation
Montreal, Quebec, Canada
Scott Armstrong, Business Development Manager
scott.armstrong@interfacing.com, +1 514 737 7333

NORTH AMERICA

Silver Award
San Joaquin County Information Systems Division
Stockton, CA, USA
Shakir Awan, PMP Information Systems Analyst V
sawan@sjgov.org, 209 953 7804

Nominator:
Oracle
Falls Church, VA, USA
Linus Chow, Principal Consultant
linus.chow@oracle.com, 703 203 2178

PACIFIC RIM

Finalist Award
AEGON Religare Life Insurance Company LTD
Vile Parle (E), Mumbai, India
Srinivasan Iyengar, Director - IT & Operations
srinivasan.iyengar@aegonreligare.com, +91 22 6729 3000

Nominator:
DST Global Solutions
Central, Hong Kong
Andy Wong, Head - AWD Solutions Asia
andy.wong@dstglobalsolutions.com, 852 2581 2880

PACIFIC RIM

Silver Award
Reliance Life Insurance
Mumbai, Maharashtra, India
Anuprita Daga, Chief Manager - IT
Anuprita.Daga@relianceada.com, +91 22 3088 3444

Nominator:
Progress Software Corporation
Progress | Savvion BPM
Bedford, MA, USA
John Stewart, VP of Corporate Marketing
jstewart@progress.com, 1 408 330 3491

PACIFIC RIM

Gold Award
South Australia Department of the Premier and Cabinet
Adelaide, South Australia, Australia
Ray Dennis, Director, Cabinet Office
dennis.ray@saugov.sa.gov.au, 61 (08) 8226 3661

Nominator:
HandySoft
Falls Church, VA, USA
Garth Knudson, Director
gknudson@handysoft.com, 703 645 4515

SOUTH AMERICA

Gold Award
QUALA SA
Bogota, Colombia
David Enrique Moreno, CTO
dmoreno@quala.com.co, +571 770 0100

Nominator:
Pectra Technology
Houston, Texas, USA
Juan Chacon, Marketing Manager
jchacon@pectra.com, 713 335 5562

	2010 BPM & WORKFLOW HANDBOOK ***Spotlight on Business Intelligence*** Linking BI and BPM creates stronger operational business intelligence. Users seek more intelligent business process capabilities in order to remain competitive within their fields and industries. BPM vendors realize they need to improve their business processes, rules and event management offerings with greater intelligence or analytics capabilities. **Retail $75.00**
	2009 BPM & WORKFLOW HANDBOOK ***Spotlight on BPM in Government*** The question, "How can governments manage change organizationally and be agile operationally?" is answered in this special spotlight on BPM in Government with specific emphasis on the USA government where agencies, armed forces, states and cities are facing almost insurmountable challenges. **Retail $75.00**
	BPM EXCELLENCE IN PRACTICE 2009 ***Innovation, Implementation and Impact*** Award-winning Case Studies in Workflow and BPM These companies focused on excelling in *innovation, implementation* and *impact* when installing BPM and workflow technologies. They recognized that implementing innovative technology is useless unless the organization has a successful approach that delivers—and even surpasses—the anticipated benefits. **$49.95**
	BPMN MODELING AND REFERENCE GUIDE ***Stephen A. White, PhD, Derek Miers*** **Understanding and Using BPMN** Develop rigorous yet understandable graphical representations of business processes Business Process Modeling Notation (BPMN™) is a standard, graphical modeling representation for business processes. It provides an easy-to-use, flow-charting notation that is independent of the implementation environment. **Retail $39.95**

www.ingramcontent.com/pod-product-compliance
Lightning Source LLC
Chambersburg PA
CBHW051409200326
41520CB00023B/7165